MAKING THE LAST DINOSAUR

MAKING THE LAST DINOSAUR

B. Harrison Smith

BearManor Media

2023

DEDICATION

For Richard Boone.
He was the last.
There are no more.

TABLE OF CONTENTS

Few men have ever done what he has done
Or even dreamed what he has dreamed

His time has passed
There are no more
He is the last dinosaur
Few men have even tried what he has tried
Most men have failed where he's prevailed

His time has passed
There are no more
He is the last dinosaur
The world holds nothing new in store for him
And things that startle you and me
Are just a bore for him
The spark of life has gone
His light grows dim

Can there be something left in the world to challenge him?
Few men have ever lived as he has lived
Or even walked where he has walked

He is the last
There are no more
He is the last dinosaur

FOREWORD BY RICK GOLDSCHMIDT

When I think of *Rankin/Bass'* television film, *The Last Dinosaur*, many things come to mind. As the official historian and biographer for *Rankin/Bass Productions*, I know it has a devoted following, as so many of the *Rankin/Bass* TV specials, TV series and films do.

The Last Dinosaur comes from a series of films *Rankin/Bass* produced for the *ABC Friday Night Movie*. Arthur Rankin, Jr., my closest friend and supporter at *Rankin/Bass Productions*, had a very close tie to the network. It began in the fifties, when he was hired as the art director for the network. At the time, most of television was filmed live and in New York, later moving to the West Coast.

Arthur was working with legends in the entertainment field on television shows such as *Tales of Tomorrow* with actors like James Dean, Rod Steiger and Lon Chaney, Jr. In fact, Arthur worked on the famous production of *Frankenstein* starring Lon Chaney, Jr., where Lon famously got drunk and didn't break the prop furniture during the television broadcast, because he was confused and thought it was another run through. I believe that Arthur may have met Richard Boone during this era.

Fast forward to the early Seventies. Rankin/Bass already had several network television specials under their belt, most for the *NBC* television network, including *Rudolph the Red-Nosed Reindeer*. A friend of theirs, Larry Roemer had a connection at *NBC*, and that was how they were able to get *Rudolph* on TV. For that, they gave Roemer an honorary credit on *Rudolph* as Director, even though it was mostly directed by Tadahito Mochinaga in Japan.

In the early seventies, Arthur Rankin and Jules Bass developed a friendship with Michael Eisner, who was then in charge of Saturday morning kid's programming at *ABC*. *Rankin/Bass Productions* began producing series, as they did earlier with the 1966 series *The King Kong Show*. The new series consisted of *The Smokey Bear Show*, *The Reluctant Dragon and Mr. Toad Show*, *The Jackson Five Show*, *The Osmonds*, etc. They only did one for another network, *NBC*, *The Tomfoolery Show*.

Then they began producing their holiday TV specials for *ABC*, such as *Frosty's Winter Wonderland*, *The Year Without A Santa Claus*, *The First Christmas*, *Rudolph's Shiny New Year*, etc. Their previous specials still aired on *NBC* and *CBS*, so they covered all three networks.

Arthur's dream was to produce and direct big budget feature films. Jules' dream was to produce a Broadway musical. Rankin/Bass Productions (Then known as *Videocraft International*), made their first feature film in 1965 in "Animagic" called *Willy McBean and His Magic Machine*. It was a modest film with a modest budget.

They signed a three picture deal with legendary film Producer Joseph E. Levine. This lead to three feature films: *The Wacky World of Mother Goose* (in cel animation), *The Daydreamer* (In "Animagic" stop-motion and Live Action) *and Mad Monster Party* (In "Animagic"). Levine was disappointed with the films, so he did not get behind them with promotion, as they needed. Consequently, *Mad Monster Party*, which was the best of the bunch, took a very long time to catch on, mostly in television.

The deal with *The King Kong Show* in 1966 and *RKO Pictures* opened the door for *Rankin/Bass Productions* to produce *King Kong Escapes* (1968). This was their first fully live-action film and I am sure Arthur was excited about this. I know for a fact Arthur was on set and visited Japan often and even selected Linda Miller for the film. I recently met Linda and we both shared a great friendship with Arthur. Arthur was very fond of the film, *King Kong Escapes*. I know this, because I sent Arthur a one-sheet for the film and I rounded up some Mecha-Kong figures for him that I later saw at his memorial displayed in his office in July of 2014.

During 1968, Jules Bass received a blow that according to Maury Laws, Bass never recovered from. *Rankin/Bass Productions* decided to produce an Off Broadway musical called *A Month of Sundays*, written by genius *Rankin/Bass* writer Romeo Muller.

The songs were written by Jules and Maury Laws and an outstanding song from this musical called "Elbow Room," would later be used in the Rankin/Bass TV special "Mouse on the Mayflower." My late friend Allen Swift was part of the cast for A *Month of Sundays* and told me he thought it was very good. It closed after ten performances and so did Jules' dreams of a Broadway musical. Romeo Muller had written another musical called *Huck* (Jack Davis had done art for this as well), but this production was later produced by another production team.

The next film that Rankin/Bass Productions produced for the movie theaters was called *Marco* starring Desi Arnaz, Jr. and Zero Mostel. This combined Arthur's dream of a feature film and Jules' dream of a Broadway musical and it even featured a short "Animagic" segment for the song "Peace Berries." It was another film with a small budget and modest success.

This brings us up to *The Last Dinosaur* and the *ABC Friday Night Movie*. As I explained, Arthur had a real connection with *ABC*. This film series came around the time that Rankin/Bass' *The Hobbit*, made a big splash on *NBC* and even featured Richard Boone as the voice of Smaug the Dragon.

The sequel, *The Return of the King*, aired on *ABC's Friday Night Movie*. *The Last Dinosaur* was the first of the live-action films for the *ABC Friday Night Movie*, followed by *The Bermuda Depths*, *The Bushido Blade* (Also starring Richard Boone and his last film), *The Ivory Ape* and *the Sins of Dorian Gray* (Where Arthur met his Second wife Olga).

It had been a while since I watched *The Last Dinosaur*, in fact, the last time was before I wrote my first book, *The Enchanted World of Rankin/Bass: A Portfolio* (Miser Bros. Press), which was released in November of 1997.

It was fun to watch, as I see things much differently than I did in my youth, and I know much more about the Enchanted World of Rankin/Bass. The criticism I had heard over the years is that it was low budget and some said it wasn't very good. If you brought the film up to Arthur or Jules over the years, depending on their mood, they might have been sort of dismissive or defensive.

As I watch the film now, I can see what the fans of the film got out of it and that is fun entertainment. It was made on a television budget, so to me it looks like many series of the day, "The Six Million Dollar Man" comes to mind, as I am rewatching that series on Blu Ray.

The Last Dinosaur came at a time when *Jaws* and *Star Wars* were released to the theatres. I remember going to the theatre with my Dad and Brother to see Dino DeLaurentiis' *King Kong* remake. There was a demand for this kind of film and many were coming out. *The Last Dinosaur* is one of those films you would watch on a Friday night and talk about it in school on a Monday.

With that said, I have become a big Richard Boone fan in recent years. I love him as Paladin in "Have Gun--Will Travel," but he was very good in the TV Series "Medic" and "The Richard Boone Show." He came from the Actors Studio in New York and was a very fine Shakespearean type.

I believe Arthur not only respected and liked him, but hired him for three of his last films to try to help him too. He suffered from chronic alcoholism throughout his life and I had read that his son said when his father returned to Hollywood in the 1970s, many of the twenty year olds that were making films, did not know him. I believe Arthur helped to restore his dignity at the end of his career.

In *The Last Dinosaur*, Boone reminds me of Lon Chaney, Jr. (Who as I said suffered from alcoholism too) as the gruff and weathered Masten Thrust, Jr. The character seems to be somewhat based on John Huston (Who voiced Gandalf the grey in Rankin/ Bass' *The Hobbit*), but yet Boone puts a lot of his Paladin character into this role like calling Joan Van Ark's character a "Crazy Lady" and laughing is typical Paladin.

I believe Joan's character being named Francesca, came from Arthur, as a tribute to his Francesca character in Rankin/Bass' *Mad Monster Party*. Francesca is a quirky photographer who seems to have feelings for both Masten and Chuck (Played by Steven Keats, who I always thought looked like Don Stroud).

Speaking of *Mad Monster Party*, when I began my research on *Rankin/Bass Productions*, Rankin/Bass musical composer and conductor Maury Laws, leant me all of the rare records he had of his musical work with Rankin/Bass.

In this pile of records was the Japanese single of *The Last Dinosaur* by Nancy Wilson. Over the years, as I became a closer friend with Maury, I know he would not have shared something with me unless he was very proud of it.

In regards to the theme of *Mad Monster Party*, Maury said, "This was a spoof of the theme from *Goldfinger*. We weren't copying it, but we gave it the flavor of that theme and somewhat the same style."

After listening to *The Last Dinosaur* theme, it reminds me of the Bond theme from "Diamonds Are Forever" and some of the Roger Moore Bond themes. I think this is what Maury and Jules were going for and it worked.

I know that the *ABC Friday Night Movie* films, including *The Last Dinosaur* had a very special place in Arthur's heart and most likely Jules' too. While Arthur never quite reached the plateau he was reaching for, he made some live-action films that have a cult status.

When I went to the memorial on Arthur's Birthday in Bermuda, there was an actor from The Ivory Ape there and Arthur's son Todd wore a costume, in tribute to his dad, from *The Bushido Blade*.

When I became the official historian for *Rankin/Bass Productions*, Arthur included me in the family, because I understood him and what he was trying to do and had done.

In fact, after my first book came out, Arthur was still pushing hard for a feature film of *The King and I*. He set up another meeting with Michael Eisner at Disney, but it ultimately got made by Morgan Creek. I know that, *The Last Dinosaur*, being the first of the *ABC* films, held a special place in Arthur's heart and fans will enjoy it for many years to come.

Rankin/Bass Historian and author, Rick Goldschmidt
with Arthur Rankin, Jr.

A LAND THAT TIME FORGOT

"I will hunt that thing down and I will kill it!"

I grew up in a time when television had three major networks, and stations stopped broadcasting around midnight and didn't come back on the air until the morning. It was a time of syndicated TV shows and movies. *MTV* wasn't even an idea. VCRs were years away from being household items, and the closest you got to seeing real movies was in the theaters or *HBO*. Cable was also in its infancy.

This was a pre-Reagan era when Richard Nixon was President of the United States, then Ford, then Carter. There were no conventions for fans of any kind. If you didn't see it in theaters, you didn't see it for a long time, if ever.

It was a time when my mother sent her eight-year-old son almost a half-mile to the town general store with a note giving permission to sell me her cigarettes.

When something special came on TV, you begged to stay up. These special events included fare like the Chuck Jones animated "Rikki-Tikki-Tavi" or "The Grinch That Stole Christmas," anything Charlie Brown, "The Wizard of Oz," and the perennial holiday favorite, "Rudolph The Red-Nosed Reindeer."

Two guys named Arthur Rankin and Jules Bass formed an animation production company in the 60s and produced a stop-motion style of animation they branded as "Animagic." "Rudolph" was their first big commercial success, and it led to a theatrical feature film called "The Daydreamer" with a host of celebrity vocal talent, with Hans Christian Andersen stories rounding out the content.

It would be Rankin/Bass's *Mad Monster Party* that would make the biggest impression on me. I saw it when I was around four and it never left my life. The stop-motion puppetry brought to life a story with Dr. Frankenstein hosting a convention for the world's monsters (all send-ups of the Universal Monsters that had long since faded by the 60s) with horror legend Boris Karloff and comedienne Phyllis Diller lending their vocal talents to this musical comedy.

While the monsters had my attention, the Baron's sexy redhead secretary Francesca had my heart. She might be my first celebrity crush, and she was a stop-motion puppet. When her dress was ripped off in a confrontation with Phyllis Diller's Monster's Mate, I was hooked.

I didn't understand syndication because, you know, I was four. It was through regular TV watching over the next few years, and with so few channels, that I learned these movies cycle and come back around. While you would think *Mad Monster Party* would show up around Halloween, I found it surfaced more around Thanksgiving and post-Christmas. Sometimes it would be in the spring, but I can't remember seeing it in the fall around Halloween.

I learned to navigate the TV Guide booklet and would read it every week to see if I could find *Mad Monster Party*. I am talking like reading it for 52 weeks just to find when that movie would pop up somewhere. Usually, it was found on the New York affiliates like WOR Channel 9 and Channel 5. When I was in fourth grade, I saw it was in the coming week lineup for April 1976. The problem was it would be on TV while I was in school.

I needed a plan, but I had not mastered the art of shutting my mouth and instead asked outright if I could stay home from school that day to watch "Mad Monster Party." Again, there were no VCRs or DVRs to record it. Streaming was what the creeks did down the road from my house, and the road from my house, and

Me 1st day of kindergarten

we didn't subscribe to cable, and even if we did, it wouldn't play on there anyway.

My mother denied my request. I came up with a plan to fake an illness, get dismissed from school, and come home to watch my movie. I packed a small baggie of oatmeal in my pocket and went to school. About an hour before the movie was to air, I asked to go to the nurse.

I went to her office, told her I wasn't feeling well, and asked to use the bathroom because I felt sick. I pulled out my baggie of oatmeal, dumped it into the toilet, and made retching sounds. I put on a good act, and when I came out, she looked in the toilet to see what looked like breakfast cereal vomit.

She made the call, and I got home with thirty minutes to spare.

My mother's boyfriend came for me, and he left me alone at home while my mom worked, so I had the house to myself. I watched it on an old console with the channel dial missing. We changed the channels with a set of needle-nose pliers. I had to keep an eye on the window for my mom or her boyfriend. If she came home and saw *Mad Monster Party* was on, she would know I lied. I asked her, after all, and she was no dummy.

I got away with it. For the moment. When my mother got home, she interrogated me until I cracked, and I was grounded for the entire coming Easter vacation. Worth it just for the Francesca-Monster's Mate catfight.

Rankin/Bass might have become the first entertainment name brand I understood and recognized by their trademark style. While I was never into their 2-D animation, I caught all of their 3-D puppet stop-motion works, but nothing was closer to my heart than *Mad Monster Party*. Being a giant monster and Godzilla buff, I discovered *King Kong Escapes*, a Rankin/Bass live-action feature film that saw them work with Japan and brought my other name brand recognition: *Toho Studios*.

The film is wrongly considered a sequel to the classic 1963 *King Kong vs. Godzilla*. It has nothing to do with that storyline. Rankin/Bass worked with the studio that brought me my Saturday afternoon Godzilla fixes as well as after-school "Monster Weeks" on Channels 11, 48, 17, and 29. The *Toho* lineup introduced me to not just every Godzilla movie made to that point but also *The War of the Gargantuas, Gappa, The X From Outer Space, The Giant Space Amoeba* (Known to me as *Yog), Frankenstein Conquers the World,* and so many others.

Toho was Eastern Rankin/Bass... I understood the product their studio produced. It was my brand.

A *Rankin/Bass* animated TV show sort of entertained me after school called "The King Kong Show" and is said to be loosely based on *King Kong Escapes* in some "further adventures" kind of thing.

What I remember is that the feature live-action movie, *King Kong Escapes* featured veteran Kaiju movie actor, Hideyo Amamoto, as the nefarious Dr. Who (No connection to the British sci-fi icon) who wanted to hijack Kong to mine some radioactive "Element X" and tilt the balance of world power.

Dr. Who in the live-action movie died a haunting death that made me look away or close my eyes. It still makes me uneasy to this day. Kong attacked Dr. Who's ship, and during the sinking, Who was crushed up against a wall by a careening table as water poured in and blood gushed from his mouth. You hear him gurgling, and it was pretty graphic, even by today's standards for a kid-oriented monster movie.

When I found out that Dr. Who was in the *King Kong Show* animated series, I was relieved to see the cartoon character bore no resemblance to Amamoto's live portrayal and there was little likelihood he would be vomiting a fountain of blood.

There wasn't much to the animated series. It focused on a doofy, almost sleepy-eyed Kong who gamboled around the island with a young boy (named Bobby, of course) as a kind of family pet. He was not the Kong of the black and white film, or even the Kong of the 1967 live-action film. He was definitely not the Kong of the 1976 remake. He was more akin to the subsequent *Grape Ape* from Hanna-Barbera Studios. Again, I never responded all that strongly to Rankin/Bass's animated product. Frosty the Snowman annoyed me, and their quasi-sequel to *Mad Monster Party* was a major letdown. They called it *Mad, Mad, Mad Monsters*, and it was a pale 2-D animated retread of the 1967 stop-motion classic.

They tried their hand at animating Mother Goose stories in *The Wacky World of Mother Goose*, which I saw with my Cub Scout troop and was left not feeling much for it.

After-school TV viewing was a great way to close the book on the education day. The best lineup was on Philly's WPHL Channel 17, and I can still remember how it went. The anime *Marine Boy* kicked it off. I was never into that and would catch it here and there, mostly for the hot mermaid.

Then came the Japanese monster live-action TV shows. The best of these was *Ultraman* from *Tsuburaya Productions*, the same company that did the effects for Godzilla movies and a number of the Kaiju films I previously listed. The company was founded by effects wizard Eiji Tsuburaya.

"Kaiju," you ask? I'll get into that for those not in the know. This whole book is about Kaiju, so by the time it's done, you won't forget the word.

The other two after-school contenders were *The Space Giants* and *Johnny Sokko and His Flying Robot*. Both featured large robots doing battle with a variety of giant Kaiju monsters bent on destroying Japan. All three dealt with aliens in one form or another.

It was *Ultraman* that I couldn't wait for, and the series was my introduction to Japanese pop culture. *Ultraman* was a Japanese sci-fi television series produced by Tsuburaya. It followed the adventures of the Science Patrol, a group of humans who defended Earth from giant monsters (Kaiju) and aliens. The series features Ultraman, the giant alien superhero who merged with a human host to fight against the monsters. Ultraman possessed a variety of powers, including the ability to fly, shoot energy beams, and grow to enormous size. Each episode featured a different monster that the Science Patrol must defeat, often with the help of *Ultraman* (almost always with the help of *Ultraman*). The show was known for its practical special effects, which included miniatures, puppetry, and suitmation.

"Suitmation" is the term given to men playing creatures in rubber and latex suits, smashing miniature model buildings, and fighting other men in giant rubber suits. Japan set the standard for this type of giant monster filmmaking just as Willis O'Brien set the bar for stop-motion animation with 1933's *King Kong*. It was also a lot cheaper and less time-intensive.

Doing a weekly stop-motion monster series wouldn't become practical until "Land of the Lost" debuted in 1974, and even for as young as I was, I noticed the low-quality stop-motion work. It still entertained, but I found the costumed Sleestacks far scarier than the stop-motion and puppet dinosaurs.

By the time I was in fifth grade, both *Toho* and Rankin/Bass were staples of my childhood entertainment. They were like two ingredients of a fantastical peanut butter cup and I knew what to expect when I saw their names on my entertainment.

My father took me to see 1974's *The Land That Time Forgot*, a Doug McClure dinosaur action fest that kicked off the "strange monsters found in arctic enclave" trope. The monsters in that film were literal hand puppets and moved with sticks, shot in forced perspective and back screen projection. For a little kid, it was new and different than men in suits, and I have to admit, the effects impressed me at the time.

In 1976, the *King Kong* remake returned us to suitmation with makeup artist Rick Baker inside a giant ape outfit outfitted with an elaborate face mask that allowed a variety of expressions. The gimmick was that producer Dino DeLaurentiis allowed his marketing to create the impression that Kong in this movie was a huge animatronic robot. It wasn't, and that effect makes it into the final film for a whopping 10 seconds or maybe even less. It's not impressive even though it was designed and built by Oscar-winning effects artist Carlo Rambaldi (*Alien, ET: The Extraterrestrial, Silver Bullet*).

I was disappointed that Kong fought zero dinosaurs, save for a big, very rubbery-looking puppet snake. A T-Rex was expected, and a T-Rex I did not get. While some of the effects impressed and garnered an Oscar nomination or win, it failed to restart the giant monster craze.

In 1976, *Godzilla vs. Megalon* was also broadcast on network TV, with "Saturday Night Live" megastar John Belushi hosting in a ratty-looking Godzilla suit like some Saturday Creature Feature host.

Godzilla vs. Megalon might be the worst of the Godzilla "Showa" series. Some would give *Godzilla's Revenge* that honor. The Japanese title for *Godzilla's Revenge* is *All Monsters Attack* (*Gojira Minira Gabara: Oru Kaijū Daishingeki*).

The Showa era of Godzilla films refers to the series of Japanese Kaiju (monster) movies featuring Godzilla, produced by *Toho* from 1954 to 1975. The term "Showa era" refers to the historical period of Japanese history from 1926 to 1989, during which Emperor Showa reigned. *Godzilla vs. Megalon* was part of this original Showa timeline of films.

The Showa era is divided into three distinct periods: the early Showa period (1926-1945), the post-war Showa period (1945-1989), and the late Showa period (1975-1989). The Godzilla films produced from 1954 to 1975 are commonly referred to as the "Showa era" of Godzilla films because not just were they made during the post-war Showa period, which saw a significant shift in Japanese society and culture, it was seen as well in the film industry.

The films from this period reflected the changing attitudes and concerns of Japanese society, and the emergence of a new generation of filmmakers who were eager to experiment with new techniques and themes. It saw the introduction of many other famous Kaiju, such as Mothra, Rodan, and Ghidorah, and the evolution of Godzilla's character from a destructive force to a heroic defender of Japan.

On that note, we circle back to the 1976 *Godzilla vs. Megalon* *NBC* broadcast.

The film's reception was mixed, with some viewers enjoying the campy humor and over-the-top monster battles, while others found the special effects and plot to be cheesy and poorly executed. The showing was successful enough to inspire a new wave of interest in Japanese monster movies and Kaiju culture among American audiences.

The real fallout was being made fun of by Belushi, and the American impression that Godzilla films and all Japanese Kaiju films were just bad cheese to be laughed at when the original 1954 *Godzilla* (*Gojira*) had an entirely different message and intention.

To be fair, by the end of the Showa era, the films had become professional wrestling in monster suits. The Godzilla series was in need of retirement by 1975 and while America was arguably at peak big monster movie interest, it might have been for the wrong reasons.

For many Americans, giant Japanese monster movies held a special, campy place in their hearts. From the classic Godzilla films of the 1950s and 60s to more recent hits like *Pacific Rim* and the rebooted *Legendary/Warner Bros. Godzilla* "Monsterverse." These movies captivated audiences with their epic battles, colorful creatures, and imaginative storytelling. They had some offbeat, out there plots unlike Western monster movies which mostly stayed within the realms of reality.

1954's "Big Bug" monster movie, *Them!* is an example. This was a quality, A-list science fiction horror about giant ants created from atomic testing, rampaging the New Mexico desert and beneath Los Angeles.

This was an American film, made by *Warner Brothers* and they played it straight. They cast Edmund Gwenn as the head scientist leading a team to destroy the insects before they destroy us. No camp, no rubber suits. These were Oscar-caliber effects that still hold up today and reality was the glue that held it together. The giant ants were not gods or forces of nature, but rather the side effects of man's science-based nuclear folly.

Part of the appeal of campy kaiju monster movies lies in their escapist nature. They offer viewers the chance to forget about the problems of the real world and lose themselves in a fantasy world where giant monsters roam the Earth. I can attest to this as we get to *The Last Dinosaur*.

These movies also explore deeper themes, such as the dangers of nuclear power, the consequences of scientific progress, and the importance of teamwork and cooperation.

Another reason for their enduring popularity was their sheer spectacle. Kaiju movies are often filled with jaw-dropping or at the least, off the wall special effects, including miniatures, suitmation, and now CGI, that bring the monsters to life in vivid detail. The sense of scale is breathtaking; as audiences watch giant creatures tear through cities and battle each other in epic showdowns.

Perhaps the biggest reason for their appeal is their sense of nostalgia. For many Americans who grew up in the 1950s and 60s, the Godzilla films were a staple of their childhoods. They were a source of excitement and wonder, and they helped to inspire a generation of filmmakers and fans. Even today, these old movies continue to inspire new generations of fans, who are drawn to their timeless appeal and sense of fun.

What does all of this mean?

As a boy who came from a childhood of divorce, physical and emotional abuse (at the hands of my mother's boyfriend) these films not only provided an escape, they taught me things.

Indeed Godzilla became a protector of the earth. The rightly maligned *Godzilla's Revenge* (basically a clip show of Godzilla movies stitched together around a child-level plot) did give me hope that I too could conquer the bullies at both school and at home.

Godzilla served as a father figure in that film, guiding his son Mr. Miyagi-style to take on the bully, Gabara and keep up the Godzilla family reputation for kicking ass. The film followed a 

young boy named Ichiro, apparently fatherless, frequently bullied at school, who escaped his problems by daydreaming about visiting Monster Island (The place where all the *Toho* monsters resided) and befriended Minilla (Pronounced Meen-ya), Godzilla's son. In Ichiro's dreams, he watches as the monsters battle various foes, including the villainous Gabara. As Ichiro's fantasies become more vivid, he learns to stand up to his bullies and find confidence in himself.

I got Ichiro. I was bullied in elementary school and had a kid who was very much my Gabara. At the end of the film Ichiro kicks the shit out of Gabara in front of other kids and we assume ends the bully's reign of terror.

In fourth grade, my father taught me how to throw a punch and use it to defend myself against a kid who was bullying me. However, it was Ichiro's bravery, inspired by Godzilla and his son that ultimately gave me the courage to confront and defeat my own Gabara.

One afternoon I turned and laid that kid out in front of all his friends. I split his lip. He promptly told on me and I served lunch detention or something like that, but I never had a problem with him again. My father was kind of like Godzilla in that movie.

I didn't have the physical ability to take on my mother's boyfriend, but the universe worked in mysterious ways and he died by the end of 1976, not long after my *Mad Monster Party* skip day.

The idea of nostalgic love for these movies is a valid one. My mother and father divorced when I was around six or seven. My dad no longer lived with us. While he was at home I do remember him loving the old Godzilla films when they played on weekend afternoons.

I also remember him laughing like hell at *Ultraman* and he seemed to enjoy those episodes. I remember one episode where Ultraman rides a Kaiju bareback like a cowboy on a Bronco and the old man just laughed at the inanity of it all. It was good to see him laugh and if dad liked it, so did I.

I watched Godzilla and Rodan take on Ghidorah in *Monster Zero* and remember being moved to tears when Godzilla, Rodan and Ghidorah plummeted off that cliff and down into the ocean with only Ghidorah emerging from the water to fly away. While I knew Godzilla lived in water, I feared he died, and Rodan couldn't swim.

I found some solace when a woman spectator asked if Godzilla and Rodan were dead and one of the male stars replied in dubbed English, "Nah, they're too tough."

Worked for me.

Ultraman delivered an almost daily dose of Kaiju fun and adventure. I played *Ultraman* in my yard. We played Godzilla and Ultraman in the snow, especially the large plow mounds which doubled for cities.

Our small town of East Bangor was surrounded by old slate quarries. We would climb mountains of slate and pretend Godzilla and other monsters were buried below them. We unwittingly risked our lives spelunking the corridors between car-sized slabs of slate on those mountains, never knowing they could collapse and crush us or trap us and bury us with Godzilla and those monsters forever. No one would find us.

This was a time when we played on the train tracks over a mile from home down by a dam that held giant snails, turtles and pickerel while across the water was a sketchy trailer park. A real monster could have kidnapped us and our parents wouldn't know until dinner time.

It was a different world—a more prehistoric one, if you will.

Japanese Kaiju films and *Rankin/Bass* "Animagic" films were an important part of my childhood development. While I was pretty young when I saw *King Kong Escapes* (It was made the year I was born and I don't think I saw it on TV until I was like seven) by fifth grade, I was very aware of *Rankin/Bass* and *Toho*.

When I heard they teamed up again to make a movie called *The Last Dinosaur*, there was no question that it would be on my must see list.

⑤ ⑦ ⑨ ⑬ **MOVIE—Adventure**
Richard Boone plays a big-game hunter on the trail of ''The Last Dinosaur,'' a 20-foot-tall tyrannosaurus rex found roaming a prehistoric world beneath the north polar icecap. A 1977 TV-movie. (2 hrs.)
Supporting Cast
Frankie Banks . . . . .Joan Van Ark
Chuck Wade . . . . .Steven Keats
Bunta . . . . .Luther Rackley

A LOST WORLD!!
RULED BY THE
LARGEST MAN-EATING
MONSTER OF ALL!!
THE
LAST
DINOSAUR"
FIRST TIME ON TV!
Starring
RICHARD
BOONE
ABC FRIDAY NIGHT MOVIE
9:00PM 5 23

I saw the ad for *The Last Dinosaur* in *TV Guide*—a big full page display showed off the dinosaur and *Have Gun--Will Travel* TV star, Richard Boone in safari outfit aiming a rifle to kill it. It was *Jaws* with a T-Rex.

Damn, it was good to be a kid in the late 70s.

The movie was a world premiere *ABC Friday Night Movie*. This was a time when network television, to keep up with cable competition, offered up edited theatrical films or their own in-house developed movies. It meant no one else had *The Last Dinosaur* but *ABC*.

I can still remember waiting for school to end and for Friday night to come. I tried to catch every preview for *The Last* Dinosaur throughout the week. I talked about it all day that Friday. It was going to be awesome and I would talk about it Monday in school.

My kid brother and I had our asses glued to the floor in front of our 25-inch *Magnavox* console to watch it. We wouldn't need the pliers because no way were we changing that channel. Commercials were for snacks or pee breaks.

It wouldn't disappoint and…the female star's name was Francesca.

FILM DYSMORPHIA

I propose a new disorder: "Film Dysmorphia." We have become so conditioned to CGI (Computer Generated Imagery) we've come to accept it as the new normal. Our minds tell us that it doesn't look right; often we reject it outright in big budget spectacles like the *Star Wars* prequels or disaster garbage like *2012*. It's a detailed cartoon, lacking in style, but we have come to believe this computer generated landscape populated with digital images is what looks good.

I need to get a few things clear before we go into the making of *The Last Dinosaur*. I do not think the film is on the level of *Jurassic Park* but I think therein lies the problem.

It was never meant to be that or high cinema. The movie was meant to be fun. "Fun" is something I think the Internet has helped to kill. Our attention has been turned to what I call "picking fly shit out of pepper." We now look for mistakes, imperfections and have become obsessed with realism, yet funny enough so many reject reality today. Instead we focus on minutia, arguing online about the smallest details and now started to build series around incidental, almost background characters from movies.

I wanted to reach out to you again......remember when we talked about my idea for an Amity tv series?

Feb 12, 2022, 12:43 PM

I was wondering if you'd be interested in collaborating w me on writing.

One fan on *Twitter* asked if I would be interested in developing and pitching a series on the town of Amity from the *Jaws* franchise. The whole premise would be about the people of the town before Chief Brody moved to the island and the shark started its hijinks.

I declined. Here's why: Who the hell cares? Just because you can do something, doesn't mean you should. The town of Amity is only interesting as the backdrop to the shark attacks of the films. Do we need or want a movie about characters from the original film or any of them? Do we want a look at Amity in the early 1900s?

What is there to say? All anybody wants is for a shark to show up. If the intent is to show this island was a flashpoint for shark attacks previous to the 1975 film, you debase the whole point of that movie. The attacks in the original *Jaws* rocked the small beach community. The shark was a disruptor to a town that thrived on the longtime peace and quiet.

Chief Brody moved from New York City for this very thing and proudly proclaimed to Matt Hooper that there wasn't a single murder on Amity's books for the last 25 years.

Do we need to look at the rise of Mayor Vaughn? Do we need some kind of in-depth look at Mrs. Taft the Selectwoman who finds nothing funny? The answer is simple: No.

We might WANT it. That's different than NEED it.

We didn't need a series dedicated to Nurse Ratched from *One Flew Over the Cuckoo's Nest*. A bad idea for many reasons, but the main one would be anyone not Louise Fletcher has no business playing that role.

To bring up another franchise, did we need to see a ten year old Darth Vader before he was Darth Vader and have his path to the Dark Side fully explained in agonizing detail?

Once again: No.

We are in a new age of "The Fan." The recent *Halloween* movies from *Blumhouse* were nothing more than fan service that brought back obscure characters, gave them nothing to do but be there for someone my age to exclaim: "Oh my God it's Nurse Chambers, Tommy Doyle, Lindsay Wallace!" or "Lonnie, that kid we saw for ten seconds in the original 1978 film!"

Audiences are less willing to suspend disbelief and seem to have a "fan service habit" that needs a constant supply of fan pleasing drugs to keep up the high. It's not about story; it's about how many stupid fan details we can pack into a film.

The Last Dinosaur gets a lot of shit for its special effects or as online reviewers like to call them "not-so-special" effects. Some of it is deserved, but some of it comes from a generation of movie watchers that have no understanding of film, its history and why some things are the way they are. There were and still are things called "artistic choices."

Let me give an example from one of my own films. I shot the action-comedy *Garlic and Gunpowder* around 2017. It had a terrific comedy cast headlined by James Duval, Judy Tenuta, Vivica A. Fox, Michael Madsen, Dean McDermott, Martin Kove and a slew more.

I wanted the film to be a throwback to 1960s screwball comedies and DELIBERATELY chose an art style of "back projection" for all driving scenes. In the old days before there was blue screening, an actor sat in a car positioned in front of a screen where crew used a projector to throw up a previously filmed road scene onto a thin screen to create the illusion of driving.

Why not just film people in a car driving? Back then it was a slog to hook up giant film cameras to a moving car. You then had to contend with car noises, road noises and noise in general and the sound equipment wasn't exactly scaled down to allow a sound person in

The green screen process recreates back projection in my action-comedy, **Garlic and Gunpowder.**

that vehicle to get all the dialogue. Nothing was wireless and wired mics attached to actors were still a new thing and barely introduced.

In short, it was a big pain in the ass. Good directors used this back projection to their advantage and started to stylize the scenes that made them their own art style. Hitchcock used rear projection to great effect in *Psycho* and the Sean Connery James Bond films used it as well.

The Zucker Brothers made terrific fun of the process in 1980's *Airplane!* when they showed Robert Stack driving in front of a screen with all kinds of crazy images and action in the road behind him. The point is the filmmakers were not going for realism. They knew it looked fake but chose the style for the sake of the production. Some finessed it and made it their own like I noted with Alfred Hitchcock.

It is an artistic choice.

The comedy classic *It's a Mad, Mad, Mad, Mad World* used this process for all of its interior driving scenes and even some of the actions scenes. The car chase with Dick Shawn and Jonathan Winters was clearly in front of a screen. Audiences didn't care because it's called "Suspension of Disbelief."

I chose to use the green screen process in *Garlic and Gunpowder* to mimic the old school rear projection art style of those 60s comedies or James Bond. I WANTED it to look fake to bring back that warm feeling to people who got it.

When the film released and reviews came in, some so-called "critics" (I will address that term later) called out the "obviously fake green screen projection for driving scenes" and attributed this to a cost factor because of low budget.

It would have been easier and cheaper to shoot it live on a real road in a real car. I CHOSE to shoot the driving scenes this way.

Audiences want realism now. They don't want to suspend their disbelief like they used to. Let's note that spaceships don't explode into fireballs in the vacuum of space, let alone make explosion sounds. Sharks don't leap upon and sink 45-foot fishing boats or sink helicopters and even better, SCUBA air tanks don't explode when shot (TV's *Mythbusters* proved that one).

Steven Spielberg wanted a big finale to *Jaws*. The book ended with an anti-climactic scene of the shark succumbing to the harpoons and barrels shot into it. It just stopped swimming and sank into the depths dead. It was a dull thud of an ending.

Spielberg wanted something bigger and came up with the exploding air tank, impossibly detonated from a 200 yard range by a low-caliber rifle with a billion to one shot. Never mind that it wouldn't explode like a bomb. It would really just shoot out air like the old spray paint cans we used to pop with our BB guns as kids.

When a crew member pointed this out, Steven blew it off, saying it didn't matter. If the audience bought the shark doing all of these impossible things for almost two hours, they would buy this new ending.

He was right. No one cared. The "Smile you sonofabitch!" ending brought audiences to standing ovations, thundering applause and cheers in the theater around me. Steven knew his shit.

There was no Internet to examine the shot frame by frame and then call up every piece of scientific data and physics from what I call "The Actually Crowd," (Because they say stuff like, "Actually that wouldn't happen...") the online entertainment party poopers who just want to be the smartest negative people in the chat room.

Realism you say? Let's look at the CGI wonders of today's big screen films. Are the computer generated backgrounds or animated characters any more "realistic" than stop motion or suitmation?

Sometimes, but in the case of the first Sam Raimi *Spiderman*, I often forgot I was watching a live-action movie and felt I was in more of a *Pixar* computer animated film. The final fights and web-slinging scenes over the city looked cartoonish to me.

George Lucas and his company created incredible models, matte paintings and sets along with exotic locales that helped create his galaxy far, far away. By the time his prequels came around that was all replaced with green screen and it showed.

The fun of the original trilogy was supplanted with long "walk and talk" scenes in front of green screens with computer generated backdrops or over-produced, stunt-laden fights on green screen soundstages with cartoonish lava and other backdrops all CGI'd in later.

Every single *Marvel* or *DC* superhero movie looks like a big budget action cartoon to me. There is no thrill to them. No actor stunt people risking their lives…just computer characters rendered in a studio.

Let's go back to *Jaws* one more time because it's a lot closer to my point than science fiction or James Bond movies. *Jaws* is about a monster…a dinosaur in fact. Science and big shark fans love to point out that The Great White Shark is the direct descendent of the fabled Megalodon…the largest shark ever that existed 60 million years ago.

The largest Great White on record is a little over thirty feet, and it might be a living one known as "Big Blue." It doesn't matter; the shark in Spielberg's classic is 25 feet and weighs three tons according Captain Quint's estimates.

Look at a photo of a real Great White Shark. They don't have jowls. The round, fleshy appendages around Bruce the shark's mouth in *Jaws* were created to hide the hydraulics that controlled his mouth. Bruce was a large, early animatronic, mechanical shark.

He could not flex like a real shark, he couldn't extend his jaws and gum line like a real shark and he couldn't shield his eyes with the membrane real sharks close before they strike.

Yet we bought it…hook, line and sinker. Few, if any, agonized over jowls on a shark or even questioned the beast's intelligence. By the end of the film the shark is hunting our trio of heroes. We know sharks don't do that but we went with it because it's entertainment.

Arguments are made to "redo" the effects in *Jaws* for some special DVD release where the robot shark is replaced with a more realistic CGI rendered shark. Why? Why do we need that? *Jaws* is a story that continues to give us a great time and the shark is a piece of art.

Robert Mattey and Roy Arbogast created the technology to make the monster. Why would we replace that work, that art for the sake of realism? Should we *Photoshop* the Mona Lisa? Maybe make Van Gogh's "Starry Night" a more realistic depiction of the stars?

That is cultural vandalism.

On the flipside, someone online took the trouble to replace the mechanical shark in the dismal, *Jaws the Revenge* with a CGI one. The effect is quite good but the problem is the movie is still shit. That's because it was a cynical piece of garbage created to line pockets with no intention to entertain.

Special FX geniuses replace the original mechanical shark with a CGi rendering. Props for effort.

The new digital shark effects might look good but you can't CGI a bad script—or polish a turd.

Ed Wood is charged with being the worst director/filmmaker ever. I challenge that. I think the people that made conscious garbage like *Jaws the Revenge* are far worse. That goes for Tommy Wiseau and his film, *The Room.* Neither man intended to make a bad movie. They put their passion and belief in their art toward their respective projects. They did not cynically set out to rip people off with the creation of empty content devoid of creativity or passion.

I created a whole podcast on the subject of cynicism in filmmaking called *Cynema.* My definition of *Cynema* is when a filmmaker has the means and resources to make something truly entertaining and makes the conscious decision not to do that. *Jaws the Revenge* is the film that symbolizes *Cynema* and inspired my podcast.

Ed Wood is the antithesis of *Cynema*--his passion and love for film made him one of Hollywood's greatest directors. Say what you want about *Plan Nine From Outer Space, Bride of the Monster* or *Glen or Glenda…* bad films, yes. Bad directing? Absolutely. However Ed Wood was not a cynic.

Films *like Jaws the Revenge, Godzilla 1998* and other big

Schlockmeister, Ed Wood

budget films are far worse than anything Ed Wood ever put out, including *Plan 9.* By many accounts, including his own, *Plan 9 From Outer Space* was Wood's opus and the film that film critic, Michael Medved bestowed his dubious bad movie award upon.

Wood said this about his film: "If you want to know me, see *Glen or Glenda*. That's me, that's my story, no question. But *Plan 9* is my pride and joy. We used *Cadillac* hubcaps for flying saucers in that."

Wood was short on talent but not passion and made his films because he loved the craft. You could say he was not much different than a child that makes terrible father's/mother's holiday gift/paintings in school. To the child this is something special, perhaps even high art but to the adult it's juvenile craftsmanship at best but it's the sentiment behind it that matters.

The "worst director ever" found former horror icon and star of *Dracula* (1931) Bela Lugosi, living in poverty—a drug addled wreck of the Hollywood system. Lugosi was drained by the film industry as surely as his alter ego Count Dracula drained his victims. Lugosi was a has-been by the 1950's as the classic *Universal* monsters were replaced by aliens, radioactive monsters and budding psychopaths.

Ed Wood gave Lugosi work and made him feel like a star–infusing this ailing man with sincere enthusiasm and the hope that he could shine again. This was a filmmaker who planned to use funds made from *Plan 9's* premiere to pay for Lugosi's rehab expenses and tried to shield him from the press vultures. Lugosi died before filming commenced and wound up in Wood's film through mismatched spliced footage.

Wood knew Lugosi was a name, and indeed *Plan 9* was his last film but was said to have cried when seeing the first cut of the film and Lugosi up on that screen.

He was not just ill-equipped in the talent department to realize that dream; he was also outgunned by a film industry that was accustomed to tossing aside its tarnished stars onto the studio junk heap. Other stars will have this problem as Mickey Rooney's famous acceptance speech at the 1979 Academy Awards for his honorary Oscar put it so sadly: *"When I was 19 years old, I was the number one star of the world for two years; when I was 40, nobody wanted me — I couldn't get a job."*

While romanticized in the Tim Burton film with Johnny Depp playing an idealized version of Wood as the forever optimist (I love that movie), it does get some things right.

Ed Wood survived the Battle of Guadalcanal (with bra and panties beneath his uniform) but was unprepared for conflict in the Hollywood film industry. This was a business that saw Wood as a sideshow freak, a living example of the Grade "Z" entertainment he was pushing.

Befriending Lugosi only confirmed suspicions of lunacy and many of the distributors that Wood approached believed Lugosi long dead. Wood treated Lugosi as more than a star–he was a legend. He was driven by his loyalty and respect for this forgotten icon in his pursuit of financing.

Sources attribute Wood with soliciting Baptist church members for the financing of *Plan 9*; going so far as to have himself and members of his cast baptized to get the film made. He did this not to swindle the gullible from their funds, but under the sincere belief he would make their money back and a profit so they could pursue their dream of making twelve films on each of the Twelve Apostles.

Wood endured attacks on his sexuality when it was revealed that he liked to cross dress at the height of conservative McCarthy paranoia. His first girlfriend left him, regarding him as a degenerate and loser who surrounded himself by a coterie of the same. He was treated with contempt and with no empathy for his devotion to Lugosi. Wood battled depression, falling into the world of soft core porn and lurid pulp novels to unsuccessfully pay the rent. Evicted from his Los Angeles apartment, he died alone from a heart attack in a friend's home watching a football game in 1978 at the age of 54.

This thumbnail of a fascinating man serves as a starting point for the exploration of *Cynema*. Wood will never be compared to

Spielberg, Coppola, Shyamalan, Lucas or even Disney. Yet all of these great names have more in common with Wood than they'd like to admit.

These names and many more in Hollywood have made their share of truly awful and dreadful films and product far worse than anything that came from Edward Wood. The only problem is that most of the country and even the world didn't realize this and were duped by a cynical Hollywood hype machine–believing they were seeing something truly great.

Plan 9, Glen or Glenda, Bride of the Monster or Jail Bait are all poorly made films, but they are honest in their poor quality and also their love and passion for film and art. They are not cynical like certain films discussed later in this book.

Ed Wood: Bad director. Bad Screenwriter. Bad producer.

Perhaps. But not a cynic.

"We are going to finish this picture just the way I want it… because you cannot compromise an artist's vision."

That…is Ed Wood's legacy and it would not have displeased him.

The point of all of this is…it takes a lot of effort and work to make a bad movie. It takes far less effort to make a mediocre or cynical one. There is a major difference between "so bad it's good" entertainment and just plain bad.

The markets are glutted with just bad content--ridiculous titled films with even worse plotlines that are made to garner clicks and views for their stupid posters, titles and artwork. The actual film is far less fun and that's when some viewers realize they've been duped.

While there are more "bad" *Godzilla* films than there are good, the worst ones are the cynical ones. The ones that were managed by the studio with slashed budgets, re-used stock footage from previous or even other Kaiju films or special effects that showed little to no effort.

That's cynicism: just make the shit, the fans will eat it. This was the real danger of *Godzilla vs. Megalon*. It was a cynical movie. There was no attention to the script. Stock footage was used with some clips of previous films thrown in and attention to detail was thrown out the window.

Some can excuse this in the *Godzilla* series by blaming declining ticket sales and studio budget cuts.

What happens when a studio gives a monster movie an almost unlimited budget but hires two filmmakers completely unqualified to make a *Godzilla* movie?

That's where the 1998 American *Godzilla* film has an answer.

THE WHY OF "SUCK"

"It's not Godzilla, it does not have the spirit."
– Godzilla actor Kenpachiro Satsuma
walking out on a Tokyo screening of *Godzilla* 1998.

Let's be honest about the word "sucks." What does it really mean? It's a popular cultural euphemism for sucking dick. That's what it really means.

When you tell someone they suck, you mean they suck on a penis. When Bill Murray's John Winger in *Stripes* tells Sgt. Hulka he thinks his idea "sucks" he's really telling Warren Oates to suck a dick.

The eighties normalized the term and neutered it to become a catchall for anything we dislike. Others will argue it has a variety of meanings, but as Father Merin told Damian Karras in *The Exorcist*, "There is only one."

The first line, I believe, on the short-lived (thankfully) nineties *CBS* series adaptation of *Uncle Buck* had little girl Maizy open the pilot episode with "You suck!" yelled at the title character played by Kevin Meaney. It's believed to be the first time the phrase was used on network television.

"Sucks" is now used for almost everything and can be heard from the elementary school level up. Roger Ebert even used it to great fanfare in telling Rob Schneider his movie *Deuce Bigalow: Male Giggolo* sucked. He made it the title of his subsequent book, *Your Movie Sucks*. The same for a famous screenwriting handbook called: *Your Screenplay Sucks*.

This food sucks. This song sucks. You suck. I suck. This trip sucks.

This movie sucks.

I've read a number of reviews about *The Last Dinosaur*, relegating it to the suck bin.

Viewer comments are replete with the word. Joan Van Ark herself seemed almost astounded at the piss and vinegar the film still gets from present day reviews.

Does *The Last Dinosaur* really suck? Let's find out.

A movie's budget is the easiest target for critics. It's low hanging fruit: they didn't have enough money and that's why the film sucks. The effects budget was a dollar ninety-nine. They couldn't pay to get better names or they used D-list celebs not good enough for *The Love Boat*.

Picking on a film because of its budget is like a kick to the balls. It's the easy drop and surest way to inflict damage. This is not a pure truth. John Carpenter's *Halloween* showed what could be done on no budget. The same went for *Insidious* or arguably *The Blair Witch Project*. A lack of funds does not mean a lack of effort or passion.

It does not always mean you have the best film. There are things a budget restricts which in turn restrict the writer and director's vision of just what can be put up on the screen. Clever minds get around some of these things, but in the end, budget rarely has impact on the quality of the script. It might choke its aspirations but it never kills its talent or passion.

What happens when you have a movie that has no budget restrictions—when it's so bad but you can't point to a lack of funding to excuse its sheer awfulness? *Jaws the Revenge* is the poster child for this, but so is 1998's *Godzilla*, made by the duo that brought you *Independence Day*.

I singled out this film because *Toho*, the company that co-produced *The Last Dinosaur* licensed their most famous and lucrative character, *Godzilla* to Roland Emmerich and Dean Devlin's American *Zoetropolis* studio for an American makeover in the mid-90s after the filmmaking duo were begged to helm the project.

According to several stories, *Toho* insisted that the Hollywood Godzilla film not change their iconic monster's image. After almost 30 films, Godzilla was an international symbol. *Toho* finished off its *Heisei* series of films that restarted after 1984's *The Return of Godzilla* and ended with *Godzilla vs. Destoroyah* in 1995. Godzilla died at the end of that film, handing off the baton to the American show runners.

The Heisei era is named after the Heisei period, which began in Japan in 1989 with the accession of Emperor Akihito to the throne. The films in this era were intended to be direct sequels to the original 1954 *Godzilla* film, ignoring the continuity established in the earlier sequels. The Heisei series also introduced a number of new characters and monsters, as well as a more serious and darker tone compared to the earlier, campier Godzilla films.

In the 1990's storyline, none of the other films ever happened except for the original *Gojira* and its hasty sequel, *Godzilla Raids Again*. Everything after that was ignored until 1984 when Godzilla resurfaced after a 30 year slumber to wreak havoc on downtown Tokyo once again.

The 1998 film intended to "reboot" the entire *Godzilla* legend. It goes back to Godzilla's origin…and that's when fans knew there was a problem from the very first teaser trailer that dropped on the front of *Men in Black*.

Devlin and Emmerich had no respect for the monster's legacy. Irate fans renamed the creature GINO (Godzilla In Name Only or 'Zilla). Dean Devlin admitted he had little regard for the original 1954 film:

"Most of the public, used to watching the hokey Japanese versions, will be thinking of men-in-suits and bad models, a kind of dinosaur hybrid who lumbers about in a semi-comical fashion trashing *Lego* buildings."

created by B Harrison Smith, 2023
Tr-Star Pictures, Sony, 1998

Devlin's partner and director of the 1998 mess, Roland Emmerich said this: "I never liked Godzilla. I always thought it was a silly idea. So when they asked me to do it, I was like, 'I don't know if I'm the right guy for that." Emmerich went on to explain that he took on the project because he was interested in making a big-budget monster movie, rather than because he was a fan of the Godzilla franchise.

Sounds like *Tri-Star* and *Sony Pictures* abilities to choose the proper filmmakers to make this movie sucked.

Whereas the original Godzilla knocked down *"Lego* buildings" Emmerich's monster dry humped CGI ones.

Devlin and Emmerich paid lip service to Godzilla's nuclear genesis, but the re-design of Godzilla must be addressed. Devlin and Emmerich decided millions of fans for almost half a century would welcome a major redesign of their monster. Reports state the only instruction Roland Emmerich gave special effects designer Patrick Tatopolous for the concept of the new monster was that he wanted it to run really fast.

Emmerich justified the new design by saying, "It was basically my version of Godzilla – the way I think it should be now. For years, people have seen Godzilla in movies, but I wanted to show them something new...I felt that a lot of the responsibility was on my shoulders since we were creating the title character."

Cynema exercises a blatant disregard for the audience in the desire for profits. Devlin and Emmerich's hubris told them they would create a new and improved Godzilla for the next millennium, a streamlined creature that just happened to look pretty much like the dinosaurs from *Jurassic Park* and *The Lost World*––two films that also brought in bags of cash for *Universal*, so naturally *Tri Star* would want their own dinosaur movie while also cashing in on a tried and true brand name like *Godzilla*.

Toho's reaction to the Dean Devlin/Roland Emmerich *Godzilla* was uniformly negative; however they are not without blame. Here's what executives at Godzilla's parent company had to say about the big-budget "we spared no expense" American *Godzilla*:

- "It's like a dinosaur in a different skin." - Takashi Nakao, *Toho's* Executive Producer
- "It's not Godzilla, it doesn't have the spirit." - Shogo Tomiyama, *Toho's* Executive Producer

- "It's nothing but a big iguana." - Shogo Tomiyama, *Toho's* Executive Producer
- "It's like a Hollywood Godzilla, not a Japanese Godzilla. And it's boring. A Godzilla movie needs to have a strong story, but the story wasn't there." - Shogo Tomiyama, *Toho's* Executive Producer

Toho was so dissatisfied with the American Godzilla movie that they decided to create their own reboot of the franchise, which led to the film *Godzilla 2000.*

The American creature looked more like an iguana on steroids spliced with a Komodo Dragon. Devlin and Emmerich wanted to keep the new design under wraps from the public as a surprise. Later it was alleged that they didn't want *Toho* to see that they violated the company that created Godzilla's trust and legal agreement by the radical makeover for their monster.

Others argue *Toho* allegedly knew what was going on and just kept their mouths shut because the money was just too good to turn down. I think the truth lies in the middle.

"We should have released the image of Godzilla a couple of months before to get people used to it." Emmerich said. "I also would have changed a lot of the story points with the girl which didn't work as well as they should have. But I'm still proud of the whole look of the

movie. That's why I hired the same cinematographer, Ueli Steiger, for *The Day After Tomorrow."*

The 1998 *Godzilla* film blamed nuclear testing on THE FRENCH(?). Yes, those evil French and their Pacific islands testing did it. Iguanas were mutated from the nukes. Godzilla's trademark roar was remixed to incorporate more "animalistic sounds" according to the filmmakers. Did we really need that? The original Godzilla's roar was created from raking gloved fingers over piano strings, creating a sound that was iconic to the King of the Monsters. You can hear it in the T-Rex's roar in *The Last Dinosaur.*

During the Memorial Day weekend, *Godzilla* took in 74 million dollars. While still a good opening, *Sony* was extremely disappointed by the take. They were unsure if fans would like the redesign, and the movie in general, and were hoping that the advertising would net them a hefty sum before word of mouth killed it.

Rumors (more like threats when I think about it now) circulated Hollywood since the early 1990's of an American *Godzilla* movie. Writers and directors left the project and by 1996, *Toho* and *Sony/Tri Star* came to terms and the producing team of Dean Devlin and Roland Emmerich were anointed to bring an all-American Godzilla film to the US masses.

Godzilla would attack New York City; it would boast a big name cast and incorporate state of the art visual effects. There would be no man in a giant rubber suit in this film since *Jurassic Park* raised the bar for giant reptilian creatures.

Breathing atomic radiation was eliminated in favor of flames borne from massive breath gusts from the creature. Hazy flame roiled over cars scattered like toys when the beast roars, but hardly coming close to anything radioactive. It's very clear these are orange flames coming from this lizard.

1984's *The Return of Godzilla* showed that the monster fed on radiation after he feasted on fallout from a nuclear power plant. Devlin and Emmerich's beast eats *tuna* and is even baited by the army into a tuna trap in the middle of the city. Their new Godzilla flees from helicopters and even dry humps a building. This lizard is a hermaphrodite where the original Godzilla was clearly stated as male.

Our Metrosexual creature is said to be in search of an ideal island to lay its eggs. Out of all the islands it had to choose from in the Pacific, it swims all the way to the other side of the globe to lay its eggs in the middle of the world's busiest and crowded island: Manhattan.

There isn't an original or creative moment in this entire film. *Godzilla* is an inflated *Jurassic Park* T-Rex running around New York City. When Godzilla jumps into the water and is chased around by a submarine, Emmerich and Devlin are quick to rip off *The Hunt for Red October* and *The Beast From 20,000 Fathoms*.

When Dr. Niko Tatopoulos (Matthew Broderick), Philippe Roache (Jean Reno), Animal (Hank Azaria) and Audrey (Maria Pitillo) discover Godzilla's lair in Madison Square Garden, the film wastes no time in ripping off *Alien* and more of *Jurassic Park*.

Makes perfect sense, right? But who cares–it's a summer blockbuster and you'll see it.

In the end the monster is dispatched by a few jet missiles after clumsily getting hung up in the Brooklyn Bridge's suspension cables. Like DeLaurentiis showed, the way to get audience reaction is torture animals and this animal dies a slow, sad death in front of Broderick in an *Old Yeller* style ending invoking the famous Dino DeLaurentiis *"King Kong-Jaws"* comparison: "Nobody cry when *Jaws* die, but when my Kong die...people cry!"

Toho is often victimized by many original Godzilla hardliners, but as I said earlier and the *Godzilla Database* confirmed, *Toho* was informed of every detail of the film including plot and script. Roland Emmerich went before *Toho* studios in Japan in 1997 and it was that year that Godzilla 1998 was set into motion. Yes, *Toho* gave some guidelines but they were informed of the changes and even stuff that went against the guidelines.

Reports vary on Toho's reaction. Dean Devlin said this about Toho's reaction to the new creature design. "They took a long time in deciding and then finally said, 'You know what? We don't even want to comment on it; we'll just say yes or no.' And then they said, 'We love this look, we love your idea and we back it 100%. Go do it.' Because it was so different, it was like a whole rebirth of Godzilla. I think they liked that," Roland Emmerich said.

Toho had a different take. The executives at *Toho* initially didn't find the new monster so easy to relate. When the American team first brought pictures of their version of Godzilla to Japan for *Toho's* approval two years ago, the Japanese executives were shocked. "It was so different we realized we couldn't make small adjustments," said Shogo Tomiyama, executive producer of the past six Godzilla films. "That left the major question of whether to approve it or not."[1]

When *Toho* saw Devlin and Emmerich's film, they allegedly flipped and took back the rights, vowing to never let America get its hands on their monster again. Less than two years later *Toho* released *Godzilla 2000* to help fix the damage to Godzilla's image by Devlin and Emmerich. They introduced a redesigned Godzilla who, for the first time ever, had greenish skin and purple dorsal spikes.

---

[1]   Valerie Reitman, Los Angeles Times, 1998

"The producer of the original, Tomoyuki Tanaka, was on his deathbed when his successor, Tomiyama, went to visit to explain the changes. Forbidden from taking any pictures outside the studio for fear of leaks, Tomiyama struggled to find the words to describe the new Godzilla. "I told him, 'It's similar to Carl Lewis, with long legs, and it runs fast," he recalled."[2]

In 2003 *Toho* released a new Godzilla film that broke away from their new "Millennium Series" as a standalone picture entitled *Godzilla, Mothra, King Ghidorah: All Out Monster Attack.* The new look of Godzilla was even better, taking the creature back to his original sinister look .They even whited out his eyes to give a sense of evil to the monster. The opening of *Godzilla: GMK* shows the *Japanese Defense Force* in a lecture over the possibility of Godzilla's return to ravage the country. A conversation between two officers during the lecture slams the 1998 film:

"Didn't the Americans encounter a similar creature in New York a few years ago?" "Yes… there was a giant monster. But that was not Godzilla."

Amen.

"That's not Godzilla," growled Kasuya [a Japanese filmgoer], 38, who wore his favorite shirt for the occasion–a black short-sleeve silk number emblazoned with yellow and orange Godzilla scenes. "He got killed with four missiles, but the Japanese Godzilla is almost bulletproof. And the Japanese Godzilla is handsome, but the American Godzilla is not." [3]

Godzilla '98 was made to make money–without respect for the culture and history that created the original film. If this had been

---

2   Ibid
3   Ibid

anything but a *Godzilla* film, it would have fared better in audience and critical reaction. It isn't even artistic. This movie is expensive and hollow–devoid of meaning and reformatted into a popcorn matinee film. Ishiro Honda and Tanaka's original was art *and* entertainment.

Now…does it "suck?" Hang on.

"The decision to make *Godzilla* an expensive effects film departs from the series' aesthetic and iconographic tradition, which even resisted stop-motion (as in *The Beast from 20,000 Fathoms* or the effect Tim Burton captured so marvelously using computer-generated imagery in *Mars Attacks!*).

The onslaught of exploitative digital effects effectively removes *Godzilla* from the world of juvenile pleasure — now it would need a gargantuan audience — leaving nothing of interest for any age. It's not a good adult movie; it's not a good kid's movie; it's not a good movie; it's not a movie. It's an Event." [4]

The Japanese original offers hope and faith in mankind at its conclusion even after the real-life horrors inflicted upon that country. Devlin and Emmerich's film offers nothing, not even entertainment. It has nothing to say.

It was a masterwork of marketing, advertising and product placement with the hope of massive merchandising opportunities. It is one of the few examples where Cynema was largely rejected by the audience that was awake enough to understand the bad bill of goods being offered.

Does it suck? No.

There are a number of things extremely positive about *Godzilla 1998*. The digital and model effects are outstanding and still hold up decades later. The film would have fared better had it been a

---

4   Gregory Solman, *Film Comment*, **1998**

Beast From 20,000 Fathoms remake, which is what is closer to than *Godzilla.*

That's about the best positive criticism I can give this film. The effects looked expensive and it functions well as a big monster movie save for its namesake. A lot of people worked on those effects and it showed. The acting? Overall lackluster with the exception of Jean Reno and Hank Azaria. One quote said this about Matthew Borderick's turn as a star action hero:

"Broderick's performance as a scientist trying to save New York City from a giant monster is lackluster and unconvincing, with his character feeling more like a caricature of a scientist rather than a believable one. His attempts at humor fall flat, and his lack of chemistry with the other actors makes for a dull and unengaging performance."[5]

Here's what I just laid out for you and it has everything to do with *The Last Dinosaur*—I just laid out a critically thought out criticism of the 1998 film. I didn't just lambast it as a Godzilla fan and I didn't like it. I gave a history of the film's production and cited where things got messed up and went in wrong directions.

I acknowledge positive things and even cite sources to support my statements. A lot of people worked on *Godzilla 1998* and they worked hard. While the director and producer's hearts and heads weren't in the right place, the crew's were. They did their job and they did it well.

Making a movie is a minor miracle. A lot has to happen before, during and after to get it done. Even the bad ones. The worst films are the ones that have everything they need to entertain and squander those resources for the sake of paydays or just not caring. Installing Devilin and Emmerich, two people who admit they had

---

5   Source unavailable. Compendium

no respect for Godzilla was a cynical move. All the studio wanted was an action dinosaur flick to generate *Jurassic Cash*.

"The *Sony* executive team that took over Godzilla was one of the worst cases of executive incompetence I have observed in my twenty year career. One of the golden assets of our time, which was hand-delivered to them, was managed as poorly and ineptly as anybody can manage an asset. They took a jewel and turned it into dust."[6]

Dean Devlin admitted that the central problem with the film and its poor reception was its script. "I know I screwed up my *Godzilla*," he said. "I'd be very happy if they pull it off and do a great one."[7] He was referring to the 2014 *Godzilla* by *Legendary Pictures* that was in production at that time.

No amount of money can fix a bad script. Write a bad one then put it into the hands of two of the biggest filmmakers in the industry who share a similar contempt for their property and you have an expensive disaster.

Toho was behind *Godzilla 1998* whether they want to admit it or not. They were also behind *The Last Dinosaur*, a Japanese-American co-production 21 years before *Godzilla '98*. In many ways, the expensive *Godzilla* remake wasn't all that different than *The Last Dinosaur* that was produced for a fraction of the 1998 film's budget.

With all of that money, you still have calls of terrible acting. With all of that money you have cries of foul from die hard Godzilla fans. With all of that money you have a terrible script, tone deaf filmmakers and a total mishandling of the intellectual property.

6   Aiken, Keith (May 31, 2015). "Godzilla Unmade: The History of Jan De Bont's Unproduced TriStar Film – Part 4 of 4". Sci-Fi Japan. Archived from the original on June 12, 2018. Retrieved March 8, 2016.

7   Vary, Adam B. (July 27, 2012). "Dean Devlin on the recently announced 'Godzilla' reboot: 'I know I screwed up my Godzilla'". Entertainment Weekly. Time. Archived from the original on October 6, 2014.

The same things have been leveled at *The Last Dinosaur*, a film made by people who did care if they entertained and with far less resources.

There are plenty of people, including Matthew Broderick, who have good things to say about *Godzilla '98*. The same goes for *The Last Dinosaur* and sometimes those positive things overlap in the way of "it's so bad it's good."

This is where I disagree. *Godzilla '98* isn't so bad it's good. It's just bad. It has some positive things, but I feel it was made in contempt of its fan base and audiences. *The Last Dinosaur*, despite its flaws (and there are plenty) was made to entertain and give a good time.

Both have good things about them and this book will list a number of positive things about *The Last Dinosaur*, because in the end, it doesn't "suck."

"Suck" is a base and lazy term that is a blanket dismissive statement for the ignorant. When I hear or see it used, it tells me that someone didn't want to put in the time to level an informed critique or assessment or they just don't know what they are talking about.

I didn't care for the last two *Halloween* films and while I *want* to say "they sucked" they didn't. There were a number of good things about them, including production value with *Halloween Kills* giving us a brilliant flashback to 1978 that eclipsed the entire film and made me feel I was watching some deleted scene from the original Carpenter classic.

The score in the 2018 reboot by Carpenter and his son Cody was stellar. The lighting, the effects…a lot of good stuff. The first twenty minutes of the 2018 film, *Halloween* were great before it fell apart and went right where the trailer told us it would go.

Just because you don't like something doesn't mean you are a "hater" or if you find some things that didn't work, needed improving, etc. doesn't affix that word to you.

I wrote this book to look at a film that gave me a considerable amount of joy as a kid and holds a warm spot in my memories. *The Last Dinosaur* is not an Academy Award winner and I never made it out to be.

It is fun as hell, though and I can't say that about a lot of the cynical content cranking onto streaming channels sucking up bandwidth. Sometimes movies are just bad. That's it.

Know the difference between "so bad it's good" and "bad." One is unintentional, the other is.

THE MANDELA EFFECT

"It doesn't hold up." You hear that a lot online and on social media when people discuss old movies or TV shows. They seem disappointed that what they thought was their favorite thing made a better memory than it did an actual movie or show.

This implies there is something wrong with our memory process where we didn't remember it like we thought we did or what we saw just wasn't that good. What caused that? Something else has to factor into the "doesn't hold up" factor.

I have said that sometimes a movie made better memories than an actual film.

"The Mandela Effect" is a recent "Internet Thing" where a large group of people believe that an event or detail from the past occurred differently than it actually did. The term was coined by blogger Fiona Broome, who named it after her memory of Nelson Mandela's death in the 1980s, despite him actually passing away in 2013.

The Mandela Effect is used to describe a variety of misremembered events, such as the spelling of brand names, the lyrics of songs, and the details of popular films and TV shows. Examples of the Mandela Effect include the belief that the children's book series is called "The Berenstein Bears" instead of "The Berenstain Bears," and that Darth Vader's famous line in *The Empire Strikes Back* is "Luke, I am your father," when he actually says, "No, I am your father."

There are various theories that attempt to explain the Mandela Effect, including alternate realities, time travel, and collective memory. Skeptics argue that the Mandela Effect can be explained by factors such as collective false memories, social influence, and the fallibility of human recall.

Growing up we used to do Bela Lugosi impressions as Count Dracula, threatening each other in some bad Hungarian accent, "I vant to suck your blood!"

It's funny, but the thing is Lugosi never said those words. He played Dracula only twice in his career and neither time did those words or anything close to them come out of his mouth. It never appears in Bram Stoker's original novel.

Where did we get that from? Friends of mine today will insist they saw Lugosi say it. They will try to name a film and being a horror filmmaker and having written a book on the genre, I shake my head and tell them they won't find it because it's just not there. It never was.

The Mandela Effect says a possible explanation for this is we are caught in parallel universe fluxes or on simpler terms, experiencing a "glitch in *The Matrix*." There are infinite other universes out there or a "multiverse" where things that happen here happen in endless combinations and outcomes in other planes of existence.

Sounds cool but I think the simpler explanation is remembering things wrong. We got the "I vant to suck your blood" thing from comedic parodies that went as viral as they possibly could back in the day. Syndicated comedy routines, a TV show, whatever…that was the line that caught on. Throw in *Count Chocula* of the monster breakfast cereals and other satire and we create some kind of collective wrong memory.

Cary Grant, the legendary actor, is often impersonated in his clipped delivery saying "Judy, Judy, Judy!" It is believed that the phrase may have originated from a scene in the 1940 film *Too Many Husbands*, in which Grant's character says "Judy, Judy, Judy" in reference to the character played by Jean Arthur. However, Grant's actual words in the scene are slightly different, and he never used the phrase again in any of his other films.

Grant's image as cool, suave and debonair helped further the impression as comedians and animated fare have all done send ups of Grant. Somewhere along the line, thanks to television, we adopted this as a mass false memory.

I will give my own personal account. I could swear when I saw *Jaws 2* in 1978 in movie theaters that the attack on the SCUBA diver toward the end of the film in the seaweed looked a certain way. I could swear the scene showed the guy swimming along to this giant underwater seaweed garden, chasing a lobster. The crustacean shot into the seaweed garden and the diver stuck his arm into the wall of green vegetation to grab his prey.

He withdrew his arm in the mouth of the giant Great White Shark. The shark was really white and it had the guy by the arm and wouldn't let go. When I saw the film again two years later, that's not what happened at all.

The shark never touched the diver. It did a quick jump scare and barreled out of the seaweed crop (more like dropped down out of it by the mechanical arm that held it), opened its mouth and left him alone. A *Boo!* moment.

It never touched the guy, let alone took him by his arm. The subsequent scenes showed the diver suffering from The Bends (air bubbles in the blood issue that can result from rising too fast to the surface). No one mentions or shows a wound to his arm.

I remembered it wrong. Nothing in the universe shifted and put me into another timeline. I was eleven years old and was already scared in that movie. I likely closed my eyes or saw only a flash of the scene and my mind reconstructed what I missed if I jumped or startled or whatever.

If you saw the film, you also know the shark is a two-toned grey and not bone white or anywhere near a solid light color. I remembered the scene wrong, but by repeating that incorrect image in my mind for two years I expected it for the repeat viewing and found myself surprised.

The Mandela Effect is bullshit. It's just something fun for people to throw around online.

So much for that.

Nostalgia. That is what colors our perceptions and expectations and shades our memories. Ever feel a warm way for a person or group of people you haven't seen in a long time, then when you get together you start to remember why you haven't seen them in such a long time? Maybe you feel even stronger about loving to see them. No matter which feeling is evoked, nostalgia fueled it.

Nostalgia is that longing or feeling of missing a certain time, people, things, events that triggers your brain into thinking about the things that brought you pleasure and positive thoughts. It's also where the "we walked uphill in snow for miles both ways to school" mentality comes from.

I am a nostalgic person. I was a nostalgic kid. By the time I was ending my eighth grade year I was missing it and even seventh grade. Middle school was a very positive time in my life. I was only 14 and believed those years were my good old days.

There were no good old days. My grandmother used to go on and on about how great the 30s and 40s were. When I got older I threw some critical thinking at her. "Nanny, you had Polio, Tuberculosis, Iron lungs, The Spanish Flu, The Great Depression, Hitler, World War II…" I went on with my list.

Yeah, those sounded like great times. War, disease, unemployment and starvation were a grand old time. She would wave an angry hand at me which told me to just shut up. She didn't want pesky facts clouding her nostalgia.

I was always aware of time and its passing. Once my life stabilized when we moved to Stroudsburg, PA, I didn't want that stability to go away. I preserved every moment that I could. I walked around our development with a *Kodak* film camera taking pictures of the sky, the clouds and mountainside knowing it would all look different one day. I was preserving those memories in case I didn't sear them into my brain.

By ninth grade I missed late night *HBO* programming. Old horror films, holiday specials like *Rich Little's A Christmas Carol* and *Emmett Otter's Jug Band Christmas*. It was only a few years since I saw them for the first time, but for me it felt like decades.

These movies and shows brought warm feelings, good memories, just like old family reunions and positive personal events. Over time it's scientifically proven our brains suppress bad memories and unpleasantness. It's a survival technique.

This is why my grandmother looked back on the 30s and 40s with affection. Her brain filed away all the bad stuff. I have found mine doing the same thing as I grew older too.

We do the same thing with our movies and TV. We have deep affections for things that made up our childhood. Some of these things "hold up" after years of not seeing them.

For me, a show like *The Mary Tyler Moore Show* doesn't just hold up, it might be even better now than when it was made. I understand the humor better, but now as an adult I also appreciate just how damned good the writing was.

The movie *Network* still "holds up." In fact, it's more important in its message of media and entertainment's fusing than ever. *The Bride of Frankenstein, King Kong 1933, Jaws, Star Wars, Invasion of the Body Snatchers 1979*...I can keep going...these films are still fantastic and powerful. There are so many more and I am sure you can add to this list.

I was just talking to someone the other day who said he revisited the old 70s *Incredible Hulk* TV show with Bill Bixby and Lou Ferigno and found that it "wasn't as good as I remembered. Actually, it was pretty damned bad." He was saddened to tell me this because the show brought him such joy as a kid.

I told him I got what he was saying as I decided to catch some old *Six Million Dollar Man* episodes. They were once awe inspiring to me. Now they were laughable.

They didn't "hold up."

Stick with me here, because all of this leads to *The Last Dinosaur* and I think some of you know where I am going with all of this.

Movies are not just content to be consumed. They are experiences. Even the so bad they're good ones. *Mystery Science Theater* understands this.

It's not about watching something on a phone or computer. It's about sharing an experience with others. My first book, *This Time It's Personal* is about that very thing. Some of the horror films I wrote about didn't "hold up" decades after I saw them. Some were just not scary anymore, but that's because

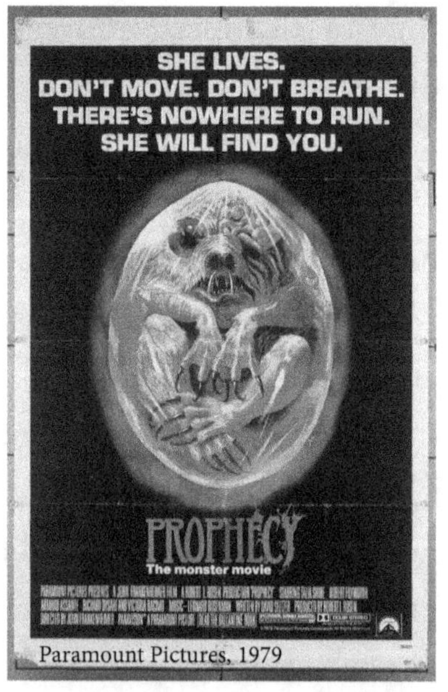

Paramount Pictures, 1979

my experiences changed and shaped me into someone different than the kid who saw those things for the first time.

A few of the "so bad it's good" ones still held up. The one I am going to use to underscore my enjoyment of *The Last Dinosaur* is 1979's monster movie, *Prophecy.*

Unlike *The Last Dinosaur* (which premiered two years before this mess) *Prophecy* had a healthy studio budget. Its screenwriter, David Seltzer, was coming off the massive success of *The Omen* and penned this eco-horror monster movie.

Both *Prophecy* and *The Last Dinosaur* shared some interesting similarities. They boasted big, rubbery, dopey monsters. They had well-known male stars obsessed with the creatures in their films. The actors of both films are chased through dense forests and nature. Nature strikes back and man vs. nature are their themes. They had high profile men known for their drinking. *Prophecy's* director, the legendary John Frankenheimer of *The Manchurian Candidate* fame was said to have been shitfaced every day onset. Before his death he confessed he didn't remember a whole lot about making the movie due to his drunken state.

The Last Dinosaur's star, Richard Boone was well-known for his alcohol consumption. It's said his wife smuggled watered down vodka to him onset and he took more than three-martini lunches and was almost checked out after lunch time. The filmmakers tried to get everything they could out of Richard before lunch.

Director Tom Kotani knew about the vodka but backed up Benni Korzen in saying it had little to no effect on Boone's performance. It made him even more natural. Kotani said watching Boone act you could see "the wheels turning" in his head. [8]

I saw *Prophecy* in the theater during the summer of 1979, a year seen as a golden one for horror movies. The giant mutant bear

---

8   *The Last Dinosaur, Special Edition DVD.* Commentary by Masumi Sekiya, Tom Kotani. 2009. *Toho Video.*

movie kicked off a summer filled with *The Amityville Horror, Dawn of the Dead* and *Alien* for me.

I walked five miles one way with some friends to catch the first, opening day matinee of *Prophecy*. Our pockets had money; we bought too much popcorn, candy and soda and found ourselves to have the theater almost to ourselves.

I thought for sure it would be sold out. Instead there might've been fifty people aside from us in that theater. We got our money's worth because the film went from something we thought would scare the shit out of us to something that had us outright laughing and applauding at the end.

To this day it is the best movie-going experience I ever had because those other people in the theater were laughing just as loud and hard as us. By the time it was over, I knew I would see it again. I saw it two more times in the theater and when it hit *HBO* a year later, I watched it every time I could on that schedule. It was that much fun.

Now, does it "hold up?" I watched it again before writing this book and I can say it does indeed hold up and is just as good-bad as the time I sat in that dark theater 40 years ago. I still laugh, I still enjoy and most of all…I still remember that hot, bright sunny afternoon walking a busy highway to go see it at the mall with good friends.

I still remember the cool, orange burned fall skies and nights when it came on *HBO*. I was in love with a girl named Dina White and I was making my first feature film with a wonderful teacher who taught filmmaking at our school. Life just couldn't have been better and I associate those times with *Prophecy*.

That's the power of nostalgia.

I associate similar warm and good feelings with *The Last Dinosaur* just as I associate those positives with after school watchings of *Ultraman*, *The Space Giants* and *Johnny Sokko and His Flying Robot*.

When I think of those shows or Godzilla movies I think of climbing those slate mountains; destroying giant snow skyscrapers at the edge of my yard and the road, pretending to be some Kaiju while a friend was Ultraman, Goldar or Giant Robot. I was always Godzilla and I would use the cold air to create frosty exhales which served as my atomic breath.

I remember innocence and being carefree.

Reality painted a different picture. Those times as a kid, loving Godzilla and those Japanese Kaiju shows took me away from the abuse inflicted on me from my mother's boyfriend. They distracted me from rats in our basement and pantry, our constant financial problems and being bullied in school.

The Good Old Days weren't always so good.

The movies and TV shows however helped make it that way in retrospect.

Prophecy came at a time when life was turning around for me. I moved to a new school the summer before, had all new friends, was finding my way and my mother's abusive boyfriend was dead. I had a great, new stepfather who saved my childhood.

THAT'S why I love *Prophecy*. That dumb monster movie reminds me of hope and enjoyment from a time when I really enjoyed being a kid.

That's not a Mandela Effect. No events changed. It's just how I chose to remember things and how my brain worked to keep me surviving. It made me love things like these bad movies because they brought me comfort and while my mind worked overtime to file away the bad memories; these films helped to fill in the gaps and keep me balanced.

When I think of *King Kong Escapes* I think of my grandmother's warm house, the smell of toast and cocoa in the air, lying on my belly under an end table with my feet warming on the heat vent while the furnace forced hot air over me.

I remember watching it on her color console TV which was way better than ours at home. I remember her sitting in this big, blue chair watching the film with me while crocheting and talking with me. She would say she loved me at least several times throughout the film.

How can you dislike *King Kong Escapes* with those memories attached to it?

If you're watching movies in solitude, crunched on tiny screens or worse yet, skipping through them in 10, 20 or 30 second intervals, you're not getting the full experience and that's sad. Maybe that's why you forget about a lot of what you watched because these things have no connection with you and your life.

That's not how film should be experienced.

The Last Dinosaur takes me back to a certain time when things in my life were changing for the better. The movie is a movie of transition for me.

I am excited to share these feelings with you as we go forward because *The Last Dinosaur* "holds up."

★★★★☆ **Classic B-Movie**
Reviewed in the United States 🇺🇸 on January 8, 2020
Verified Purchase
Hard to believe Rankin/Bass did this. Love my Sci-Fi, Horror, Monster, etc... B-Movies.

THE DINOSAUR MOVIE

America has had a love affair with the dinosaur movie, which could be argued that the Kaiju film was actually born in the United States. ("Actually…")

The dinosaur movie genre dates back to the silent era of cinema, with 1925's silent film *The Lost World*, directed by Harry O. Hoyt. Based on the novel by Sir Arthur Conan Doyle, the film tells the story of an expedition to a remote plateau in South America where prehistoric creatures still exist. *The Lost World* is the first American film and perhaps the first in the world to use stop-motion animation techniques as the central effect to bring its dinosaurs to life, creating a sensation at the box office. Seven years earlier, the 1918 *Ghost of Slumber Mountain* employed stop motion pioneered by a young man named Willis O'Brien who went on to do the effects for *The Lost World*. O'Brien was royally screwed by the film's producer Herbert Dawley who hijacked O'Brien's work, claiming it to be his own and failing to pay O'Brien properly after hacking the original dinosaur movie to pieces.

The Lost World is a dinosaur run amok in a city movie. It's not a Kaiju film but it hints of things to come in the Japanese monster genre. It starts with the discovery of a "land lost in time" complete with cavemen (called an "Apeman" in the film), a T-Rex and a brontosaurus that ends up in the streets of London, creating havoc until it falls into the Thames River and swims away.

Stop motion animation was the CGI of its time. The technique was used to create the illusion of movement by animating physical objects frame-by-frame. It involves taking photographs of a physical model or puppet, moving it slightly, and then taking another photograph. When these photographs are played back in sequence, the model appears to be moving.

In the case of 1925's *The Lost World* and 1933's *King Kong*, stop-motion animation was used to bring prehistoric creatures to life on the screen. The process involved creating physical models of the creatures, often made of metal armatures covered in foam latex, and animating them using stop-motion techniques.

To create a stop-motion animation sequence, the animators would first develop a storyboard or script for the scene, detailing the movements and actions of the creatures. They would then

Young Willis O'Brien (top) and crew animating dinosaurs for *The Lost World*.

create a miniature set, often consisting of detailed backgrounds and foregrounds that would be used as a backdrop for the animation.

The creature models were placed on the set, and the animators would take a photograph. They would then slightly adjust the position of the creature, take another photograph, and repeat this process until they had captured all of the necessary frames for the sequence.

In order to achieve the illusion of movement and fluid motion, the animators would often shoot at a lower frame rate than the standard 24 frames per second used in most films. For example, in

King Kong, animator Willis O'Brien shot at a rate of 12 frames per second, which allowed for more subtle and nuanced movements.

Once the stop-motion animation sequences were complete, they would be combined with live-action footage using a process called compositing, which involved layering the animation on top of the live-action footage and blending the two together using various techniques, such as matte painting or rear projection.

The animation was later processed to be superimposed into real human actor action mixed with fake sets and even large prosthetic limbs that helped convince the audience this was the real deal.

While seen as cartoonish and laughable by today's standards, it was setting the standards when it all debuted and revolutionized filmmaking special effects.

Almost 30 years before *Godzilla*, a giant brontosaurus attacked a modern city with the authorities trying to dispatch it. *The Lost World* was a hit and that success brought imitators.

One of those imitators was the 1933 classic *King Kong*, directed by Merian C. Cooper and Ernest B. Schoedsack. While *Kong* is not a true dinosaur movie, as the titular creature is a giant ape, it does feature several dinosaur-like creatures that inhabit the mysterious Skull Island including (you guessed it) a T-Rex.

That Willis O'Brien "kid" who did the stop motion effects for *The Lost* World hit his peak with *King Kong*. Once again modern-day explorers find a land (this time Skull Island instead of a South American mountain plateau) populated with prehistoric flora and fauna.

They also found a "Big Bad" in the form of a giant ape called King Kong who is worshipped as a god, subdue him and bring him back to a city; this time around it's New York instead of London.

Kong breaks free, runs amok, and destroys some property before being shot off the top of the Empire State Building by airplane gunners. Not technically a Kaiju film, 1933's *King Kong* does have the elements that will be hallmark of the coming Japanese genre.

Kong is considered a god, a spiritual beast and even a punisher of men who go against nature. The ape exhibits no supernatural abilities. He has no laser or flying power, but he is powerful and strong and he has a weakness for blondes.

The film's groundbreaking special effects, which again blended stop-motion animation and live-action footage, were a major influence on the dinosaur movies that followed. For me, it's still the best *King Kong* movie with *Legendary Pictures Kong Skull Island* right behind it.

One of those imitator films was the real inspiration for *Godzilla 1998--The Beast from 20,000 Fathoms,* a 1953 creature feature directed by Eugene Lourie. The film features a prehistoric creature, awakened by a nuclear bomb, rampaging through New York City. The *Beast from 20,000 Fathoms* is notable for its use of a live-action model for its monster, rather than full reliance on stop-motion animation.

This film hit less than a year before 1954's *Godzilla.* While *The Beast from 20,0000 Fathoms* was a flesh and blood beast and not seen as a god; the creature does have a mythic kind of aura to it, awakened by atomic power and imbued with the ability to poison humans with radiation as a super weapon.

It will be 1954's *Gojira* (The proper spelling pronunciation of the monster's name) that will officially kick off the Kaiju genre. *Godzilla* is seen as a punisher for the sins of man. Born of atomic testing or reawakened by it, *Godzilla* was seen as a god by the residents of Odo Island. His rampages through Japan invoke the horrors of World War II and allied fire bombings as well as the two nuclear bomb drops that happened less than five years before the film's release.

While stop motion was used for some parts of 1954's *Gojira* (*Godzilla*), the cost of the process was prohibitive to *Toho Studios* who turned to "suitmation" as the best way to realize their monster.

The suitmation process involved creating a physical suit or costume for the monster, and filming an actor in the suit interacting with miniature sets and models.

To create the Gojira suit, special effects artist Eiji Tsuburaya and his team sculpted a foam rubber body and head over a metal framework, with the details and textures of the suit added using various materials such as latex and paint.

Accounts vary, but the suit was estimated to weigh over 200 pounds, requiring an actor of physical substance to endure being inside of it. Holes were drilled into the fingers of the creature to allow the actor's sweat to drip out. Ventilation pipes were snaked inside the suit to allow cooling and actor Haruo Nakajima is said to have lost over 20 pounds playing the legendary monster.

The costume had limited vision and restricted movement for the actor inside. Despite these challenges, Nakajima was able to bring a sense of realism and personality to the character through his movements and expressions.

The miniature sets used in the film were meticulously crafted, with great attention to detail in order to create the illusion of a massive scale. These sets were filmed separately from the actors in the suit, with the camera and lighting carefully positioned to match the perspective of the suit actor.

Puppetry was also employed to give detailed close-ups of the beast as the suit's head was not able to deliver detailed animation. This was still before remote robotics were developed to give animatronic realism to otherwise stiff and single expression masks and prosthetics.

Toho Studios employed Eiji Tsuburaya's special effects company and both would go on to produce *The Last Dinosaur* 23 years later.

After reading all of this and processing it, do you still think these monster movies "suck?" There's a lot of energy and resources put into "suck" don't you think?

An autographed still from the original *Gojira* autographed by original suit actor Haruo Nakajima hangs on my office wall as I write this. I once taught high school history and used Godzilla as part of my post-World War II lessons. I taught how the Japanese created the monster as a metaphor for their suffering in the wake of the atomic bombings of Hiroshima and Nagasaki.

I showed them the original 1954 *Gojira* in its native Japanese language with subtitles. I did not show the bastardized American 1955 cut, *King of the Monsters* with actor Raymond Burr edited into make him a central American character appeal to American audiences.

I showed the film like a theatrical experience, complete with widescreen LCD projection, surround sound and a dark room. When the lights came up these teenagers had a very different impression of Godzilla.

One girl simply said, "It was so damned sad. I wasn't expecting that."

She expected to laugh. While they were too young to have seen John Belushi (most didn't even know who Belushi was) host *Godzilla vs. Megalon,* the after effect of that and years of Saturday afternoon creature features with their parents and people my age brought them up believing Godzilla was Grade Z entertainment. It existed only as comedy and the stuff of *Mystery Science Theater.*

Perhaps the worst explanation was they grew up with the 1998 *Tri-Star Godzilla* (GINO or Zilla) as their only example of Godzilla. The original 1954 film hit them in ways they did not expect, especially in the wake of 9-11 which was only a few years earlier.

Godzilla didn't suck anymore to my students. Just like that. They watched a film filled with allegories to the horrors of war, national tragedy and human suffering. When I explained the scene of the woman holding her children, preparing to die as Tokyo goes up in flames around her, they sat silent. Director Ishiro Honda said that scene came from his own experience in the war, when he saw a similar scene of a mother about to perish with her children during the allied fire bombings of the city.

"It was so damned sad."

They got it. They saw past the old effects. They even got through the subtitles and the whole film being black and white. The story transported them into the Kaiju world and they suspended their disbelief.

Again…you can't CGI a bad script.

RISE OF THE KAIJU MOVIE

It's time to properly define the "Kaiju" genre although most of you reading this book know what it is. You know its origins and that hundreds of books have been published on it. This brief history is for those who think it "sucks" and find the effects and results laughable and easily dismissed.

I have posited that nostalgia is the driving force behind our love for B-movies. B-movie monster movies have played an important role in the history of cinema and popular culture. They have shaped our movie going experience. They have also given us great, Oscar-winning filmmakers who cut their teeth and made their bones on B-movies.

Without Roger Corman and his ultra-cheap *Little Shop of Horrors* we might not have had Jack Nicholson. Without B-movie schlockmeisters like Corman, William Castle, and Samuel Z. Arkoff, we might never have experienced Francis Ford Coppola, Jonathan Demme or the legion of actors and filmmakers hired or inspired by all of these people, their companies and films.

While many B films may not be critically acclaimed, these movies often hold a special place in the hearts of moviegoers and genre fans, and have inspired countless filmmakers and artists. Without *Godzilla* Spielberg may never have come to *Jaws* or *Jurassic Park.*

Aside from nostalgia, one of the key reasons for the enduring popularity of B-movie monster movies is the way in which they allow for a creative exploration of the unknown and the fantastic. These movies often feature imaginative creatures and scenarios that push the boundaries of what we consider being possible, and can serve as a way for viewers to escape the mundane realities of everyday life.

B-movie monster movies often feature a level of camp and absurdity that is hard to find in other genres. Whether it's the cheesy special effects, the over-the-top acting, or the ridiculous plotlines, these movies have a charm and personality that is all their own, and can be incredibly entertaining to watch.

This was the case for me with 1979's *Prophecy*. It still is.

Furthermore, B-movie monster movies have been influential in shaping the horror and science fiction genres as we know them today. Many of the tropes and archetypes that we associate with these genres, such as the "mad scientist" or the "giant monster rampaging through the city," can be traced back to the B-movie monster movies of the 1950s and 60s.

Amazing what you can get from just a little bit of history, isn't it?

**Japanese puppeteers work their magic onstage
with the artistry of Banraku.**

To understand the influence of Kaiju movies, we must look to the traditional Japanese art of *Bunraku*. Bunraku is a form of puppet theater that has been performed in Japan for over 300 years and involves intricate puppets, or "ningyō," operated by puppeteers who are visible on stage.

This art form originated in Japan in the early 17th century, during the Edo period. Its ningyō were fused with those multiple puppeteers, who worked together to bring the characters to life. Bunraku plays often dealt with themes of honor, loyalty, and the struggles of the common people.

Puppetry is highly valued in Japan for its craftsmanship and attention to detail. Puppet makers spend years honing their skills and creating intricate designs, resulting in puppets that are often considered works of art in their own right.

In the world of Japanese film and television, puppets and animatronics are often used to create creatures and characters that would be impossible or impractical to film using live actors or computer-generated imagery. This has led to a long tradition of puppetry in the realm of science fiction and fantasy, including the Kaiju films that feature giant monsters like Godzilla and Gamera.

I saw something like this as a kid in elementary school for a puppet stage production of *The Nutcracker*. Live actors worked onstage around puppeteers dressed all in black, like movie Ninjas, who held marionettes and other intricate puppets by black poles with invisible strings to create the illusion the things were alive. I was fascinated by it and never saw anything like it.

Bunraku has had a profound influence on Japanese culture and art, and its impact can be seen in a variety of mediums, including Kaiju movies. Godzilla, the most famous Kaiju, has been described as a modern-day version of the Japanese dragon, or "ryu." Like the dragon, Godzilla is powerful, destructive, and difficult to control.

Other Kaiju, such as Mothra and King Ghidorah, draw on other Japanese myths and legends. I will lay that out in a moment.

One of the key figures in this influence was the Bunraku Japanese puppet master, Takeda Tetsuya. Takeda was known for his innovative use of puppetry techniques, which included the use of mechanisms to create realistic movements and expressions in the puppets. His influence on Kaiju movies can be seen in the way that filmmakers have used special effects to bring their monsters to life on the big screen.

I mentioned in the previous chapter that the 1954 *Gojira* implemented hand puppetry along with stop motion and suitmation to bring its Kaiju monster to life. This is the influence of Bunraku. Puppetry will be used through all Kaiju films to the present day.

The intricate movements and expressions of the puppets, combined with the live narration and music, create a captivating and immersive experience for the audience.

Another important figure in the influence of Bunraku on Kaiju movies is the artist, Kawanabe Kyōsai. Kawanabe was a prolific artist who was known for his depictions of demons and other supernatural beings. His artwork was a major influence on the design of Kaiju monsters, which often feature fantastical and otherworldly characteristics.

The Eastern preference for our giant monsters and dinosaurs seems to be born of realism. The goal of 1925's *The Lost World* and O'Brien's *Ghost of Sleepy Mountain* was to recreate the extinct beasts as accurately as possible. O'Brien went to such lengths he consulted with the archaeologist who discovered the first T-Rex bones.

1933's *King Kong* went further. It was reported some filmgoers fainted when Kong first appeared onscreen, overwhelmed by the realism playing out on a 60 foot movie screen. While O'Brien's sets have their own feel, they were always meant to blend in with the actors and evoke realistic jungles, mountains and cities.

This would continue through the 1940s and 50s where Ray Harryhausen's stop motion work would also lean more toward realism than surrealism. Both the monsters and their backgrounds would lean more toward realistic depictions than abstract. Even Harryhausen's work on the foreign *Sinbad* and *Jason and the Argonauts* films went for a matchup of real vistas with the ones created for his animated creatures and figures.

I was exposed to Russian filmmaking as a boy when some channel aired a movie based on Russian tall tales or fairy tales that went for a cartoonish, abstract look for its miniatures and creatures. The filmmakers were not trying to mimic reality and instead went for a more artistic approach as some big, pink whale moved through an ocean that was clearly a pool with a hand painted backdrop of pastel colors and odd lighting for sunset.

Japanese filmmakers and audiences have a long history of preferring surrealism over realism, especially in the Kaiju genre of filmmaking. This preference for surrealism is rooted in several cultural and historical factors, including Japan's unique relationship with nature, its history of trauma and disaster, and its tradition of myth and folklore.

One of the key reasons Japanese audiences are drawn to surrealism is their deep connection to nature. Japan is a country that is both geographically and culturally isolated, with a rich tradition of animism that sees all things as imbued with a spiritual essence.

This has led to a fascination with the natural world, and a desire to explore its mysteries and complexities. In many ways, Kaiju films are an extension of this fascination, as they allow filmmakers to create fantastical creatures that embody the awesome power and majesty of nature.

In the 1954 *Gojira* the eponymous monster is portrayed as a force of nature, a symbol of Japan's trauma and a warning against the dangers of nuclear power. The film's surreal elements, such as the giant monster rampaging through the streets of Tokyo, are used to heighten the sense of dread and horror, while also underscoring the destructive power of nature.

The Japanese had enough realism just nine years before in the wake of the fire and atomic bombings of their country. The filmmakers took a more abstract approach to their monster movie.

The first time we see Godzilla onscreen is when he rises over a beach hillside in front of Emiko Yamane, and it is…a puppet. It's not Nakajima in the suit rising up, but rather a puppet used for Godzilla's debut.

Kaiju films often tap into these themes of natural disaster by depicting giant monsters that destroy cities and wreak havoc on human civilization. However, they also often include surreal or fantastical elements, such as time travel, alternate dimensions, or alien invasions. By blending these elements together, Kaiju films allow audiences to explore their fears and anxieties in a safe and controlled environment, while also offering a sense of catharsis and release.

Japanese audiences are drawn to surrealism because of their rich tradition of myth and folklore. Japan has a long history of storytelling, with a vast array of myths, legends, and fairy tales that have been passed down from generation to generation. Many of these stories feature fantastic creatures and supernatural beings, such as dragons, oni (demons), and yokai (spirits).

The Kaiju genre draws on this tradition by incorporating elements of myth and folklore into their stories. For example, in the film *Mothra* (1961), the female monster is portrayed as a guardian of the natural world, a kind of divine protector who battles against evil and destruction. By tapping into these mythic elements, Kaiju films offer audiences a sense of connection to their cultural heritage, while also allowing them to explore their imaginations and push the boundaries of what is possible. Mothra herself was a giant, elaborate puppet-marionette.

The new *Legendary Pictures* "Monsterverse" continues in this Kaiju tradition. Godzilla is here to bring balance to the earth in these new films. Ancient pictures depict these creatures as gods and Godzilla is the king of them all…a Kaiju Zeus that all other monsters bow before. The 2014 reboot kept his nuclear origins, but also made his foes two creatures that were a threat to the natural balance of the earth.

At the conclusion of 2019's *King of the Monsters*, the end credit sequence shows the Kaiju restoring the earth with their radiation. Green areas reappear, waters are cleaned and the negative impact of man on nature is mitigated.

Mothra is seen as "The Queen of the Monsters" in the 2019 film; with mysterious resurrection powers that bring Godzilla back from the dead with Mothra sacrificing her own life-- martyrdom, to save her fallen king and…our savior.

Ghidorah is a disruptor in this film. He's been one through the previous series as well with the exception of one film. He is also seen as a god that came from the sky—a space alien that does not belong here, making him Godzilla's ultimate foe.

2003's *Godzilla: GMK* reinvented Godzilla as a true supernatural beast, infused with the spirit of Japan's war dead, seeking revenge on the society that sent them to their doom. Mothra, Baragon and

Ghidorah were reinvented as "Guardian Monsters" to protect Japan and the world from a resurgent Godzilla.

The religious aspect is clear and where the Kaiju genre dovetails with Shintoism.

Shintoism, a traditional religion in Japan, plays a significant role in this genre. Shintoism is based on the belief in *kami*, or spirits, that are present in all natural phenomena. These spirits are often associated with specific places or objects, such as trees, rocks, or mountains. Again, *Godzilla: GMK* illustrates this beautifully.

Shintoism does not have a single founder, nor does it have a holy book or creed. Instead, it is a complex and diverse set of beliefs and practices that have evolved over time. The religion espouses the idea that there is an inherent divinity in all things, including animals, plants, and natural phenomena such as mountains, rivers, and the sun.

While there is not a direct correlation between Shinbutsu-shugo and Kaiju films, it is possible to draw a connection between the two based on the idea of blending different elements.

Harmony…that's what the religion stresses. Harmony with the *kami*, or spirits, that are believed to inhabit the natural world. These spirits are revered as protectors and guardians, and are often associated with specific places such as shrines or natural landmarks.

The Last Dinosaur made it clear Masten and his troupe are not supposed to be there. They are a threat to natural harmony. They are invaders, intruders and they defiled the land from the moment they popped the hatch on that Polar Borer.

Shintoism also places great importance on ancestral worship, with many families maintaining household altars or visiting ancestral gravesites to pay their respects.

Its influence can be seen throughout Japanese culture, from its architecture and art to its festivals and traditions. While it has traditionally been a part of Japanese life, it is not exclusive to the Japanese people, and many people around the world have found value in its teachings and practices.

Buddhism and Shintoism have coexisted in Japan for centuries, and as a result, the two religions have influenced each other in various ways. This blending of the two religions is sometimes referred to as Shinbutsu-shugo and refers to the blending of Buddhist and Shinto beliefs and practices, which has resulted in a unique religious tradition in Japan. Similarly, Kaiju films blend different elements together, such as science fiction, horror, and action, to create a distinctive genre of Japanese cinema.

The Kaiju genre gives us monsters often depicted as embodiments of natural forces, such as earthquakes, typhoons, or volcanic eruptions. They are not simply mindless beasts, but rather powerful, supernatural beings that are intimately connected to the natural world. The destruction that they cause is not simply a result of their size and strength, but also of their connection to the powerful forces of nature.

It is clear that *The Last Dinosaur's* T-Rex is more than just a dumb animal as Richard Boone's Masten Thrust first believes. Only later in the film does Thrust come to realize he just might be the one being tracked and hunted. The T-Rex is a force of nature and maybe even the embodiment of all the dinosaurs that lived in that arctic oasis.

1991's *Godzilla vs. Biollante* gave us a Kaiju created from the DNA of both a rose and a human being, fused with Godzilla's cells. She is explicitly referred to as a "god" in the film in which she appears.

In 1963's *King Kong vs. Godzilla* the two monsters are portrayed as being akin to two ancient gods, locked in an eternal battle for dominance. This was repeated in the recent *Godzilla vs Kong* remake from *Legendary's* "Monsterverse."

Similarly, in the non-*Toho* Kaiju film *Gamera: Guardian of the Universe*, the titular giant, flying turtle (*Daiei Studios* answer to Godzilla) is described as being "born from the Earth" and is depicted as a guardian spirit, protecting the natural world and children from human threats.

One of the earliest Japanese Kaiju movies was *Jigoku no Kengō* (1938), which featured a giant squid attacking a ship. However, it was not until the 1950s that the genre truly took off with *Godzilla*, which became a cultural phenomenon and spawned a long-running franchise.

The Kaiju genre took a gradual turn toward kid entertainment throughout the Showa series. This is seen with the *Godzilla* franchise. 1963's *King Kong vs. Godzilla* was mostly played for laughs with the focus being on two franchise characters, symbols of their respective cultures, in a battle royale to the finish. It went downhill from there with monster mash ups and the focus moving more toward children audiences for a wider appeal.

The original dark tones of the 1954 film faded along with the memories of the war as Japan rebuilt and became incredibly prosperous and powerful in the post-war era.

Kaiju movies took on a darker tone in the late 80s and 90s and focused more on the human characters and their struggles to stop the monsters. This can be seen in films like *The Return of Godzilla* (1984) and *Godzilla vs. King Ghidorah* (1993). The latter was a damning indictment of post-war capitalism and American imperialism and was deemed on this side of the Pacific as "Anti-American" by some politicians and Godzilla fans. Godzilla was seen in that film as a protector of Japanese troops during the war and then mutated by the American atom bomb to return as an angry god to the Japanese.

I'll bet you never gave much thought to this very cursory overview of the Kaiju film. Keep all of this in mind and go back to revisit *The Last Dinosaur* and I guarantee you're gonna see it differently. It still might not transform into a "good movie" but I'll bet it "sucks" less.

This chapter closes out with Japanese society's affinity for the surreal and abstract in their entertainment. Puppetry is part of it for sure. The Japanese film industry has a long history of utilizing theatrical sets and visual effects in their movies, rather than striving for strict realism. This preference for artifice and stylization in Japanese film can be traced back to various cultural, historical, and artistic factors.

Many Japanese found the 1998 *Godzilla* "too real" and devoid of spirit. Their perception was a monster made of digital bits and bytes with no anthropomorphic characteristics like the original films. Devlin and Emmerich wrongly kicked the concept of making their *Godzilla* with human characteristics to the curb. This was a fatal mistake in the film's reception Stateside as well.

No one on either side of the globe wanted to see Godzilla as a giant lizard running AWAY from the military while trying lay eggs. Just what the hell was that shit?

One factor for the Japanese love of style is the influence of traditional Japanese theater, such as Noh and Kabuki, which heavily utilize stylized sets and costumes to create an otherworldly and dreamlike atmosphere. Japanese filmmakers have often drawn inspiration from these theatrical traditions and have carried over their use of visual stylization and artificiality to their films.

Another factor is the role of film in Japanese culture. Japanese cinema has often been seen as a form of escapism and entertainment, and audiences have traditionally been more interested in the emotional resonance and artistic expression of the film, rather than strict realism. This has allowed Japanese filmmakers to experiment with different styles and techniques, and to create fantastical, dreamlike worlds that are more representative of their artistic vision and emotional impact, rather than strict realism.

Japanese filmmakers have often been constrained by limited budgets and resources, which has led them to rely on visual effects and stylized sets as a cost-effective way to create visually striking and memorable films.

It is worth noting that this preference for stylization and artifice is not unique to Japanese cinema, and can be seen in many other artistic traditions around the world (like the Russian whale movie I mentioned). In many cases, the use of stylization and visual effects can actually enhance the emotional impact and resonance of the film, creating a heightened sense of reality that is more effective than strict realism.

Many Americans grew up watching Kaiju films on television, and have fond memories of the characters and stories. For some, these films represent a simpler time in their lives and watching them can be a way to reconnect with their childhood. This makes American audiences more accepting of the surreal sets and soundstage work, but this is seen more as "allowing for" poor quality instead of understanding that it's not.

Throw the following ingredients into the nostalgia stewpot and you get a great recipe for monster movie enjoyment:

1. Spectacle: Kaiju films are known for their spectacular special effects and over-the-top action sequences. Watching giant monsters battling each other and destroying cities on the big screen can be a thrilling and exciting experience for many viewers. Many Americans love the over-the-top antics, the totally fantastical action and elements that break free from the confines of realism. In other words: fun.

2. Escapism: Kaiju films provide a form of escapism for viewers, allowing them to temporarily forget about their problems and immerse themselves in a fantastical world where anything is possible.

3. Cultural exchange: American audiences are often fascinated by Japanese culture, and Kaiju films provide a window into that culture. These films are an opportunity to experience a different perspective on storytelling and filmmaking, and to learn about the cultural influences that have shaped the genre.

Kaiju movies and the TV shows gave me my first, in-depth look into other cultures and their worlds. I got to see how Japanese families lived, ate, worked. I saw their smaller homes or apartments and I got a look at their cities (before they were stomped into dust).

Despite their fantastical elements, Kaiju films often explore universal themes such as the consequences of scientific experimentation, the dangers of technology, and the importance of cooperation and communication. In other words, there was and is something binding about these films with all of us no matter where we are across the globe.

1967's *Destroy All Monsters* was the second Godzilla film to feature American and global landmarks (New York, Moscow, Paris among others). I got a sense of a global community watching these films as a boy. Even the "bad" films had some kind of insight into Japanese life. That includes *Godzilla vs. Megalon.*

Even the much-derided *Godzilla's Revenge* showed that Japanese kids had to deal with their own shit at school. *Ultraman, Space Giants* and even *Johnny Sokko* showed me cultural life and traditions different from my own.

Not bad for entertainment labeled "Grade Z" or…"sucks."

When I sat down to watch *The Last Dinosaur* in February of 1977, I had a pretty good cultural background even if I didn't know it. I also had a good background on the American side with Rankin/Bass. I knew Maury Laws's music and as I said, Joan Van Ark's Francesca Banks was a direct nod to *Mad Monster Party's* Francesca.

Generation X knew a lot of the previous generation's culture. We had no choice. We are "The Forgotten Generation" and we had to forage for our entertainment. I knew who Richard Boone was from TV. The same for Joan Van Ark. I recognized the effects as the same company that did *Ultraman* and Godzilla.

Sitting down to watch *The Last Dinosaur* with a bowl of buttery *Jiffy Pop* popcorn was like sitting down into a warm, comfy bean bag chair. I loved it.

THE AMICUS YEARS

Japan wasn't the only country cranking out big, suitmation, and puppet dinosaur films in the 70s. The Brits were up to some big monster shenanigans as well.

Amicus Productions, also known as *Amicus Pictures*, was a British film production company that operated from 1962 to 1977. The company was founded by Americans Milton Subotsky and Max J. Rosenberg, who were both based in England at the time. *Amicus* was known for producing horror and science fiction films that were often anthology-style stories, featuring multiple segments or vignettes within a single film.

Throughout the 1960s and 1970s, *Amicus* produced a series of horror and science fiction films that became cult classics, including "*Torture Garden*" (1967), *The House That Dripped Blood* (1971), *Asylum* (1972), *Tales from the Crypt* (1972), *Vault of Horror* (1973), *From Beyond the Grave* (1974), *The Land That Time Forgot* (1974) *The People That Time Forgot* (1977) and *At the Earth's Core* (1976). Many of these films featured well-known British actors such as Peter Cushing, Christopher Lee, and Doug McClure.

The last three films on the *Amicus IMDb* listing are what interest me for this book. Without these films, there might not have been a *Last Dinosaur. The Land That Time Forgot* kicked off renewed western interest in the dinosaur movie. The "back to nature and the simple life" movie fad was kicking into high gear with Americans embracing movies about American Mountain Men, Westerns, city-dwelling families quitting the rat race and striking out into the forest to live off the land and…expeditions to mythical lands containing prehistoric beasts.

The Land That Time Forgot was based on the "fell into the public domain" Edgar Rice Burroughs book of the same title. A WW I German sub is hijacked by survivors of a ship they sunk and find their way to the lost world of Caprona.

Caprona is a continent not found on any map (of course) and shielded in ice. The interior of this lost continent is heated by

Amicus, 1974

volcanic calderas that managed somehow to keep animal and plant life thriving despite the vicious cold that surrounds the exterior of the land that time forgot.

Doug McClure, a rugged good looks leading man was known from the TV series, *The Virginian*. He found a new niche with

Amicus and starred in almost back to back big dinosaur pictures starting with *The Land That Time Forgot*. Schlock B-movie producer, Samuel Z. Arkoff's *American International Pictures* co-financed the film only if McClure signed on.

The *Mystery Science Theater* episode seven skewering this film might be my favorite out of all eleven seasons. The riffing is spot on and the love the writers had for this film shows. They got it. The film might not be great, but it doesn't suck. Treat yourself. I can't believe *The Last Dinosaur* never made it during this show's run.

The dinosaur effects bypassed suitmation and were actual puppets—hand puppets.

Some had moveable legs but they looked like motorized toy models in the wide shots and hand puppets in the close. My father took me to a matinee of this film and I remember being impressed as I was so used to suitmation between Godzilla and Ultraman. The puppets allowed a little more detail but their movement was severely limited. In most scenes the dinosaurs are just standing there, looking around or being shot while standing in place.

There were flying Pterodactyls but as *Mystery Science Theater* pointed out they looked they were strung from some child's room mobile. Their wings didn't flap and their mouths never moved. The big, full scale models were strung from cranes and whirled around. They had wide "dead eyes" from their inability to blink.

The nostalgia factor is what does it for me. Just seeing Doug McClure in his thick turtleneck sailor's sweater kicking German ass is good fun.

Director Kevin Connor said this about the film's effects: "The reason we went for the hand puppets was for a more fluid look. Roger Dicken, who created the dinosaurs did such fine details and had the movement down so well that we went with him and used that technique. Also, we developed the use of a small *VistaVision* camera to shoot the dinosaur back-ground plates which gave us great quality because the exposed frame is twice the size of a normal 35mm. Everything was shot front projection as well." [9]

The Land That Time Forgot was a boxoffice success and dove-tailed with the smash success of an American Saturday morning dinosaur series, *Land of the Lost*. The Sid and Marty Kroft show went for three seasons, right up to about the time *Amicus* released *The People That Time Forgot* and went bankrupt.

America was dinosaur crazy. The 1976 *King Kong* remake promised to be a big screen spectacle and I know I was psyched for all new dinosaur fights, and instead, I got the afore-mentioned crappy rubber snake wrestling match.

At the Earth's Core moved *Amicus* back to suitmation with the pup-petry still there but taking a back seat. Giant dino-saur and fantasy mon-ster suits chased Doug

McClure and horror legend, Peter Cushing through prehistoric soundstage jungles that looked more like the sets from *Land of the Lost*.

---

9   *Jones-Morris, Ross (7 August 2012). "The Studio That Time Forgot – An Interview With Amicus Director Kevin Connor*

The civilization living at the earth's core was ruled by the tyrannical and murderous Mahars, man-sized prehistoric flying reptiles with mind control abilities. This film is another brilliant Season Eleven *Mystery Science Theater* classic.

It's mentioned because, guess how Doug McClure and Peter Cushing mange to get to the center of the earth? If you said "giant, mechanical Iron Mole boring machine" you would be right.

Combine *At the Earth's Core* Iron Mole borer with *The Land That Time Forgot's* secluded prehistoric arctic oasis penetrated by Thrust Industries Polar Borer and you get the foundation of *The Last Dinosaur's* plot. If there IS a chance The Mandela Effect is real, then somewhere out there, in another universe, Doug McClure stars in *The Last Dinosaur* in the Richard Boone role.

I caught a double drive-in feature of *At the Earth's Core* and *The People That Time Forgot* in the summer of 1977. My aunt and uncle took my brother and me. We sat on top of a station wagon with my two cousins, a tray of snacks and popcorn and waited for the sun to drop low enough for the previews to begin.

I was ten and sitting through a double feature of big dinosaur movies was child's play. The best part was, I just saw *The Last Dinosaur* on TV earlier that year in February. I was dino-stoked

**A page from the Japanese press book for the
release of *The Last Dinosaur*, 1977**

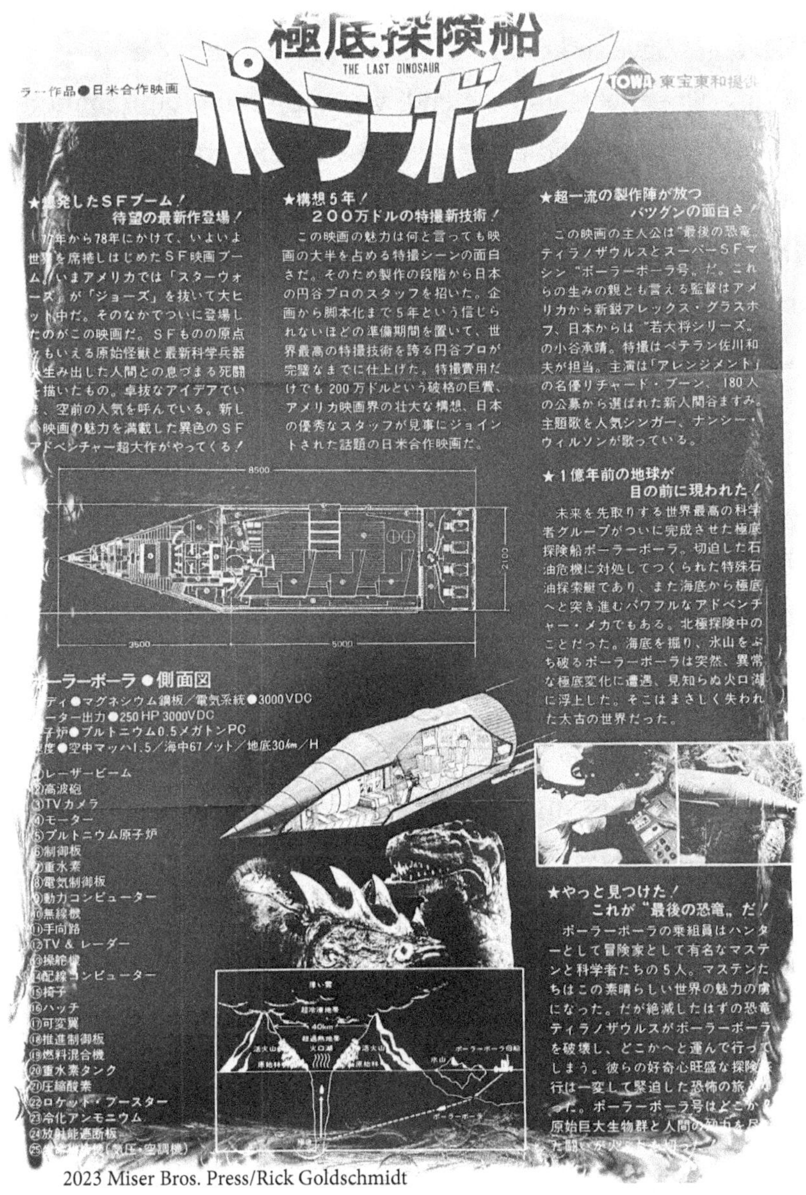

2023 Miser Bros. Press/Rick Goldschmidt

and I remembered *The Land That Time Forgot* was a lot of fun as well.

Do they "hold up" now all these years later? I have them on DVD, but I have to admit, *Mystery Science Theater* helps them to hold up. The effects are low end; without doubt, but Connor had this flair for camp and cheese and his casting was always spot on. Years later when I saw *Superman II* I recognized Sarah Douglas who played one of three Krypton villains, Ursa from *The People That Time Forgot.*

Director Kevin Connor explained the effects on this film: "We tried to get the beasts bigger so as to interact better with the actors – more one on one. We had a somewhat bigger budget thanks to the success of 'Land.' The beasts were specially designed so that small stunt guys could work inside the suits in a crouched position and on all-fours. Needless to say it was very cramped and the stunt guys had to take frequent breathers. Some worked better than others – but we were experimenting and trying something different." [10]

Connor would go on to lament the low budgets on all of these prehistoric outings, including the sequel to his *Land That Time Forgot* titled *The People That Time Forgot,* which was another Burroughs property. Amicus and the financial powers that be saw these films as "kiddie matinee" movies, not films for adults.

This was a major mistake because it was the adult demographic that gave all three films their financial success. *Jurassic Park* was less than twenty years away, but *The Last Dinosaur* was already moving into production when *At the Earth's* Core was starting to film.

---

10 *Jones-Morris, Ross (7 August 2012). "The Studio That Time Forgot – An Interview With Amicus Director Kevin Connor*

Kevin Connor's dinosaur threesome contributed to the "prehysteria" America was enjoying as the 70s moved along.

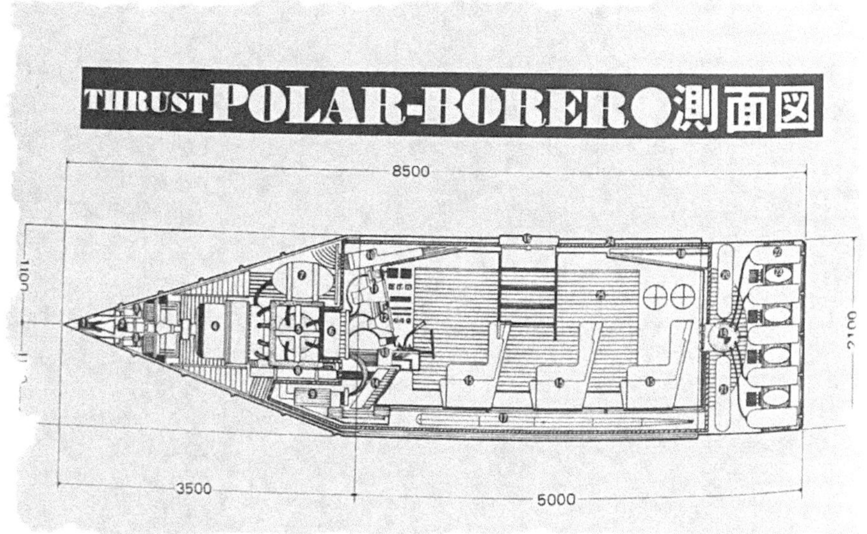

2023 Miser Bros. Press/Rick Goldschmidt

IT'S A ABOUT THE DINOSAUR
IT'S ABOUT THE MAN

THE LAST DINOSAUR

Masten Thrust has had it all: money, power, dames -- the works.
Now pushing sixty he lives for one thing -- hunting. Mounted heads
and horns march around his trophy room in great herds, and it seems
there's nothing left to hunt, then...

One of his oil drilling teams probing under the Polar Cap break
through into a pocket of suspended time. Here, in a minute prehistoric world are the remnants of a cretaceous period and the
largest predator ever to stalk the earth, the Tyrannosaurus Rex --
the last dinosaur.

A select hunting party: a Nobel prizewinning scientist, a great
woman photographer, a palaeontologist (Dr. Kawamoto) and a Masai tracker are
led by Thrust back into the dawn of time after the ultimate game.

The hunt is a disaster -- weapons destroyed, means of return cut
off, they are trapped in a nightmare of survival against elements
and animals, shadowed by a relentless tribe of early men, more
vicious than a baboon pack.

Masten defeats the tribe with a handmade crossbow and inherits
an enamored young female. He leads them to game and shelter
and thrives in the primitive confrontation.

As the others in the party go down and defect, he becomes obsessed
with one thing -- to kill the dinosaur. At the end he sits, alone in
the moonlight on a crude catapult waiting for the beast -- the earth
shakes -- the trees move -- and it is there -- he has one chance --

******

The world's richest man and most relentless hunter is projected
into a pocket of suspended time to hunt the last remaining dinosaur.
Trapped, and forced to survive without weapons, the hunt becomes
an obsession and the climax with the beast, shattering.

The hand-typed synopsis for *The Last Dinosaur* from the desks of Rankin and Bass, 1976

I have to assume you know what *The Last Dinosaur* is about and have seen the film. Why else would you be reading this? There's always a chance you haven't, and if that's the case I recommend you find it and give it a view before going any further.

When I got on the phone with actress Joan Van Ark who played Francesca Banks in the film, we touched on the subject of "passion" in filmmak-

2023 Miser Bros. Press/Rick Goldschmidt

ing. She admitted she had never watched the film from beginning to end. She never watched a full hour of any of her TV episodes of *Knot's Landing* and I'll assume probably not a lot of her other work as well.

She is an actress. She laughed and even used the word "diva" in talking about her approach toward her craft. Joan had a wonderful sense of humor and it was clear passion drives her. She had always worked and continues to work with a number of "plates spinning in the air," as she liked to say. "Dynamic" would be a proper word to describe Joan Van Ark.

2023 Miser Bros. Press/Rick Goldschmidt

We talked after she rewatched the film for my interviews. She was resolute in her assessment of the film. "It's not a good movie," she told me. "I'm sorry, but it just isn't."

I understood what she was saying. I sent her a detailed outline of my intentions for the book and a "roadmap" of sorts of where it would go and what it would cover. It seemed to me she thought I was trying to make the movie out to be more than what it was or what she thought actually ended up on the screen in the final cut.

"It's so kitschy," she groaned.

I knew that. I have always known that. Joan made it clear that whatever she had to say about the movie would be positive. She had no intention of besmirching the characters or the people no longer here to speak for themselves.

There would be no "Richard Boone was so drunk he could barely stand while filming," stories or accounts. She adored Richard and although challenging, loved working with him. When one article was referenced stating there was tension between her and Boone, she waved it away.

"There was nothing more than the usual frustrations any actor or group of people making a film under stressful conditions would have. (i.e. riding on the turtle's backs while floating upstream) "No. I loved working with Richard and we had a challenging time together."

The stressful conditions included 18-20 hour shooting days. That's enough to make anyone fray around the edges. Add in the weather conditions (heat, humidity, two nights of heavy rain and cold). Anyone would be prone to irritability now and then.

Van Ark stated someone (Associate producer Benni Korzen) would plead with the cast to keep going on those 18-20 hours days by saying "Do it for Arthur!" They meant Arthur Rankin himself. She did her impression of Korzen's Danish accent.

"Do it for Arthurrrrrr!" They did it because they had to.

She is the last living member of the four starring characters. Joan Van Ark has become the last dinosaur, so to speak. She lamented this and got choked up, and you just knew she was being honest. The emotion that came through made her affections for her fellow *Dinosaur* co-stars clear.

The previous chapters laid out why I love *The Last Dinosaur*. I love the film for what it is. It doesn't "suck." It has some noteworthy and remarkable things going for it, and in many ways, came close to being the greater film its filmmakers wanted it to be.

As we move forward I am not going to try to spin this movie into something it is not. It has a lot of flaws for sure. Joan is right in her assessment that it is kitschy, but I will disagree with her that it is bad.

The Last Dinosaur entertained me in 1977 and it does now. Even if I am laughing at some of the effects (when we get to the boulder to the head scene you'll see) or Richard Boone screaming "You DING

DONG!" with such intense sincerity, the movie is entertaining and still brings me enjoyment.

"So bad they're good" movies do that. Bad movies do not.

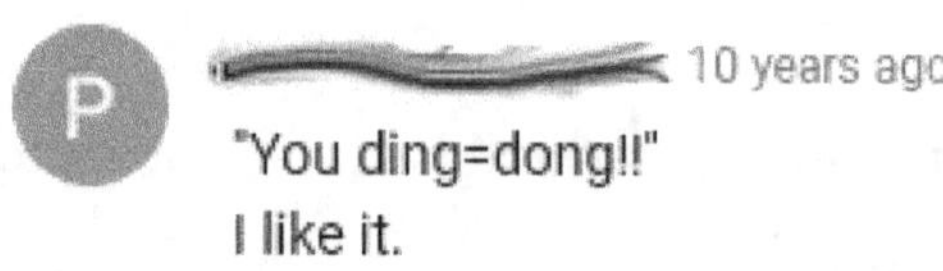

Joan and I discussed the cynicism of the industry and how it has grown over the last 40 years. There is just so much stuff coming out that people find it hard to invest their time into anything. With this deluge came a lot of really, really bad monster and creature feature movies that were not made to entertain.

These films were made to fill content demand. They often have gimmicky or hyperbolic titles to catch your attention. Some have titles like *PCP Python* or *Vampire Shark* (I made these two up, but I wouldn't be surprised if either or both get made or are in production by the time this book releases).

These are "Gotcha!" titles. They gotcha to pick it up, stream it, talk about it and watch it. They're made to get the name out there. They're made to catch a headline in horror magazines and when you watch them you realize the title or pitch sounded a lot better than the shit you just watched.

This content is just content. It has no real intention to entertain you aside from scoffing at their silly titles or concepts. They know what they are making is shit and they don't care. They gotcha.

As I illustrated with Ed Wood, *The Last Dinosaur* was not a "gotcha!" movie. It was made with every intention to entertain and while it was being made its filmmakers felt they were going to do that. *The Last Dinosaur* is not Cynema. It is not a cynical film.

When you have crew and cast working easily over ten hours a day, that's not phoning it in.

Lionsgate, 2022

The people behind the production were so sure about this they originally shot for a theatrical release both in North America and then the world. When the test screenings showed this would not be the case, the film moved to TV as a *Friday Night Movie* for *ABC* and that's where I caught it and enjoyed the living hell out of it.

There are a number of scathing reviews for the film. To quote the teen boy Snack, from my own monster movie, *Where the Scary Things Are,* "It's the Internet…people shit on everything."

Shitting on things gets clicks. Trolling, flaming, click baiting… that gets people to read your stuff. Even if it's just to get someone to post something nasty, you still got a reaction. You still got that click and that translates into advertising dollars or something of value.

Toxicity is fungible.

This is why I dismiss "trailer reviewers." A movie trailer can't be "reviewed." You can't pass judgment on an entire film based on a 30-60-90 second trailer. That's like walking into the doorway of a restaurant, taking three sniffs and declaring, "This place sucks."

Even though the teaser for 1998's *Godzilla* gave me concern, I still went to see the film to judge it on its own merit. Even today when people ask me what I thought of the trailer for this or that, I reply, "I'll see the movie."

Trailer reviews are like asking someone what kind of a winter we're going to get. My response is always, "Ask me in June."

The previous chapters were written to inspire critical thinking for when we get to this movie. Now we are here and it's time to appreciate the work that went into a film that's been summarily dismissed by many.

Two reviewers for the online *DVD Talk*, John Sinnott and Stuart Goldbraith IV took balanced assessments of *The Last Dinosaur* and serve as a kickoff to understanding how this movie was made.

Sinnott was less enamored, but wrote a review based on critical thinking and solid understanding of film history.

"The dialog is horrendously bad, a lot of the acting is atrocious, and much of the plot makes no sense. Still, if you enjoy hokey SF movies and especially Kaiju (giant monster) films it's worth a look." [11]

Sinnot goes on to lay out his thoughts in a fair way.

"There are some good parts to the film. The special effects generally work very well, and look much more impressive than the usual lizards with fins glued to their backs that was the standard not too long before this film was made. The scene where the T-Rex catches a giant fish and devours it on screen is quite impressive. While it's obvious that the dinosaurs are guys in suits, it's fun to watch them fight and chase Thrust and company.

It's just too bad that the script didn't go through a couple of rewrites to get the rough edges off of it. It could have been a classic, but as it is, it's perfect *MST3000* fodder." [12]

Sinnot gets it and notice the word "sucks" doesn't pop up once. He sees the positive and negative and also the film for what it is.

---

11   Sinnot, John, 2011. https://www.dvdtalk.com/reviews/52607/last-dinosaur-the/
12   Ibid.

Film reviewer Stuart Galbraith IV had this to say.

"*The Last Dinosaur* may be the most undervalued work in the entire *Kaiju eiga* (Japanese giant monster movie) genre, a film that transcends its rubbery monsters and timeworn story and into something mixing familiar sci-fi adventure and suspense with a beguilingly authentic, haunting melancholy. Though its special effects vary from comparatively excellent to inadequate and completely unconvincing, its central character is conceived with enormous intelligence and almost poetry, and played at that same level, uniquely, by Richard Boone in a role suited to his unusualness. The film is way above average in other ways, too: some of the sets are imaginatively designed and generate a strange dream-like atmosphere, the film's haunting theme song (quoted above), the direction and supporting performances are, for the most part, spot on."

Reservations aside, *The Last Dinosaur* is one of the best science fiction pictures ever to come (primarily) out of Japan - for my money it's way better than *Jurassic Park*. The inspired screenplay and especially Richard Boone's character and performance raise it many notches above the usual Lost World adventure. It certainly made a strong impression on me when I first saw it, and images and scenes first experienced 33 years ago have stayed with me all these years.

The Last Dinosaur made a strong impression when I saw it on *ABC* back in 1977, and I'm pleased to report it holds up extremely well even today, despite all the technological advancements in terms of digital effects. Indeed, genre screenwriters today could learn a lot about story and characterization from this underrated, long-lost minor classic. Highly recommended." [13]

---

13 Galbraith, Stuart, 2009. https://www.dvdtalk.com/reviews/45612/last-dinosaur-the/?___rd=1

REVIEWS

Scenes from THE LAST DINOSAUR, telecast on ABC. *1*: Toho carpenters build scaffolding to operate the full-scale prop Tyrannosaurus foot. *2*: Steven Keats in The Polar Borer. *3*: The team is attacked by a Tyrannosaurus as soon as they enter the lost land below the polar ice cap. *4*: Luther Rackley and full-size Tyrannosaurus.

THE LAST DINOSAUR

THE LAST DINOSAUR An ABC-TV Movie World Premiere. 1/11/77. In Color. 100 minutes. A Rankin/Bass Production. Produced by Arthur Rankin, Jr. and Jules Bass. Directed by Alex Grasshoff and Tom Kotani. Associate producer, Benni Korzen. Screenplay by William Overgard. Music by Maury Laws, arranged and conducted by Ken Hirose. Title song sung by Nancy Wilson, lyrics by Jules Bass, arranged and conducted by Bernard Hoffer. Special effects by Kazuo Sagawa. Producer for Tsuburaya Productions, Noboru Tsuburaya.

Masten Thrust .... Richard Boone
Frankie Banks .... Joan Van Ark
Bunta .... Luther Rackley
Chuck Wade .... Steven Keats

The producers of lost world films keep trying to get it right but seldom seem to succeed. There are exceptions of course with such films as the original KING KONG, one of the few features which deserves to be called a classic, but generally this sub-genre staggers along usually failing in the plot or special effects departments. The Rankin/Bass production of THE LAST DINOSAUR has the spirit of adventure and the idea of a modern big game hunter tracking down a tyranosaurus is appealing, but as with most of its predecessors the film is only moderately successful. The film was intended for theatrical release and will be seen worldwide that way, however U.S. rights went to the American Broadcasting Company for a television premiere. Plans by Rankin/Bass to release the film domestically to theatres after first being shown on the tube will probably fail to materialize.

Craggy faced, gravel voiced Richard Boone stars as Masten Thrust, the world's richest man; an ill tempered ruthless character who seems to lack feeling for anyone or anything outside the hunt. Boone's performance, especially in the later scenes, appears to be under the influence of something other than the hand of the director.

Dan Scapperotti covers New York City.

by Dan Scapperotti

16

When one of Masten's oil exploring teams accidentally discovers a lost world beneath the polar ice cap he assembles the now familiar team to return to the primitive world. The group is composed of Masten, a female photographer who seems to have melted some of the ice in Masten's character, a Japanese Nobel Prize winning scientist, Bunta, a Masai tracker and friend of the industrialist, and a paleontologist who was the only survivor of the previous expedition. The party sets out in the polar borer, a rocket-shaped vehicle which uses a laser power beam to burrow into the earth, and once again modern man thrusts himself into a prehistoric world.

The opening shot of the primitive landscape is impressive with the polar borer breaking the mist covered surface of the lake with a mountain range matted in the background and a pterodactyl drifting across the distant sky. The effects were filmed in Japan in the Toho style and are predictably uneven. These "man in the monster suit" effects are unconvincing even in multi-million dollar productions, however some of the composite shots are interesting. The sequence where Joan Van Ark darts between the legs of the tyranosaurus is nicely done.

The character of Masten has several contradictions. The hunter seems to be genuinely concerned with the fate of his party and has left orders that if the mother ship doesn't hear from the expedition they are to leave and no further lives are to be risked, but at other times he is a ruthless killer who threatens to kill Wade and Frankie when they decide to return to the outside world until Bunta stops him. He's like an addict fighting the compulsion for a fix, in this case the desire to hunt. He promises Dr. Karamoto that the animal they search for will not be harmed and he wants to keep his word but fires on the beast on their first encounter. When Karamoto is killed, Masten proclaims bitterly: "This animal, this eight ton animal is a carnivore. It eats meat. Us. This forty foot monster with the brain the size of a dried pea has just destroyed a man with one of the great minds of this century. I will hunt this thing down and I will kill it. I will not leave until I destroy that thing." Maston is now completely obsessed with the hunt.

The film's conflict is between the dinosaur and Masten with the title referring to both. Masten, the rugged individualist and ruthless big game hunter is becoming as extinct in the modern world as the prehistoric animal he hunts. The roles of the hunter and the hunted are interchangeable between Masten and the Tyranosaurus.

Masten and Bunta represent the primitive, the savage able to live in the bush and survive off the land while Frankie Banks and Chuck Wade are of the modern world where interdependence is necessary. The film's final confrontation is not between the man and dinosaur but between the two worlds with Masten, who has everything modern society can offer, deciding to remain in the Jurassic world while the remaining members of the expedition return to the familiar world they know.

THE LAST DINOSAUR has been cut for its television premiere with as many as twelve scenes deleted, most of them dialogue and non-effects scenes. The only scenes cut that involve the dinosaurs are parts of the fight between the triceratops and the tyranosaurus which contained bloodletting in excess of network standards outside the evening news, and the death of Dr. Karamoto where a mockup of the dinosaur's foot comes down on the doomed scientist in a closeup.

Midway through the film it would appear that an extensive sequence was deleted but incredibly it was *never filmed* leaving an abrupt change in the action that an amateur filmmaker wouldn't permit. Following the discovery of the destroyed camp the action abruptly shifts to the expedition's confrontation with the aboriginal tribe. Four months have elapsed since the previous scene and there are several references to the *first* encounter with the savages. The change in unsettling and must leave the audience feeling that they've missed something.

THE LAST DINOSAUR is one of the few theatrical films produced by Rankin/Bass, known mainly for their holiday specials which utilize puppet animation. The organization did produce KING KONG ESCAPES some years ago and is currently preparing an animated version of THE HOBBIT which is anxiously awaited by devotees of Tolkien. ∎

Cinefantastique Vol 6 No 1 1977

Cinemafantastique review for *The Last Dinosaur*, 1977

Juni 1977 „NEUES FILMPROGRAMM" Preis öS 2,50 / DM —,50

Eigentümer, Herausgeber, Verleger und Druck: NEUES FILMPROGRAMM. Für den Inhalt verantwortlich: Herbert Weiss, alle 1070 Wien, Lindengasse 43, Telefon (0222) 93 64 53. Für die Bundesrepublik Deutschland (nur für Filmtheater) NEUES FILMPROGRAMM, 8000 München 21, Agricolastraße 16, Telefon (089) 56 25 00 — Anschrift für Einzelbestellungen und Abonnenten für Österreich, die BRD und das übrige Ausland nur: Filmprogrammdienst, Postfach 126, A-1071 Wien, Abonnementpreis für Österreich S 50 — inkl. Porto für jeweils 30 Nummern, für die BRD DM 12,— Einzelpreis für Österreich S 2.50, für Deutschland DM —,50. Für Sammler sind im Einzelverkauf derzeit etwa 2000 Titel vorrätig. Gesamtverzeichnis dieser Titel inkl. Zusendung S 15,— DM 2,—

2023 Miser Bros. Press/Rick Goldschmidt

Foreign press announcement for
The Last Dinosaur, 1977

Galbraith got it too and went as far as to say it's far more enjoyable than *Jurassic Park*. This is what I wanted Joan Van Ark to understand when she expressed her contempt for her own film. There is something endearing about this movie, despite its kitsch, and that's because real passion and work went into it. No one phoned it in making *The Last Dinosaur* and these two guys from *DVD Talk* saw that and used the term I dropped earlier…the movie "holds up."

The full reviews talk of the "melancholy" tone of the film. There is sadness to it, and both Boone and his dinosaur quarry are at the center.

People made this movie. People with lives off set. People with histories. Some of these people, like Joan Van Ark, took the project because their agents recommended they do so. It was a job or a "gig" as many like to say. It was a good paycheck, a trip to exotic Japan and sounded like fun. For Joan, it was the chance to work with her father's hero, Richard Boone. Boone's role as Paladin in *Have Gun--Will Travel* made him a minor legend. His later experience with *The Richard Boone Show* and its unceremonious cancellation turned him into a folk hero. He died on a hill and left Hollywood as a result of his growing disenchantment with an industry he felt was changing too fast and not for the better.

Sounds a hell of a lot like his character, Masten Thrust in *The Last Dinosaur.*

Let's start with the title song. There is hardly a review, positive or negative that fails to mention the title song, belted out in Shirley Bassey fashion by singer, Nancy Wilson.

"I loved that song," director Tom Kotani admitted.

Masten Thrust is a skilled hunter who has dedicated his life to pursuing rare and dangerous big game. He is fearless, determined, and willing to take risks to achieve his goals.

The Tyrannosaurus Rex is a fearsome predator who is driven by instinct and the need to survive in a hostile environment. Both Masten Thrust and the Tyrannosaurus Rex are characterized by their strength, intelligence, and single-minded focus.

The two characters are also very different. Masten Thrust represents the human desire to conquer nature and assert dominance over the environment, while the Tyrannosaurus Rex represents the primal forces of nature itself. The song "The Last Dinosaur" captures this tension between human ambition and natural power.

Few men have ever done what he has done
Or even dreamed what he has dreamed

His time has passed
There are no more
He is the last dinosaur

Few men have even tried what he has tried
Most men have failed where he's prevailed

His time has passed
There are no more
He is the last dinosaur

The world holds nothing new in store for him
And things that startle you and me
Are just a bore for him
The spark of life has gone
His light grows dim

Can there be something left in the world to challenge him?

Few men have ever lived as he has lived
Or even walked where he has walked

His time has passed
There are no more
He is the last dinosaur

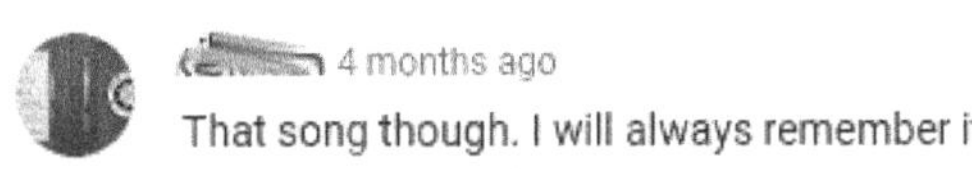

"I don't remember a lot about that project. I just remember that I was asked to sing the song, and I went in and did it. It wasn't something that I had a strong connection to, but it was a job and I was happy to do it." That's not exactly unbridled enthusiasm from Nancy Wilson, but we got a pretty nifty title song that burned into viewer's brains.

I remember seeing it the first night it debuted during prime time on *ABC* and I had that song in my head for the next several days. The score was composed by Maury Laws who was kind of like Rankin/Bass's John Williams. He scored almost everything of theirs.

Laws was just as identified with Rankin/Bass movies as the "Animagic" process. His music had its own sound. It's a Laws score and he gave us a number of memorable tunes over the decades.

His score for *The Last Dinosaur* IS melancholy. The title song evokes sadness. This is supposed to be an adventure flick and yet it is a swan song.

It's about Richard Boone's Masten. It's not about the dinosaur.

I love when I read this revelation in the reviews. Sometimes it's tongue in cheek with the writer poking fun at the heavy-handed metaphor. Other times, especially in comments on the film beneath the reviews or on *IMDb* you can tell some feel impressed that they figured that part out. "Hey! The song isn't about the dinosaur! It's about Richard Boone!"

Find the song on *YouTube* and tell me you can get it speedily out of your head after listening.

When I watched this as a boy, I felt bad for the dinosaur and I also felt bad for Boone's character. I didn't want Boone to kill the dinosaur because they were on its territory. They were the invaders and the dinosaur just wanted to be left alone to do its dinosaur things. While I knew he wasn't "the last one" because of lots of other dinosaurs running around that caldera, I did think he was probably the last of his kind. The last T-Rex.

Masten's name invoked "Mastadon" to me. If I am right, Boone's name represents another extinct animal. Both are two prehistoric beasts making their last stands.

Masten Thrust outlived his usefulness.

"His time has passed. There are no more…"

Thrust is a relic in an evolving world moving on without him. Animal rights activists harass him. Women's rights activists deplore him. Economic awareness has made him an icon of capitalistic evil. His body has grown old. His interest in this world has faded.

"The world holds nothing new in store for him…"

All of this was pretty heavy shit for a ten year old. I didn't get anything like that from Godzilla or any of the Japanese Kaiju after school TV shows. The movie also was kind of a last dinosaur because America just wasn't making big dinosaur films at this time.

I go back to the 1976 *King Kong* remake, but that doesn't count as a dinosaur film. Maybe if there had been some damned dinosaurs in it that could have helped. Kong is an ape and he didn't really smash down New York City and plow through buildings.

The Last Dinosaur was the kind of stuff they made in Japan and had been making in Japan, but this was an even sweeter treat for American audiences.

American filmmaking was also like this big stew pot. The titan major studios weren't the only companies. You had *American International*, Roger Corman's low budget company *Concorde* and then *New World, Sunn-Classic Pictures* and their faux-documentaries on cryptids and supernatural topics, and a variety of low to mid-budget companies all cranking out some pretty interesting product. It's not like today's post-pandemic, Internet world where the studios stay at the top by cranking out big-budget, giant spectacle product (Martin Scorsese calls films like these, especially superhero movies "theme park rides") while a handful of low budget companies fight to flip their product for a profit on streaming channels that pay shit.

I could argue that the decision to put it on free network television enhanced its viewing potential versus people plunking down money for movie tickets. The trouble future *Friday the 13th* producer Steve Miner would go through not long after *The Last Dinosaur* aired to get an American Godzilla movie made underscores the lack of interest by studios or even the public to pay for giant reptiles smashing cities.

Put it on free TV, and people will clear their schedules for it.

There could've been a shot on the drive-in circuit. That's where I caught *The People That Time Forgot* and *At the Earth's Core* as a wildly fun double header. I could see *The Last Dinosaur* playing with one of those *Amicus* films like *Warlords of Atlantis* or even a revival of 1974's *The Land That Time Forgot*. It would be almost like watching one single movie with the things they shared in common.

1977 was the year *Star Wars* released and changed movie special effects forever. *The Last Dinosaur* going up against *Star Wars?* Only a ding dong wouldn't know the outcome.

Going to see a movie in the 70s meant heading to the growing chains of multiplexes to see whatever was advertised on TV. People don't usually pick a movie when they get to the mall or the chain. They already know what they want to see.

There was a lot of stuff to see besides *Star Wars*. You also had *Close Encounters* as space and sci-fi movies were back. While *The Land That Time Forgot* was financially successful in the United States, it was still a British film and seen overall by exhibitors as a kiddie movie.

There was a stigma to that, and some kids likely would have known they would have had better luck with a Disney film over some cheesy looking dinosaur film. It's hard to say how *The Last Dinosaur* would have performed theatrically, but I think I can say that putting it on as a special "Network Presentation" made it more unique and sought after.

I saw the ad in *TV Guide* while poring through the magazine in search of *Mad Monster Party*.

Going into this TV movie as a boy, I expected the dinosaurs to be stop motion. That process went part and parcel with Rankin and Bass. When I saw the TV previews for *The Last Dinosaur* I was a bit amazed. They showed the dinosaur in the commercials but it's interesting to note they showed a lot of the dinosaur in natural lighting scenes.

Instead of a hand painted backdrop of sky under studio stage lights, some of the dinosaur action scenes were shot outside using natural sunlight and real sky. Many of these shots were taken from the ground up to give the dinosaur suit height through forced perspective.

They were quick shots but I remember to this day thinking, "Wow! That looks REAL!" The whole movie is not that way. The shots where real lighting was used played well and if you watch it today, you'll agree. This is that weird nexus of Western and Eastern art styles. An all-American cast that represents an audience wanting realism is in the hands of Eastern filmmakers whose audiences prefer stylistic surrealism.

It was a tough mix.

The Last Dinosaur hits a number of "TV Tropes." The word "trope" has become a more specific entertainment term for "cliché." A trope is a commonly used literary or rhetorical device or figure of speech that conveys a particular meaning or effect. It is a recurring motif or theme that is used in various forms of artistic expression, such as literature, film, television, and music, to convey a specific idea, emotion, or message. Tropes can take many forms, such as a metaphor, a simile, an archetype, a symbol, or a cliché, and are often used to help the audience understand or relate to the work in question.

The Last Dinosaur checks off quite a few.

TROPEASUARUS REX

Whether you saw *The Last Dinosaur* or not, it's worth going through the plot "tropes" that give background on the film, film history and help understand the production of the movie as we get into how it was made.

We discussed the trope of the double meaning of the song. This is designed to give some elevation to the material. It doesn't always work, but damn, Nancy Wilson's torch singer bluesy voice makes it all worthwhile.

The film opens with Richard Boone's Masten Thrust, the "richest man in the world" who is an avid big game hunter. How do we know that? The walls behind him are filled with stuffed heads and bodies of the prey he's killed, for starters--right down to the animal skin rugs on the floor his latest female conquest sits upon.

We find out this is not a mansion room or even some expensive penthouse. No, it's a JET! Masten's own private jet and here is a trope right out of the gate, not even 30 seconds into the movie. All "world's richest men" have a super jet of some kind. This one even has a fireplace but where the smoke goes, I don't know. Smoking was still allowed on planes at this time, but I can't imagine an open flame in an airborne, pressurized aluminum cylinder is all that safe.

2023 Miser Bros. Press/Rick Goldschmidt

We have the nameless female conquest to show Masten's virility. She's a silly red-haired floozy, right down to her polyester, flair bottom leisure suit and tiny dog in a purse motif.

She looks at another trope on a coffee table, the "Major News Magazine Cover" trope that has Masten on the cover of *Newsworld* as the filmmakers likely didn't want to pay or wrangle for the right to use *Newsweek* unless the magazine declined participation.

Before we are even out of the opening scene we roll into the "Photo Album Used as Exposition" opening titles. Masten tells us what the set dressing of dead animals told us: he's the Great White Hunter so to speak, as if we needed him to vocalize this while in safari bush attire. Verbalizing what's already been shown is another trope.

Masten drops his one night stand off at the airport and before he leaves delivers what might be one of the best lines in the film. The red-haired ditz questions why he gave her a solid gold bullet as a parting gift or token of his "appreciation."

He replies, "Well, if times get really tough, you can bite on it." It's delivered in perfect Richard Boone style. Off he goes to his new and final adventure.

Masten walks into the "Opposites Attract" trope when introduced to Joan Van Ark's Francesca Banks. She's apparently the greatest journalistic photographer ever and she makes it clear she is a staunch feminist and raised to be tough by her tough father.

These two are diametrically opposed, but she's beautiful and the mentioning of her tough father and knowledge of guns lays the ground work for the "Daddy's Issues" trope. Her inevitable attraction to Masten will come from said "Daddy Issues."

The hits just keep coming when Masten introduces Chuck Wade and Dr. Kawamoto to a large international press corps that has gathered for *Thrust Industries* big announcement.

It's here where the "Fluid Science" trope starts. The only survivor of a previous polar expedition, Chuck Wade (Steven Keats), is said to be some kind of geologist, botanist or biologist. He describes his encounter with a T-Rex discovered under the polar ice cap and how it ate the rest of his crew. From there Chuck shows he is also an adept in paleontology and will continue with this all the way through the end of the movie.

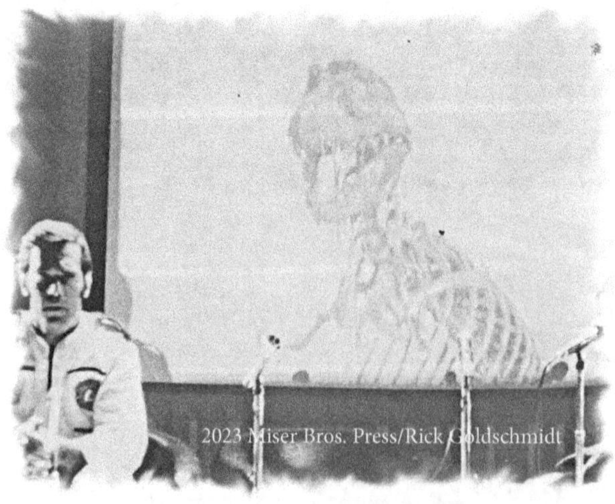

The same goes for Dr. Kawamoto who is (of course) a Nobel Prize winning scientist whose credentials seem to cover just about everything in science.

What could be a trope but I've read accounts of "racism" (which I don't think qualify here) The Great White Hunter and embodiment of Western Civilization introduces his faithful sidekick and animal tracker, Bunta (Luther Rackley) who is of course as tall as a dinosaur, black and silent.

He seems to be on display before the press corps, who seems more amazed by Bunta's height and masculine prowess than the news of a living dinosaur just announced.

That's okay, we have Richard Boone telling everyone to shut the fuck up and they do.

We have the "Reverse Trope" of the independent woman who uses her feminine wiles as needed when Francesca seduces Masten to ensure he doesn't boot her from the expedition.

From performing a strip tease at a sendoff party to making her move after showing him her field and action photos (which show no signs of being incredible or why she was "unanimously" picked the press pool to go with Thrust). It doesn't matter, it's the trope tool needed to establish the romantic connection between the two and of course, Masten relents and "Frankie" is cleared for entry.

We have more "Fluid Science" tropes with the Polar Borer, a drilling machine that looks a lot like the phallic Iron Mole from *At the Earth's Core* that uses lasers (?) without any explanation to its mechanics, to drill through rock and strata. It doesn't matter; it gets us to where we need to go.

We have a "Lost World in Ice" trope. A land unfound by satellites, jet fly by's or any kind of modern technology. All we needed was some old map from the 1700s leading us to this legendary target.

Our land that time forgot is underneath the polar ice cap but it is brought to us by a dormant volcano whose radiant heat makes the whole place warm enough to support the prehistoric life that somehow got isolated here.

The "Fluid Science" trope is our narrative friend. Don't ask a lot of questions, just go with it.

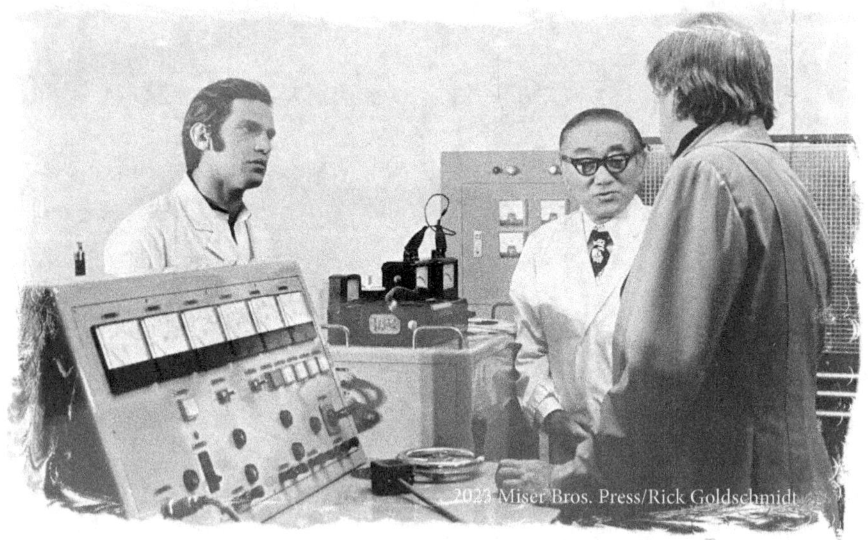

2023 Miser Bros. Press/Rick Goldschmidt

2023 Miser Bros. Press/Rick Goldschmidt

2023 Miser Bros. Press/Rick Goldschmidt

2023 Miser Bros. Press/Rick Goldschmidt

When our intrepid explorers arrive in the land that time forgot (which looks pretty cool instead of the tropish tropical jungles used in these films) Chuck Wade wrongly identifies a species of charging prehistoric beast and Dr. Kawamoto never corrects him. This leads to Frankie almost being run over (why she was still tak-ing pictures only feet from a giant animal that would give

2023 Miser Bros. Press/Rick Goldschmidt

no real interesting photo at that close of range) is saved by Masten.

The "Couple Falls in Mud and Laughs" trope kicks in which allows us to see there's going to be a love triangle with Keats, Boone and Van Ark. Rackley never gets in on the action and Kawamoto is too old and will succumb to a trope even if he had expressed interest.

There is the "Who Dies First" trope coming up. Trope history tells us it will be "The Black Guy." The *Scream* films brought that trope to popular audience attention. However it won't apply to Luther Rackley's Bunta.

Dr. Kawamoto will be the first to die, which of course gives Masten the excuse to declare war on the T-Rex as it snuffed the flame of one of the greatest scientific minds of our time.

This leads right into the "Ahab or Quint" trope (they're the same thing) where our lead character becomes obsessed with killing the creature and will stop at nothing and spare no expense (including the lives of those around him) to do it.

2023 Miser Bros. Press/Rick Goldschmidt

The T-Rex is the embodiment of trope. One of the best, and noted by almost every reviewer, is the giant beast's uncanny ability to go into stealth mode. It can just sneak up on people like Dr. Kawamoto and then Trope Stomp him to death with the obligatory shot of a giant dino foot coming down into the camera as the good doctor throws up his arms and screams helplessly.

But wait! That's not all. Bunta is supposed to be the greatest tracker on the planet, yet he fails to find the dinosaur before it finds him. Each encounter between Bunta and T-Rex comes after the damned thing tip-toes, without breaking a single tree within feet of Bunta. Now you see him, now you don't until he stomps the shit out of you. Bye, bye, Bunta.

The "No Way Out" trope follows to ratchet up the suspense. The dinosaur seems intelligent and snatches the Polar Borer which Chuck Wade surmises acted as a "shiny thing" in the way crows are

2023 Miser Bros. Press/Rick Goldschmidt

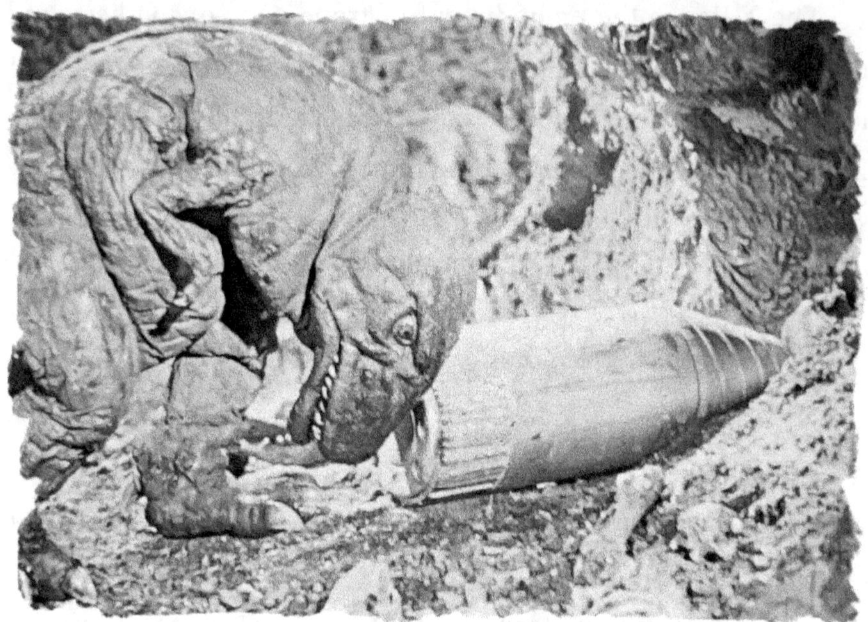

2023 Miser Bros. Press/Rick Goldschmidt

attracted to stuff like that. Not bad for a geologist/botanist. Add saurian psychologist to his repertoire.

Our stealthy T-Rex hauls the Polar Borer to its evil monster lair which must be populated with the bones of its victims to let us know this dinosaur is badass. This is "The Lair Trope" and it dovetails with the "Over the Top Monsters" trope that puts our T-Rex into direct conflict with a Triceratops that, for some reason, is buried alive in the side of the mountain lining our Rex's lair.

When Masten and the gang find the Polar Borer gone, Masten reveals the "No Way Out Trope." He made this a one-way mission without the knowledge of the others. He says the reasoning is to not allow one more life lost. They will live out their days under the polar ice cap with their prehistoric friends.

2023 Miser Bros. Press/Rick Goldschmidt

The "Caveman Trope" adds more friends for Masten and company. We get the standard caveman icons with Japanese actors filling out the roles to give, I assume, some kind of exotic look or to fill out jobs on the Japanese end of the co-production. This opens the door to the "Man vs. Primitives" trope showing Masten constructing a cross bow even though he threw his rifle away during his first confrontation with the T-Rex. Why? It doesn't matter.

Fashioning the crossbow shows civilized man falling back on his primitive roots in a fight for survival. Since we are going backwards in time to a more primitive version of man, we roll right into the "Women Belong in the Kitchen" trope where our staunch feminist and independent female journalist, Frankie, becomes the cook and kitchen cave wench while the men go out to hunt and gather.

When cavewoman Hazel comes into the picture Frankie immediately turns her into a replacement cook to serve the men. So much for women's rights throughout time.

The "Final Confrontation" trope comes on the heels of all of this where Masten forces a showdown between himself and his saurian enemy. The only thing that doesn't make this a full trope is

2023 Miser Bros. Press/Rick Goldschmidt

that Masten doesn't perish at the hands of his enemy.

Where Captain Ahab was strapped to the side of his white whale and drowned to death and Captain Quint slides into the mouth of his shark quarry, Masten survives his climax battle only to lead us into the final trope.

The "No Way Out" trope brings us full circle where Masten tells Frankie he is not returning to civilization. Chuck found the Polar Borer in the T-Rex lair and somehow the dinosaur didn't sneak up on him in there. The group rolls the thing out of there and a good several miles back to the lake. How? Doesn't matter. The vehicle still works, despite being tossed, smashed and buried by heavy falling rock. Of course there's just enough power to get them back, but they have to leave NOW.

2023 Miser Bros. Press/Rick Goldschmidt

2023 Miser Bros. Press/Rick Goldschmidt

Masten knew all along this was a one way trip. When he fails to convince Francesca to stay with him, she begs him to leave the dinosaur be. "It's the last one!" she shouts at him.

"So am I," he sadly replies.

Boom! The double meaning of the song is fulfilled.

It was here that Joan Van Ark choked up with me again in describing the day they shot that scene. The way Boone delivered the line was so raw, so personal; she knew he felt in his soul what those words meant.

He saw himself in real life as Masten—a last dinosaur.

She said that while rewatching the film and that scene, Boone's performance took her right back to that moment as she felt heavy emotion on the set that day and it rushed back to her. "He's so sad in that shot," she said. "It was a powerful and emotional moment for Richard."

Francesca joins Chuck and they leave Masten behind. Hazel approaches the alpha male cautiously and his body language lets her know he's okay to approach. They will become this land's Adam and Eve, walking off into the distance as the T-Rex lets out a roar that echoes over the land.

Nancy Wilson's song kicks in as we roll end credits.

That's a complete movie synopsis using tropes to walk you through it. Kaiju lovers can add more, I am sure.

What comes through this trop-ish summary is the film is indeed melancholy. It is rare to see this kind of thing in big monster movies. The original *Godzilla* struck that depressing, hopeless tone, but that 1954 *Gojira* wasn't made as a true action-adventure movie. There have been other Kaiju films, even the British *Gorgo* that have somber tones but these emotions usually focus on the monster.

At the end of *Godzilla 1985* (the American version of 1984's *The Return of Godzilla*), American TV star, Raymond Burr, who headlined the American re-cut of 1954's *Gojira* called *Godzilla King of the Monsters*, gives a speech at the end of the film that underscores the somber nature of the beast.

When the Japanese military and scientists drop Godzilla into an active volcano through exploding ground devices that blow a rock shelf out from under him, Burr's speech is laid overtop as the monster screeches and plummets into the molten lava below:

"[Nature] occasionally throws up the terrible offspring of our pride and carelessness to remind us of how puny we really are in the face of a tornado, an earthquake or a Godzilla.

For now, Godzilla, that strangely innocent and tragic monster, has gone to earth. Whether he returns or not, or is never again seen by human eyes, the things he has taught us remain."

I watched that movie in theaters in 1985 as a senior in high school and while the American cut went for camp and laughs, Burr took the whole thing seriously. He made it clear that if he returned to the role he originated in 1955, he didn't want to be funny. His somber eulogy to Godzilla brought tears to my eyes along with that operatic music.

Burr told the *Los Angeles Times*, "I think the important thing for any actor is to take whatever role you do seriously. It doesn't matter what it is, whether it's a comedy or a drama. If you don't believe in what you're doing, the audience won't either."

It reminded me of *The Last Dinosaur* only eight years previous. The difference between the two films is that Burr's words and the filmmaker's intent was to make Godzilla tragic. No human in the story is presented as a kind of dualism with the beast.

The Last Dinosaur lets us know from the opening song that this is about a man and his eventual connection with a beast, but that song is about Masten Thrust and Richard Boone's somber delivery at the end, tells us he knew it was also about himself.

Boone was like Raymond Burr. He took his craft seriously and he took this role seriously. Whether he was pleased with the final result or even how it all went down, according to everyone who worked with him and an adamant Joan Van Ark, he did his job and he did it well.

Those three words: "So am I," illustrate this beautifully.

His time has passed. There are no more. He is the last dinosaur…

RICHARD BOONE

OPEN LETTER TO THE MOTION PICTURE INDUSTRY FROM RICHARD BOONE

To those who seek to hire me:

You are engaged in a business that by its own terms is intended to entertain. It is not intended to reform or improve the human race, although it has often been used for those purposes.

Your responsibility is not to me; it is not to the public; it is to your stockholders. Your first obligation is to produce profits. If your profits are produced by good entertainment, fine. If they are produced by bad entertainment, that is regrettable. But either way, so long as the public will pay for it, you will go on making pictures.

In the past few years, however, it has become increasingly apparent that the public is becoming restive. It is bored with slick pictures which have little or no human interest. It is tired of mechanical plots and predictable situations. It is weary of violence, violence in any form. It has had its fill of gangsters and the "police crime" stories that support them. It has even shown signs of weariness with sex, which is a tribute to its own maturity.

There is only one kind of picture that is exciting to the public, and that is a good picture. It is, of course, possible to make a good picture about violence or sex, but these things cannot be the point of the picture. They cannot be the reason for the picture's existence. They can only be incidental to the story.

But how can the industry make good pictures? It can start by dealing honestly with its actors. Actors are not cattle; they are not machines. Actors are people, and their primary motivation, like that of any other human being, is to do good work. They want to do good work because it is an end in itself. If their work is good, they are happy; if it is bad, they are miserable.

What makes work good? A good script. A good director. A reasonable shooting schedule. Adequate compensation.

But you say you can't afford good scripts, good directors, reasonable shooting schedules, or adequate compensation? If that is the case, you are in the wrong business.

You are living in a fool's paradise if you think that you can continue to make cheap pictures and still sell them to the public. You are living in a fool's paradise if you think that the public is going to keep on subsidizing your business because you are too cheap to give it what it wants.

Your business is dying because your product is bad. It is not the fault of the public; it is not the fault of television; it is not the fault of the critics; it is your fault.

The public has a right to demand good entertainment. If you can't give it to them, get out of the business.

Sincerely,
Richard Boone

This open letter to the motion picture industry placed in a January, 1960 issue of *Variety* from Richard Boone says a lot about the man himself and sheds a little light as to why the role of Masten Thrust appealed to him.

Boone saw the entertainment industry (specifically television) changing quickly around him and not for the better. He had little regard for television and felt that the industry was practicing what I call Cynema. It had the ability to make better stuff, it was choosing not to. He never felt Hollywood was on the artist's side.

More and more he saw himself as the last of a dying breed—actors who cared about the art and delivered top quality to their fans and audience. His commitment to quality was seen by some as an obsession—something he hunted constantly.

He was also every bit the hell raiser that *The Last Dinosaur* makes Masten Thrust out to be. While at Stanford University he and some frat buddies took a lifelike dummy and orchestrated a plan to mess with one of their frat brothers from another Greek organization.

Boone called their friend and told him to get over to their frat house. They hid out in the bushes along the route they knew their friend would come. When they saw his car, they threw the dummy out into the road, with the car striking it.

It might seem like boys being boys, but the issue was the car matched the make and model of their friend's, but it wasn't their friend's car. It had been driven by none other than former First Lady of the United States, Mrs. Herbert Hoover.

Mrs. Hoover swerved the car after hitting the dummy. She leapt from the vehicle, panicked that she just hit and killed someone and twisted her ankle in the process. The practical joke had gone way wrong and it resulted in a college investigation that saw Boone "invited not to return" or expelled in common vernacular.

RICHARD BOONE

RICHARD BOONE, one of the entertainment industry's foremost individualists.

He is a man of many lives. Oilfield roustabout, fisherman, prize fighter, aerial gunner, artist, bartender, writer and actor are among the many real-life roles he has played. He drew on all of these diverse experiences to make such successful TV series as "THE RICHARD BOONE SHOW" and his earlier TV successes such as "MEDIC" and "HAVE GUN, WILL TRAVEL" and, more recently, "HEC RAMSEY".

Boone was born in Los Angeles to Cecile and Kirk Boone and is a seventh generation nephew of Daniel Boone. His father was a corporation lawyer, a field his father hoped his son would follow. Boone received his primary education at the Army and Navy Academy at San Diego and during the summers worked as a crewman on a charter fishing boat. He enrolled at Stanford University as a liberal arts major with emphasis on drama.

Coupling art with action, Boone went out for the boxing team at Stanford and won the amateur light heavyweight college championship. After graduation, he worked as an oilfield laborer in southern California and studied at the Art Students League at night.

**The hand-typed press background on
actor, Richard Boone for the film.**

He left Los Angeles to take up painting and was about to try to make a living as a professional artist when World War II forced him to drop his artistic plans and enlist in the Navy. He spent four years in the Pacific as an aerial gunner in a torpedo squadron, narrowly escaping with his life several times after being torpedoed on the carrier Intrepid, bombed on the Enterprise and kamikazied on the Hancock.

Following his discharge in 1946, Boone decided on an acting career and enrolled at New York's Neighborhood Playhouse under the G.I. Bill. After leaving School, he worked in the Saratoga (New York) Playhouse, appeared on and off-Broadway and racked up more than 75 starring roles on TV in 18 months.

Then Boone was signed for his motion picture debut in the 1951 "HALLS OF MONTEZUMA" under a long-term contract with 20th Century-Fox. He parted company with 20th after 10 pictures to freelance. Then came his TV successes.

His other films have been "CALL ME MISTER", "THE DESERT FOX", "RETURN OF THE TEXAN", "RED SKIES OF MONTANA","KANGAROO", "THE WAY OF A GAUCHO", "MAN ON A TIGHTROPE", "VICKI", "THE ROBE", "CITY OF BAD MEN", "BENEATH THE TWELVE MILE REEF",

"THE SIEGE AT RED RIVER", DRAGNET", THE RAID","BATTLE
STATIONS", "MAN WITHOUT A STAR", "TEN WANTED MEN",
"ROBBERS ROOST", "STAR IN THE DUST", "AWAY ALL BOATS",
"LIZZIE", "GARMENT CENTER", "THE TALL T", "I BURY THE LIVING",
"THE ALAMO", "A THUNDER OF DRUMS", "RIO CONCHOS", "THE
WAR LORD", "HOMBRE", "KONA COAST", "THE NIGHT OF THE
FOLLOWING DAY", "THE ARRANGEMENT", "MADRON", "THE KREMLIN LETTER",
"BIG JAKE" and"AGAINST A CROOKED SKY".   He has also starred
in the made-for-television movies "IN BROAD DAYLIGHT"
and "A TATTERED WEB".

Boone's outstanding performances also include the title
role in William Faulkner's "THE OLD MAN" on Playhouse 90
and a Broadway role as Abe Lincoln in "THE RIVALRY".

His most recent role was in "THE SHOOTIST" as the killer
gunman determined to do away with John Wayne.

****

He kicked around in an artist's colony and found his way into the US Navy when World War II broke out. He served as a gunner in the South Pacific and saw enough to exacerbate an already healthy liking for alcohol that turned more into a coping mechanism for the horrors he experienced during the war.

The world holds nothing new in store for him. And things that startle you and me Are just a bore for him…

After the war he tried his hand at writing short stories in a Hemingway kind of vein only to find his dialogue needed work. Boone looked into theater as a way to find how actors worked on their dialogue and caught the acting bug.

Boone began his film career in the early 1950s, appearing in movies such as *Halls of Montezuma* and *The Robe*. He also appeared on television, starring in the anthology series "Climax!" and guest-starring on shows like "The Twilight Zone" and star in "Have Gun – Will Travel."

However, Boone's most iconic role came in 1958, when he was cast as the lead in the Western television series "Have Gun – Will Travel." Boone played the character of Paladin, a gunfighter and adventurer for hire, for six seasons and became one of the most recognizable and beloved actors of the era. He also was beloved by future *Last Dinosaur* star, Joan Van Ark's father.

He moved to Hawaii with his family and became an advocate for more television series to be produced there. His enthusiasm for the state encouraged the producers of *Hawaii 5-O* to base their entire production there. They even offered Boone the lead and iconic role of Detective Steve McGarrett but Boone turned it down. Jack Lord stepped into the role.

Boone created, directed and acted in his own *NBC* series, *The Richard Boone Show* which was a unique anthology type of series that received critical acclaim but according to the network, didn't bring the ratings. The show was cancelled after one season with Boone finding out through the Hollywood trades instead of anyone from the network telling him directly.

"I think the way they did it represents what they are," Boone stated. "They did it in the most chicken, gutless way possible. They leaked it to the trade papers. As long as the business remains in the hands of the graduates of the advertising business, creative people don't have much of a chance. I'd hate to be the next man who comes up with a creative idea." This mishandling of Boone pushed him to leave Hollywood and relocate to Florida.

"It's harder and harder to do your best work in TV. There seems to be no reversing the trend of commercial control over the creative side, which is becoming weaker and weaker."

By the late 1960s his career was starting to fade while he popped up in feature and TV movies as well as series episodes.

"A series should get better every year," he said. "I resent it when it stands still or goes back. We're doing five shows this year and we've got two good shows and three that I would call silly. But this is some of the toughest acting I've ever done in my life. There's a scene where I told off a punk who had killed a friend of mine. That was hard, but the silly stories will kill you."

It's claimed he smoked between 60-100 cigarettes a day. His drinking was well-known with some attributing it to his reputation for being difficult. The smoking and drinking took a toll on him physically, and aged him well ahead of his years.

Few men have ever done what he has done. Or even dreamed what he has dreamed.

By the early 1970s, Boone was taking on low budget films and keeping the bills paid. By the time he crossed paths with Arthur Rankin and Jules Bass, he knew he was in the twilight of his career.

Boone returned to Los Angeles in the mid to late 70s looking for work and found that most of the industry executives, producers and directors were in their 20s. A number of them didn't even know who he was. There was no *Google* to just look up his *IMDb* or *Wikipedia* him.

He was crushed by the way things changed.

He is the last. There are no more...

It makes sense as to why he would be attracted to the role of Masten Thrust. They were one in the same.

"People think of acting as a profession," he once said. "It's not. It's a way of life. Talent is not a golden rarity among humans. There is more talent walking the streets of the world than there are pretty girls and bald men. Unfortunately, most talent lives and dies unrecognized. People who become good actors really don't have any other choice. They *have* to do it. They have to act. It's more important than security, more awesome than fear of failure, and has a more voracious appetite than any other passion."

Boone went on to do the voice of Smaug the dragon in Rankin/Bass's animated production of *The Hobbit* and his last onscreen appearance was another Rankin/Bass live action feature, *The Bushido Blade*.

A dental visit revealed a lump that turned out to be cancerous. When he was diagnosed with esophageal cancer, he refused treatment, knowing it would put him through hell. He succumbed to the disease in 1981.

The spark of life is gone. His light grows dim...

2023 Miser Bros. Press/Rick Goldschmidt

The man was larger than life (although he's said to have been 6'2 he claimed to be 6'0) and a direct descendent of frontier legend, Daniel Boone. He witnessed Kamikaze attacks in the Pacific during the war but there are numerous accounts of friends and those who knew him stating he never talked of his wartime experiences. He wrote poetry both during and after the war but kept those to himself and as far as I've been able to find, never been published.

His drinking was a way of dealing with the demons he brought home from World War II.

He admitted he had interest in directing feature films, but he was by then in his mid-fifties and felt…his time had passed. While he demanded great work, and many found him difficult as a result, they also wanted to work with him because they knew Richard was about quality.

Arthur Rankin, Jr., who produced *The Last Dinosaur*, summed up the actor. "Richard Boone was the one actor who was really cooperative. He worked hard on it. He was a pro. He had a hard time getting around. He had bad hips. He was always in pain. He was a heavy smoker. He was a tough guy. He was a man's man. He was very cooperative, but he knew that the movie wasn't very good. He knew that it wasn't his best work, but he did the best he could."

This will come up later in discussing the production of *The Last Dinosaur* and the stories of Boone's script demands, frustration with the direction of the film and its final result.

Few men have ever lived as he has lived. Or even walked where he has walked.

His time has passed. There are no more.

He is the last dinosaur…

JOAN VAN ARK

Joan played intrepid, Pulitzer Prize winning journalist, Francesca "Frankie" Banks. She was unanimously chosen by her fellow press corps to join Masten on his journey to find the last dinosaur. She becomes emotionally entwined with Masten while also developing feelings for Steven Keats's Chuck Wade.

Photo Courtesy of Joan Van Ark

Van Ark shared the same passion for quality in her craft. She doesn't see her career as work. She would watch the dailies of *Knot's Landing* episodes to study her performance to know if she delivered. More on that later.

The Last Dinosaur's journalist got her real-life start as a student at age 15. Her father, a photographer/writer for *Time/Life Magazine* locked an interview with actress Julie Harris. After the interview, Harris suggested Joan try acting at the Yale School of Drama which gave her the focus on acting, which is all she cared about.

In line with Francesca's fiery spirit, Joan was accepted to Yale's graduate program straight out of high school and was the only female undergrad student on campus at that time.

Van Ark began her acting career in the 1960s, appearing in small roles in various television series as well as Broadway and London stage work. Her TV credits included "Perry Mason," and "Bonanza." Much later, in 2004, she landed her first major role in the soap opera "The Young and the Restless," where she played the character of Gloria Fisher for three years. Van Ark's other notable television credits include "Love Boat," "Fantasy Island."

In 1977, Van Ark landed the role that would make her a household name - Valene Ewing on the CBS primetime soap opera "Dallas." She played the character for three seasons before leaving the show to star in her own spin-off series, "Knots Landing." Van Ark portrayed Valene for almost 14 seasons of "Knots Landing," (earning six nominations) and later made a reunion episode where she reprised her character.

In addition to her work in television, Van Ark is most proud of her stage work on Broadway and London, playing the female lead in *Barefoot in the Park*, directed by Mike Nichols. She was nominated for a Tony for *Rules of the Game* on Broadway.

Van Ark has been recognized for her rich and varied work throughout her career. She has worked with a number luminaries including legendary actor, Dennis Hopper. She received a Daytime Emmy nomination for Outstanding Supporting Actress and was also a multi-nominee and winner of the *Soap Opera Digest Award* for her role on "Knots Landing."

She became an acclaimed director and continued pushing boundaries within the industry.

Joan directed an Emmy nominated short documentary on homelessness and domestic violence for the Directors Guild of America. The woman doesn't let any grass grow under her feet.

"Leave it be!" her Francesca screams at Masten in *The Last Dinosaur.* "It's the last one!" She is the only person on the team aside from the late Dr. Kawamoto to express any concern for the T-Rex's welfare.

In real life, she is an animal lover and a supporter along with Hollywood legend, Tippi Hedren of the animal welfare organization, The ROAR Foundation in support of the *Shambala Animal Preserve* for exotic big cats and elephants that have been abused and neglected. Not sure what Masten Thrust would think of that but I think if there was an endangered T-Rex out there, Joan would work toward saving it.

She also served on the advisory board for the *Barbara Davis Center for Childhood Diabetes.* Add to this impressive list of social causes and career, she is a member of the *Celebrity Action Council* of the *Anne Douglas Center* for homeless women in Los Angeles.

Joan is also an accomplished and sought-after voice-over artist, lending her talents to such varied material as playing *Spider-Woman* to guest spots on the popular animated hit, *Archer.*

What served her well in staying alive against a rampaging T-Rex is the fact that Joan is also a renowned long-distance runner and has participated in various marathons for charitable causes. Most proudly—The Boston Marathon.

All of this lays out a resume that would give Francesca Banks a run for her money. Joan Van Ark embodied everything in real life that her *Last Dinosaur* character reflected. It's no wonder she connected well with Richard Boone. They are two artists cut from the cloth and dyed with a deep passion for whatever they took on.

Laying out her life's accomplishments and unique childhood aptitude and talents illustrates what drives actors to certain roles. In short, Joan Van Ark was and remains a go-getter so no wonder she responded well to the role of Francesca when given the project.

She received the offer for *The Last Dinosaur* from her agency, *William Morris* (Now *William Morris Endeavor*) and was told it would be a feature film with Richard Boone in Tokyo and Japan. When she heard that Bonne was her co star, knowing her father was a huge Boone fan from *Have Gun-Will Travel*; it closed the deal.

As a woman who managed an interview with a major star as a teenager, the fact that there was zero prep time for the role and production didn't daunt her. After accepting the part she winged off to Japan to start the film knowing all of the details of what she was walking into.

"I never looked at *The Last Dinosaur* as anything like a monster movie or Godzilla. I looked at it all as a chance to be in Japan, in another country, another environment with a great actor that my father adored (Boone)."

The production offered two tickets, one for Joan and the other for her award-winning (Emmy, Golden Mike) *NBC* anchor husband, John Marshall. "Jack took limited time to be with me. He wasn't there the entire shoot, and he and Luther Rackley (the tracker Bunta) had a ball. They got along unbelievably."

Joan saw the film as an acting part, not a creature feature and as a tribute to her father by working with Richard Boone. "Unfortunately, and God bless everyone involved, but *The Last Dinosaur* to many, and rightly so, is a joke."

Joan lamented the reception of *Dinosaur* over her other horror creature feature, *Frogs*. She felt that film had a better reception which led to her labeling *Dinosaur* as a joke. It was a fun thing to have with such a mix of actors and all of the special effects, but it's not something Joan takes seriously on her long filmography.

"I wanted to do this film, most of all, for reasons that are an actress's reasons and less "Joan Van Ark the person" reasons. Overall, it was more Joan Van Ark, the actor."

I found that quote to be a defining statement of a true professional who knew how to guide her career and understood the parameters of what she getting herself into. While I see Joan's point on a number of things, I don't share the supposition that the film is a joke to everyone.

The first several chapters of this book lay out my reasoning for this, but I see where Joan is coming from because she was there. She lived it and she had other expectations for the final product.

Van Ark responded well to the character of Francesca being an aggressive, "doesn't take no for an answer" type of woman. "She's chasing a story and most of all, chasing this legendary character that Richard Boone plays and then ends up in this nightmare once they got the destination and realized the challenge of the last dinosaur—there was something about her that was feisty, energetic and professional in what she did. She went after a story, and I know that from my husband. The bottom line was she knew what she wanted and she was gutsy."

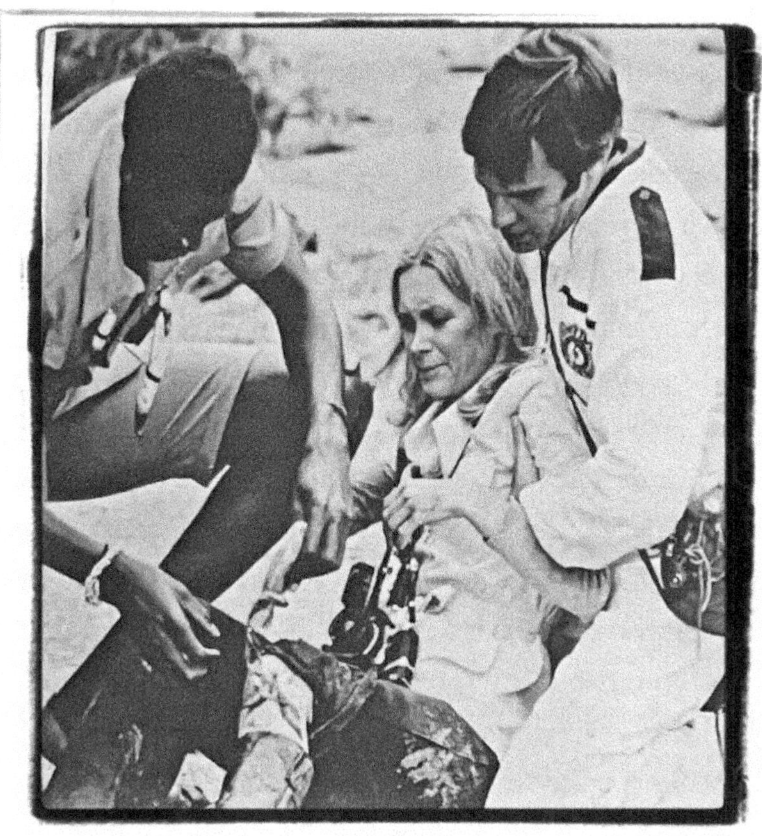

2023 Miser Bros. Press/Rick Goldschmidt

Joan Van Ark reacts to Bunta's (Luther Rackley) leech salt treatment after falling into yet another mud pit as Steven Keats lends support.

Combine this appealing character with the chance to wing off to a new location in a different part of the world seemed like the perfect package deal. She got to have her husband with her, throw in Richard Boone and it all looked like something worthwhile to her.

Word has it that Candace Bergen, also a *William Morris* client at the time, was originally offered the part but had to pass because of scheduling problems. The project moved to Joan who snapped it up and headed off to Japan to chase a renegade T-Rex alongside a renegade big game hunter.

True to her intrepid nature, Joan said the entire "pre-production" consisted of "pack your stuff, get on a plane and go to work."

"Basically that's what it was," she agreed. "I just knew that Francesca had levels and layers and she had an arc (pun intended). I wish she had been even gutsier in the middle of all her challenges. If I played her now, I would've had her feet on the ground because women have come to the fore in such a magnificent way and are starting to get their due. I wouldn't have been as vulnerable in some of the acting choices that I had on the film."

Van Ark re-watched the film the night before we had this conversation, seeing the movie in its entirety for the first time since she completed it back in 1977. "I did "Knot's Landing" for almost 14 years and I never saw any of the final TV episodes. I went into the projection room and with no sound, looked to see if my face, my body language, everything I did that I hoped told the story."

The editor would run the show's daily footage at lunch hour for the writers and or producers. Joan would take her lunch, hiding in the projection room to view the footage.

"My lunch was usually a banana and honey because that's my go-to food on a set. It's quick and it does the trick."

She would go the next day to watch the dailies with the producers and writers who never knew she was above them watching in the projector room.

"I see that as part of the work of a caring actor," Joan stated. "Go big or go home." She took note of the mach speed the way things move nowadays. Now it's more about making your days and staying on schedule and budget. And actually that's valid and appropriate under current conditions. The new normal, post-COVID."

She had no contractual power to change anything she might not have liked in those dailies. "Never," she was adamant. "It was done. It was in the can. Moving on. Editing is the producer's work."

That level of commitment sounds just like Richard Boone's commitment to make the best possible art that he could. One could look at this as two actors from a different process that would be out of place in a brave new world of streaming content and instant celebrity.

"I wanted to see what I looked like performance-wise last night watching *The Last Dinosaur*. I wanted to be gutsier in the scene where I realized we were going to stay in that place, maybe for eternity until we died."

There was no pre-meeting with anyone of the cast while in the United States. *William Morris* did all the talking and negotiation for Joan, set up all the details, handed her two tickets and off she went to Japan.

"Rankin and Bass were also *William Morris* clients so the agency did all the talking with them. I did not."

The only time Joan ever met Arthur Rankin and Jules Bass, the producers of the film, was at the wrap party at the end of production. Her husband had long left. "And I was introduced to sushi as well! I never had that before! It was champagne and sushi. It was an AMAZING wrap party," she remembered. "I wish the film had been that good."

It was held in an opulent Tokyo hotel with first class everything. Including the film's starring actress.

A cast photo at *The Last Dinosaur* in Japan, 1976.
Notice Richard Boone's positioning to ensure he's never cut out.

CREATION: THE SCREENPLAY

A Prehistoric Beast Is A Cartoonist's Concept

By John Stanley

THE MOVIES have their new overpowering King Kong, but television is about to enjoy its own version of a ferocious monster — and not just a man in a hairy suit knocking over cardboard cities with a swipe of its arm.

This is a *real* movie monster. That is, it was achieved through the stop-motion process first developed by Willis O'Brien in the 1933 "King Kong" and perfected by the ingenious Ray Harryhausen in recent fantasy films like "The Golden Voyage of Sinbad." It falls into the category of special effects by craftsmen who must spend months manipulating their tiny models, a frame at a time, just to get a few seconds of film.

"The Last Dinosaur," Friday at 9 p.m. on Channels 7, 11, 13, is a collaborative effort between ABC and Toho Pictures of Japan (famous for Godzilla and other Oriental monstrosities) to bring to life a ferocious tyrannosaurus rex, largest and most deadly of prehistoric carnivorous beasts.

The creator of this bulking entity is cartoonist William Thomas Overgard, who has been drawing the popular "Steve Roper" comic strip since 1952, and who is now making his initial foray into film. Overgard looks upon screenwriting as merely an extension of cartooning.

"A cartoonist," he says, "has to have the mind of a camera, see things from different angles, different perspectives. Each cut is simply another panel. I enjoy writing immensely because it allows me to escape the mold of the comic strip and stretch my imagination by dealing with themes

Roper would never touch upon. And it keeps me from feeling I've turned stale."

Overgard first conceived "The Last Dinosaur" two years ago as a story about a modern hunter who travels back in time to track down the last of the tyrannosauruses — but ABC had plans to do an updated "King Kong" and the project was shelved. When Dino deLaurentiis snagged the rights to the giant ape first, the network jealously felt it too needed a monster and asked Overgard to come up with another concept. This time Toho agreed to co-finance and co-produce.

At first ABC frowned on Overgard writing the screenplay. "If you don't have several credits," he explains, "they start running scared. But the producer, Arthur Rankin, insisted that I not only do the scenario, but also be available for rewriting in Japan for four weeks, where most of the film was shot."

"The Last Dinosaur" is the story of a rich industrialist (Richard Boone) who is in possession of a new laser drill. His expedition bores under the polar cap in search of new oil deposits, and after cutting through a volcano, discovers a 25-mile area of foliage forgotten by time. Joan Van Ark plays the girl photographer, Stephen Keats is the young geologist and Luther Rakley the black scientist.

* * *

OVERGARD, who will be 51 in April, grew up in Santa Monica. From the time he was 12 he was writing letters to

See Page 37

S.F. Sunday Examiner & Chronicle

'The Last Dinosaur'

Continued from Page 36

Milton Caniff, praising "Terry and the Pirates." After serving in the Navy at Okinawa, Overgard sought out Caniff, who became his mentor and encouraged him to pursue cartooning as a profession.

"Occasionally, when Caniff fell ill, he would allow me to sketch the backgrounds and the bodies, but never the faces. Later, when he felt I was more competent, he allowed me to do two Steve Canyon comic books."

Although Overgard regarded comics as "shabby," preferring flesh and blood characters over superheroes, he joined the thriving comic book empire of Charles Biro in New York. "It was very primitive material — Boy and Black Diamond comics."

In 1952 Publishers Newspaper Syndicate was revising its "Steve Roper" series and, on the advice of Caniff, Overgard submitted samples. "It was conducted like a contest, with dozens of us trying for the position. I overwhelmed the competition by doing five strips and huge sheets of characters, girls, anything I could think of to make me look better than I was."

Immediately he began to update and upgrade the strip, introducing attractive women and a new character named Mike Nomad.

Since then Overgard has collaborated with writer Allen Saunders (and his son John) in the development of the strip. After they have agreed on outline, Saunders writes the text and dialogue while Overgard does the blocking and the final inking.

Overgard works 13 weeks ahead of print schedule, usually four days a week from 8 a.m. to noon. The rest of his free time is devoted to writing novels.

Three have been published — all paperbacks which have been moderately successful. The first, "Pieces of Hero," was purchased by a major studio for Lee Marvin, but the actor was disenchanted with the studio and refused to do it, even though James Poe had developed a screenplay at great expense. Overgard is currently at work on a book about cocaine smuggling in Mexico and three new TV movie outlines.

The question most often asked about "Steve Roper" is whether Steve's wife died in an explosion or is still mysteriously alive. "Allen and I are divided on that issue," reveals Overgard. "I personally think she should stay in the shadows, but Allen wants to bring her back. I don't know what the hell we're going to do."

Datebook, Sunday, February 6, 1977

'THE LAST DINOSAUR'

WILLIAM THOMAS OVERGARD

It all starts with a script. What happens when you hire a cartoonist to write a live-action movie about hunting a dinosaur?

Arthur Rankin and Jules Bass came from the world of animation. It's what they knew best but it's also what they did best. Producer Benni Korzen was brought to the live-action arm of Rankin/Bass because he was known as producer who could get things done on the right budget and get them done on time.

Rankin and Bass were on firm ground with animation. Korzen came from the live action feature world, and this was the world Rankin/Bass wanted to conquer next.

Korzen moved to the United States from Denmark, and has produced, line-produced or executive produced over 20 feature films. He is 85 today and still producing with A-list filmmakers and studios.

Korzen was introduced and teamed up with Rankin/Bass toward the end of the 60s as the duo looked toward live-action films. "My connection with Arthur and Jules started when they came to Copenhagen. They came to Denmark because they were doing a Danny Kaye special. I spent a lot of time with Danny Kaye as were friends. That's where I met Arthur and Jules. I had lived in New York as well and went back and forth."

These were basic details, however. Benni went on to say, "HOW they met me isn't as important as to WHY they needed me. At that time, I thought they had done about all they could in animation. They had annual holiday hits that started with *Rudolph the Red-Nosed Reindeer* in '64 and *The Daydreamer* with a lot of the stop motion stuff written by Romeo Muller and pretty much everything scored by Maury Laws," Benni reflected.

Photo Courtesy of Benni Korzen

Korzen laid out the Rankin/Bass formula—they preferred to use talent that produced results which made life easier for everyone. It was kind of "production shorthand" when you knew who to bring on board and would be reliable and get the job done.

The guerilla, indie horror movement starting in the early 70s with Tobe Hooper and running through its heyday with John Carpenter and George Romero (Romero was already running rogue with his *Night of the Living Dead* ten years before Hooper) established the common sense formula of finding good people in front and behind the camera and hanging on to them for as long as you could.

This is why in John Carpenter's early days you will see he used the same director of photography for most of his earliest (and best) work. The same goes for cast. It's no coincidence faces like Jamie Lee Curtis, Tom Atkins, Charles Cyphers, and Donald Pleasance rolled over into numerous Carpenter productions, especially in his early days.

It makes sense. George Romero did the same thing with his cast and crew. He and Carpenter often shared inside jokes with each other on their productions, naming characters after each other and crew members. It was tight-knit and close and allowed these film-makers to make their best product.

Rankin and Bass did the same thing before all of them. "They were very relaxed," Benni reflected. "They would bicker with each other, but almost always in a kidding kind of way. They would nag on each other."

"Busting balls," I replied and Benni laughed. "Yeah, something like that."

Rankin/Bass historian Rick Goldschmidt told me that he felt Jules Bass was more of "a loner" and the less social of the duo. Benni said there was some merit to that but felt the word "private" was a better word to describe the aloof director.

"Arthur was always very showy with his family and friends. When he was courting his wife, he had no problem with showing her about and talking openly. He socialized a lot and he was like an open book. Jules was different. I don't think in all the years I knew and worked with him did I ever see much of his family life. His private life was private and he didn't share much in that respect."

Fair enough.

"I was an eyewitness and can tell you exactly how they (Rankin and Bass) did it." Benni referred to how the duo sold their projects to network TV. They had a formula and it was as relaxed and casual as the two of them. This is how *The Last Dinosaur* came to be.

At this time Rankin/Bass were dealing exclusively with the *ABC* network.

"We had an office in New York City, just off fifth and 52nd in Manhattan. What they would do…one of them had a personal relationship with the *ABC* head of development. They would invite four or five executives to come to the conference room on the fifth floor.

They would sit them down in the middle of the room. In the middle of the room was a large artist's easel and it was covered with a cloth. Then after everybody had a bit of chat they would lift the cloth revealing a poster that basically explained the movie they wanted *ABC* to finance."

These are the early days of "The Pitch Session." Rankin and Bass did not go at it like carnival barkers or hucksters. The atmosphere was relaxed from the beginning of the meeting. "There was a lot of "So, how are you and how are things going? How's the wife, the kids?" That kind of thing."

However at the head of the room was that covered easel and underneath it was business and no matter where you were in the room your eyes could not escape what was under that cloth. That

The original artwork used to pitch the film to the ABC executives in New York. This was later used for a Variety announcement that the film was finished.

was why everyone was here and it built up everything for a terrific Rankin/Bass anticipatory set.

When the time came, Arthur and Jules would remove the cloth (without a "Ta da!") and show the group their latest project pitch.

That one day in early 1976 the poster revealed artwork for *The Last Dinosaur*.

"They had a team in-house, in Japan who created the poster art. It not only had the title but also had some images that explained exactly what the story was. To the extent a poster could. They were very well put together."

Korzen went on to say that these kind of pitch meetings rarely went longer than 45 minutes. The executives would walk out after shaking hands after basically saying, "Okay, this is what we will do."

That's how easy it was for Rankin/Bass to sell a project. Now, why? How do two guys herd some suits into a room and less than hour later convince a network to spend money on an idea represented by a single poster?

The answer is: past history. Arthur Rankin and Jules Bass had a track record. The product they made for *ABC* and even other networks (like *CBS* with *Rudolph*) were still making money. Their previous works had become annual holiday traditions and advertising cash cows.

Arthur Rankin and Jules Bass were "Quiet Cool." They didn't have to use bombast or hyperbolic language. When they said they would get something done, they got it done. Their track record in wildly successful animation (both stop-motion and 2-D) was legendary.

If these two guys said they could make a live-action dinosaur movie, then they could. They laid it all out from concept to execution and let the executives decide.

They approved *The Last Dinosaur* and they did it without a cast attached or even a script.

"At that time there was no screenplay. The basic idea they had was then handed over to Bill Overgard, who was an in-house writer for Rankin and Bass."

Overgard hailed from the world of comics. He was famous for his syndicated serial comic strip, *Steve Roper*. He started early with assisting on the adventure serial comic, *Steve Canyon*. (I am old enough to remember I had a *Steve* Canyon set of slides for my *Viewmaster* in the early 70s). His penchant for adventure stories would lead to various ups and downs with that strip, a

William Overgard at work drawing.

brief cult "failure" with a noir-ish short-lived strip about a talking ape with *Rudy* from 1984-1985 and then moved into animated Saturday morning cartoons like the *Rankin/Bass* produced, *Thundercats*.

He moved into screenplays by the late 70s with *The Last Dinosaur* being his first for Rankin/Bass. He transitioned from comic work to novels to screenplays.

Looking at Overgard's life and his background, adventure was at the center. He brought innovation to *Steve Roper's* angles and perspectives in those panels. He even believed his work was "ripped off" by famed pop artist Roy Lichtenstein and addressed it in a *Time Magazine* piece. He wrote this:

"Sir: As a cartoonist I was interested in Roy Lichtenstein's comments on comic strips in your article on pop art. Though he may not, as he says, copy them exactly, Lichtenstein in his painting currently being shown at the Guggenheim comes pretty close to the last panel of my Steve Roper Sunday page of Aug. 6, 1961. Very flattering ... I think?" [14]

He spent 31 years, almost half of his life on *Steve Roper*.

Three years after *The Last Dinosaur*, another famed cartoonist turned screenwriter, Jules Pfieffer would turn the comic strip *Popeye* into a feature screenplay. Jules made the leaps from cartoonist to playwright and screenwriter (He wrote the script for the classic Mike Nicholls film, *Carnal Knowledge* which was adapted from Pfeiffer's play).

The result would be mixed in the same way it was mixed for Overgard. The mind of an artist working in a visual medium should translate well into a screenplay one would think. In the cases of both *The Last Dinosaur* and *Popeye* it's perspective.

Popeye has been assailed by critics who point fingers first at its screenplay—or lack thereof. Some reviewers stated it was less a screenplay than it was a list of characters and events and the 1980 Robin Williams film was "incoherent, boring, a mess."

What's been said about *The Last Dinosaur's* script?

The Last Dinosaur was written by William Overgard (*Steve Roper*) and combines elements from Sir Arthur Conan Doyle's *The Lost World*, Edgar Rice Burroughs' *At the Earth's Core* and Universal International's 1957 science fiction film, *The Land Unknown*. [15]

On the surface, it's goofy junk in the vein of *Unknown Island* or *The Land that Time Forgot*, but then it invites us with a straight face to think about aging and regret and the inevitability of change, and how the passage of time eventually takes everything away from

---

14 Overgard, William. 1963. Letter to *Time Magazine*, May 17, 1963.

15 *The Good, The Bad and Godzilla,* May 12, 2009. http://augustragone.blogspot. com/2009/05/last-dinosaur-strikes-again-toho-video.html

all of us, no matter how much we might have started with, or how much we might amass on the way.

Even the Tyrannosaurus, rightly the best developed of the valley's prehistoric fauna, is hampered by screenwriter William Overgard's inability to make up his mind about what its capabilities are. Instead of being *The Last Dinosaur*'s Moby Dick, the T-Rex comes out more like its white buffalo. Ultimately, this is another case in which you'll have to decide which weighs more— the uncommonly ambitious stuff that it tries to do, or its inability to do very much of it in a satisfying manner." [16]

"Our film opens in the den of our antihero, industrialist and big game hunter Masten Thrust (!). That name should give you some idea of the script's quality… One can just imagine the screenwriter convincing himself that all this 'subtext' somehow justified the crappy script." [17]

"The thumping development of William Overgard's script is that the title applies as much to Thrust as the T-Rex: the millionaire is at his happiest when shipwrecked, deprived of the trappings of wealth and even modern weaponry, forced to rely on his own inventive smarts (he whips up a crossbow and a giant catapult) as he sets out on a naturally-inconclusive quest to bring down the T-Rex. Thrust is a broadly cliché character, but still the most interesting person to be pitted against a dinosaur in a film since Robert Armstrong's Carl Denham, and his contrary antics mean that at least this doesn't stick to the formulae of every other Lost World movie made up until 1977." [18]

---

16 Ashlin, Scott. *The Last* Dinosaur review. http://1000misspenthours.com/reviews/reviewsh-m/lastdinosaur.htm

17 Beg, Kenneth. *The Last Dinosaur. Jabootu's Bad Movie Dimension.* Dec. 10, 1998. http://jabootu.net/?p=592

18 Newman, Kim. *The Last Dinosaur (1977). The Kim Newman Website.* April, 13, 2020. https://johnnyalucard.com/2020/04/13/film-review-the-last-dinosaur-1977/

"Writer William Overgard originally developed *The Last* Dinosaur as a time travel story about a hunter traveling back to the Cretaceous Period to stalk the last Tyrannosaur. With hype building for Dino DeLaurentiis` big budget *King Kong* remake (1976), Rankin/Bass saw the potential in Overgard`s story and hired him to rework *The Last Dinosaur* into a "lost world" tale set in the modern day." [19]

"The film was written by first time screenwriter William Overgard and it shows.

He has exchanges like this take place when the group first encounters the T-Rex and barely escapes even though Thrust shot at it:

Wade: You told me! You swore to all of us that we were not going to harm the dinosaur! We were only supposed to take film and study it!

Thrust: You ding-dong!

I don't know what's worse, the fact that Wade is upset that Thrust tried to defend them or that the

worst insult the hunter can come up with is "ding-dong." "[20]

"William Overgard (not Overguard) was diversely talented much like frequent *Kaiju eiga* writer Shinichi Sekizawa. Primarily a cartoonist and novelist, he penned the strip *Steve Roper and Mike Nomad* for a while, and as a protégée of Milton Caniff was heavily influenced by *Terry and the Pirates* and *Steve Canyon*, an attitude carried over into *The Last Dinosaur*. (*Reader Sergei Hasenecz notes*, "He didn't pen (write) *Roper/Nomad*, he drew it. And it was for quite a while, from 1954 to 1985, just short of 31 years. After he

19 *Sci-Fi Japan.com The Last Dinosaur on DVD From Warner Archive.* 2023. https://www.scifijapan.com/dvd-blu-ray-digital/the-last-dinosaur-on-dvd-from-warner-archive

20 Sinnot, John. *The Last Dinosaur. DVD Talk.* Mar. 22, 2011. https://www.dvdtalk.com/reviews/52607/last-dinosaur-the/

left *Roper/Nomad,* Overgard did some ghost-writing for the *Kerry Drake* comic strip, then wrote and drew the oddball and original *Rudy.* He also did scripts for two cartoon series, *Silver Hawks* and *Thunder Cats.*) Overgard later wrote *The Bermuda Depths, The Ivory Ape,* and *The Bushido Blade* for Rankin/Bass, but none of these ever comes close to approaching the poetry of *The Last Dinosaur.*" [21]

As a screenwriter, what's my take on Overgard's work? I am biased because you are reading someone who loves 1980's *Popeye* and believes it is Robin William's best movie. I didn't say his funniest, but his best because *Popeye* is art. The main reason for that is the script and its loose love for the characters.

Overgard might've aped some dino adventure stories for sure, but in the center of it all he creates this somber tone, this swan song for a man and beast. I might go as far to say that he put a nice spin on man vs. nature where it turns to Man vs. Himself.

As noted before, this is that rare Kaiju film that allows the human character to be a sympathetic major character that is on equal footing with the monster.

Overgard's dialogue can be silly, sure. The effort to establish Frankie as a fiercely independent woman only to reduce her by the third act to a prehistoric housewife and sex object is counterproductive.

"You ding dong!" I don't have to say much more about the dialogue at times.

Yet, in this low budget movie is a great one under the layers. It's a true adventure story and it works with all the elements it borrows.

---

21 IV Galbraith, Stuart. The Last Dinosaur. DVD Talk. May 22, 2009. https://www.dvdtalk.com/reviews/45612/last-dinosaur-the/?___rd=1

The pacing is overall tight for an almost two hour film. Overgard gets points just for his "Golden Bullet" line alone.

The script for *The Last Dinosaur* is fun. Coming from a cartoonist, *Tsuburaya Productions* visual effects go hand in hand with the world Overgard created on film. It lacks realism, it lacks proper execution of effects that would be considered primitive by today's standards.

That's all okay, because here we are, 50 years later still talking about it.

CREATION: PRE-PRODUCTION

Rankin and Bass made it all look easy. Just go in, pitch what you want, get a check, go off and make your movie. It's not exactly that easy, but according to producer, Benni Korzen, their productions were some of the most easy-going he'd ever worked.

Let me give you a basic rundown of what pre-production entails. It's the same for any movie despite the budget. The scale of it is the only variable.

It starts with the idea, which we saw with the unveiling of the poster for the *ABC* brass. From there it moves into actual development. This is where a writer is attached (William Overgard) and producers start hiring staff: Location scouts/managers, cast, crew, services…it all starts to kick in before the cameras start to roll.

Benni Korzen was brought on board because of his work in low budget features and having the mindset of stretching a dollar to cover complex productions. While Rankin and Bass were on animation terra firma, this was a new landscape for the partners and Benni was there to help guide them through the live-action territory.

"Schedules were created and what I then did as part of the team was put together an action plan for where we would do this or that. Arthur had, at that time, worked out a very strong connection to filmmakers in Japan. Masaki IIzuka was this important connection."

Rankin/Bass had long used Tadahito "Tad" Mochinaga to head their "Animagic" productions in Japan throughout the 60s. I remembered seeing his name on the opening credits of *Mad Monster Party* every time I got to see it. His name stood out.

Tadahito Mochinaga, was a prolific stop-motion animator and director, who made significant contributions to the animation industry throughout his career. His collaboration with *Rankin/Bass*, was characterized by a string of well-received productions that many went on to be timeless classics and as popular as when they debuted over half a century before.

Mochinaga served as Animation Director/Supervisor for "The New Adventures of Pinocchio" (1960–1961), a charming television series that saw him working closely with a talented group of animators to bring the beloved character to life. His technical proficiency and attention to detail earned him a reputation as a skilled animator, which led to his work as Animation Supervisor on 1964's "Rudolph the Red-Nosed Reindeer" and "Willy McBean and his Magic Machine" released a year later

Mochinaga's expertise in stop-motion animation also earned him a role as "Animagic" Technician on *The Daydreamer* that entertained me as boy on TV even though it had a theatrical release a year before I was born in 1966; with a dark adaptation of Hans Christian Anderson's original *The Little Seamaid (Mermaid)*.

He continued in this role for *Ballad of Smokey the Bear* (1966), a short film that promoted fire prevention and safety measures. Mochinaga's technical prowess was also evident in his work as "Animagic" Technician on *Mad Monster Party* (1967), and the film that made his name known to me as a boy.

Rankin/Bass Productions collaborated with several animation studios, such as *Toei Animation, Eiken* (formerly known as *TCJ* or *Television Corporation of Japan*), Mushi Production, and particularly *Topcraft. Topcraft*, established on February 1, 1972, by Toei animator Toru Hara, was responsible for providing animation supervision for some of *Rankin/Bass'* specials. Despite *Topcraft's* dissolution, several of its staff, including Hara and industry stalwarts such as Hayao Miyazaki, went on to establish *Studio Ghibli*. Others formed *Pacific Animation Corporation*, which continued to produce *Rankin/Bass* titles until the latter's eventual closure.

They met future *Last Dinosaur* associate producer, Masaki Iizuka when he started as a production assistant on their 1973 film, *Marco*, the odd live-action/animated musical adventure film starring Zero Mostel. Benni Korzen helped produce this film as well.

Iizuka would become an associate producer on *The Last Dinosaur*. He worked with Rankin/Bass on the quasi sequel to *Mad Monster Party*, *Mad, Mad, Mad Monsters* and since became a major part of the *Rankin/Bass* fold.

This would lead to their fusion with *Toho Studios*, its distribution subsidiary company *Toho-Towa Pictures*, *Tsuburaya Productions* and other animation production companies. The *Rankin/Bass* partnership with Japan ensured *The Last Dinosaur* would be a total co-production between East and West.

"Masaki was the key person who got into contact with all the local key people in Japan," Benni Korzen said, and stressed Iizuka's contribution to the film cannot be overestimated. "While Masaki got to work on the Japanese "To Do List" we got started on the casting."

"The key cast would come from the United States. That's how *The Last Dinosaur* started its development around 1975-76 with 100% of the movie shot there."

Benni took pause to go reflect again on the relationship between Arthur Rankin and Jules Bass. "It was a fascinating partnership. I had worked with numerous people before and with other partnerships but Arthur and Jules were very different. Since they were so very smart and knew what they were doing, they tested each other. It was a positive criticism kind of thing."

This will be important in the actual production of the film.

Arthur and Jules could move simply and quickly because their in-house team just rolled over into the next project. Arthur had an apartment in Tokyo and to accommodate composer Maury Laws for *The Last Dinosaur* they went through a lot of trouble to move a piano into that apartment.

"Arthur felt that Maury should have constant access to this room where the piano was stored and should be allowed to walk around this film and "sniff it out" because he would be more creative and inspired for the score of the film." Benni admired Arthur's commitment to quality and is another piece of evidence to show the film was not a cynical one.

While writer Romeo Muller was their staple writer, they threw the opportunity to William Overgard. With all of these key players in place and with Benni Korzen as the contractor aligning all of the Japanese sub contractors, the casting phase for *The Last Dinosaur* could begin.

"I wish I could say that the pre-production or even production of *The Last Dinosaur* was troublesome or difficult. It really wasn't from a producer sense. The actors had to go through some things with being in a difficult location, but Arthur and Jules were so smart and elegant. It was not like other productions I worked with. It did not compare to the standard studio executive kind of thing."

Korzen went on to talk of the East Coast vs. West Coast attitude toward filmmaking which I subscribe to as well. There is just a different way the east coast filmmakers do things in comparison to their west coast counterparts.

Things happen faster and more efficiently than the sometimes bloated and lumbering way films get made in California. Whether it is urgency or a disdain for what many call "Hollywood Bullshit," Arthur and Jules were east coast all the way and this fortified their reputations as men who got things done and done well.

"There's a slightly different way of conducting business between Hollywood and New York, especially back then." Benni was resolute. "It impressed the shit out of me, and never saw anything so simple and direct as the way Arthur and Jules ran their productions. When you can express an idea for a movie in a poster, and just a single poster in a relaxed atmosphere--that's incredible. Super, fast and simple. That's how they worked."

THE LAST DINOSAUR

Hunting is the name of the game for Masten Thrust, the world's richest man. When one of his oil drilling teams probes under the Polar Cap breaking through into a pocket of suspended time they discover a minute prehistoric world ruled over by the largest predator ever to stalk the earth, the Tyrannosaurus Rex - THE LAST DINOSAUR.

Obsessed with killing the dinosaur Masten recruits a select hunting party and leads them into the dawn of time after the ultimate game.

The hunt is a disaster - one by one the party go down and defect. At the end Masten is alone. A solitary figure but still a relentless hunter, awaiting his one chance - to kill THE LAST DINOSAUR.

An original Rankin/Bass pitch sheet for the film, 1976.

CREATION: CASTING

2023 Miser Bros. Press/Rick Goldschmidt

Rankin and Bass were no neophytes when it came to casting talent for live-action films. They combined live stars with animation with their earlier productions of *The Daydreamer* and *Marco*. Casting for *The Last Dinosaur* would follow their template.

Represented by William Morris, the talent agency that could be considered among their "in-house" staff packaged up the film and took it out for the casting directors to match up candidates for the roles.

Did they have anyone specific in mind? I could not find any information to corroborate that. With Benni Korzen's description of their cool, relaxed business model, it's likely they turned this part over to the agency and let the Hollywood machine take over.

Richard Boone sealed the deal for Joan as she said previously. She had no prep time, got tickets for her and her husband to go to Japan. "William Morris did all the talking," Joan said.

When Joan arrived in Japan, the actors were first put up in a first class hotel in Tokyo and treated royally. Rankin and Bass knew how to take care of their people.

"The real adventure was when we headed out to the location in the Japanese Alps (in Kamikochi, Japan). I t was…remote. Let's just say that. Remote."

The hotel in the Kamikochi Prefect might've been the only hotel in that area and was "lacking" to say the least and a major contrast to the luxury hotel in Tokyo. "It was not quite the best hotel in Japan." Joan laughed at that one. She referenced giant green apples that became a staple of her diet.

"I lived on them, and I can't find them here in the States--these apples were the size of grapefruits. They were huge and amazing. That would be "go food" for me during the shoot. It was quick and pure energy for me. They didn't have garbage and salt, MSG and all that stuff. I loved them."

I asked about Luther Rackley who played Bunta, Richard Boone's big game tracker. Joan laughed when I asked if she flew on the same plane with him over to Japan. "This story is great. I did not fly on the same plane with Luther. He was a basketball player as you know for The New York Nicks, but he also had this side job as an actor. He made me laugh because he was on a plane out of New York. I flew out of LA. He read the script on the flight. He hadn't read the script because they'd just offered it to him."

2023 Miser Bros. Press/Rick Goldschmidt

Joan couldn't remember if it was *William Morris* or whatever agency that brought him the project. "He was with *William Morris*. They said something like "They want you to do this tracker in this movie, blah, blah, blah…"

She chuckled again. "He hadn't read the script and he might've been cast at the last minute, I'm not sure, but he gets on this plane and flies from New York to Japan and finds out from reading the script he doesn't have one line in the entire thing! He's just tall and thin and just tracker looking."

2023 Miser Bros. Press/Rick Goldschmidt

This memory brought her a lot of giggles as she reflected on her husband and Luther bonding and becoming close friends during the time he was in Japan with Joan. "They enjoyed some Asahi Beer. I'll just put it that way. It was almost like my husband was in the treetops with Luther having fun while I was literally praying under my breath that we got the shot and we got it right and I was giving the goods on a day's work."

She did reflect to in a similar interview with Kaiju writer, Brett Homenick, "Luther is just hysterical to me, and almost comical to look at, even though that's not the way he came off in the movie, by any means. But it was so funny because he never really said a word! He's just such a personality. That's where Alex Grasshoff (the film's director) and all of us would get the giggles because there were so many difficult situations." [22]

When I offered that on one hand Luther had it good—he had no lines to learn and just ran around the forests of Japan. On the other hand, he could've easily asked, "What the hell am I doing here?"

"Exactly!" Joan exclaimed. "You nailed it! It was double-sided. I am sure he had a great time one way or the other."

Despite the challenges shaping up on arrival to set, Joan was adamant when she said, "I have to say this—in watching the film last night in its entirety, which I may have done before but I don't recall, I saw that the actors on the set and starting with Richard Boone, God bless him; when it came time and we heard "action" out of the two directors (we had two directors, one Japanese (Tom Kotani) and the other *William Morris*--Grasshoff) I was pleasantly surprised with the work by the three principals: Steven, Joan and Richard Boone. The work was there. We gave it the best effort."

It's here where Joan got deeper in reflection and opened up about Richard Boone. This moment started a pattern of affection by Joan for Richard and dispelled the numerous (I now believe false) online stories that Boone and Van Ark had conflict.

---

22 Homenick, Brett. Chasing the Dinosaur! Conversation with Joan Van Ark. Vantage Point Interviews. Aug. 18,, 2019. https://vantagepointinterviews. com/2018/08/19/chasing-the-last-dinosaur-a-candid-conversation-with-joan-van-ark/

2023 Miser Bros. Press/Rick Goldschmidt

There are reports out there, mostly in reviews of the film (as so little has been written about *The Last Dinosaur* until now) that Boone was condescending and dismissive of Van Ark, living up to his character's misogyny and contempt for women.

Joan was firm that none of this was true. She did and still does hold Richard Boone with the utmost respect and affection.

"The looks between Richard and me—there was a softness that I recognized, and it was pure male and it's *ageing* male, which I now know that because you look in the mirror and it ain't quite what you hoped for. And that's not Richard necessarily but..."

She paused there and chose her next words carefully and you could hear the emotion in them as she spoke again. "He was a true dinosaur in a way..."

He is the last. There are no more...

Producer Benni Korzen summed up Richard Boone in one word: "Fascinating." He was a larger than life actor and man. His persona on *Have Gun--Will Travel* was part of his real makeup. The Richard Boone that demanded quality, that demanded actors give their best to whatever they were doing and wrote that industry letter to urge the powers that be to shun cynicism in entertainment, was the same man on the set of *The Last Dinosaur*.

There is a scene in *Star Trek II: The Wrath of Khan* where Admiral James T. Kirk needs to find his way out of a no-win scenario. *The Enterprise* was just attacked by his long ago enemy, Khan who demands Kirk surrender his ship or have it blown away with his entire training crew on board.

Kirk stalls for time and starts pushing buttons and touching controls, perplexing Vulcan Commander Saavik. When she asks him what he is doing, Kirk tells her that a captain of a starship should know how everything works for the kind of situation they were facing. He demonstrates by exploiting a little known code to force the enemy ship to drop its shields and give them a window to fire back and escape.

2023 Miser Bros. Press/Rick Goldschmidt

Richard Boone was very much like James T. Kirk. He was a writer. He was a director. He knew how to move lights and he knew how things on a set should work. He was vocal when he lost confidence in directors and once walked off a set and never finished his dialogue because of what he felt was unprofessionalism and ineptitude.

Korzen supported and described Boone's ability to size up any situation right down to something as simple as a group photo shoot for a press release.

"He knew everything, not just being an actor but everything that takes place on a movie set," Korzen told me. "At one point we were out on a location for *The Last Dinosaur* and there was a still photographer lining up some stuff for a PR shot. This guy lined up people and Boone said, "No, no, no, I don't want to be there.""

Richard was saying he didn't like where he was placed for the group shot. "He just said, in English, and I heard it, "I don't want to be cut off."

Boone knew the place where the photographer put him could have him cut off when the photos printed in various sizes or aspect ratios. He was the star of the film and there was no way he was going to get cut out of his own press for the movie.

 "He knew where he should be in that photograph," Korzen was impressed. "It took just ten seconds to rearrange Boone in the shot and that was it."

Korzen did address the "drunk on set" rumors that seem to pock nearly every review of *The Last Dinosaur*. Keep in mind the film was made at a time before The Internet and before 24 hour news and smothering "infotainment" coverage of every move a star made.

There have always been gossip columnists but the dreaded gossip harpies of Old Hollywood, Louella Parsons and Hedda Hopper, who could destroy careers with just a few lines in their columns, would pale against today's online vultures and bottom feeding predators.

The *National Enquirer* was nearing its peak but the gossip tabloid afforded little attention to a faded star like Boone and something as banal as drinking on set. The late 70s were a time of wanting more shocking revelations: cocaine, heroin, outing closeted stars and AIDS was just around the corner.

The production could control the information that got to the press because of the limited pipelines but also by the physical isolation of the location. If Boone was staggering around drunk, no one would know except the crew and cast and there were no cell phones or places to upload the footage like what happened to Christian Bale and his now infamous tirade on the set of *Terminator Salvation*.

Boone's wife was along for the production, but served as a kind of assistant, according to producer Benni Korzen. She was there to dilute his vodka with water and keep it handy for him throughout the shoot day. "Yes, diluting the vodka that accompanied Boone wherever we shot."

Benni laughed at this but made it clear that while Richard Boone liked to imbibe he was always on his mark and professional when the cameras rolled. "I never saw him drunk during the production, no."

He did add that he was impressed with the amount of vodka that vanished from the bottles that made it to Richard through the dilution process. "There was no reduction of his craft on camera."

Joan Van Ark echoed similar accounts. "It was always best to get everything you needed from Richard before lunch," she chuckled. "He liked to take…a liquid lunch, shall we say."

Van Ark supported Korzen's account that Boone's drinking was no secret and part of his legend; however he was there for the shoot and to get things done right.

"He was always professional," Joan told me. "He was isolated, though." She described that not a lot of interaction between her and Boone or Boone and anyone went on between scenes. When the action was done Richard secluded himself to his trailer until he was called for again.

Korzen agreed but added that this was not an anti-social thing, but rather how Boone handled himself. There was a lot going on inside of him, and while the timeline of his cancer diagnosis is unclear, there is the possibility that he knew he was not well. That is not confirmed and Korzen admitted that could be a possibility but Richard never spoke of it with him.

There are several accounts that Boone's drinking was a coping mechanism for the horrors he endured in World War II. He was seen as a man who carried some heavy burdens with a lot of inner turmoil. It's interesting to note that this internalization of things seemed to come out or was remedied by his love to paint. He once wished to be a famous painter and the art is said to have brought him serenity and some kind of peace.

2023 Miser Bros. Press/Rick Goldschmidt

"He wouldn't have talked to me of such things," Korzen said. "Richard kept things very close to him."

Korzen did admit that the production was not equipped to handle an aging legendary star like Boone, which will be discussed later. "Joan Van Ark is right about her memory of her time with Boone. He was a professional and I never saw any issues between Richard and his co-stars. They seemed to be having a fun time. I never saw his alcohol consumption impacting his performance or impact his capacity to do his job."

I did ask if Boone had any issues with a particular piece of dialogue. He is rumored to have been irritated with the script and would halt production to change lines or rewrite whole scenes. The writer in him was as much in tune with the production as the actor.

"Ding dong," I asked Benni. "Richard wanted acting to be the top of his craft but he calls Steven Keats a "Ding Dong" and reviewers latch on to that. Did he ever bring up this line or complain about it to you?"

"No, I don't remember him doing that." Korzen had to give it some thought. He did follow it up by saying that when Richard did offer up a complaint, "He wasn't wrong in what he was saying."

Korzen knew Richard was committed to quality and his few complaints 

were never with his cast mates but rather with the logistics of shooting in such rough terrain and during a several day spate of monsoon rains. "It was monsoon season," Benni laughed. "You can imagine how that went."

2023 Miser Bros. Press/Rick Goldschmidt

Steven Keats was his own legend. Keats was rumored to be both a hot head and a ladies' man on the set of *The Last Dinosaur*. "Both accounts are correct," Benni Korzen confirmed.

"Steven was very successful at being a ladies' man. I remember that there was a young woman, part of the Japanese crew who was stunningly sexy and the minute we stepped off the transport that took us to the location, both me and Keats saw this woman and started talking about how beautiful she was. It was no more than 24 hours before they had sex. That was far faster than I could operate."

<u>STEVEN KEATS</u>

STEVEN KEATS portrays Chuck, the young palaeontologist recruited into the hunting party to track down 'THE LAST DINOSAUR'.

This fast-rising young actor is also to be seen as an Israeli commando in Paramount's BLACK SUNDAY. He also played key roles in DEATH WISH, THE FRIENDS OF EDDIE COYLE, THE GAMBLER, HESTER STREET, SKY RIDERS and GUMBALL RALLY.

His Broadway credits include OH CALCUTTA!!, ONE FLEW OVER THE CUCKOOS NEST and WE BOMBED IN NEW HAVEN. Keats has also been seen on television in several series episodes and TV movies - ANYTHING GOES, ADAMS OF EAGLE LAKE, THE DREAM MAKERS, PRETTY BOY FLOYD and THE MONEYCHANGERS.

****

Keats was seen as surrounded by a bevy of female admirers and potential conquests. He was the popular guy on set who got the attention of the women and he welcomed it. "Steven was a wonderful part of the family and we loved having him there. We really did."

2023 Miser Bros. Press/Rick Goldschmidt

Joan remembers him as having incredible energy. "Between takes he was a motor mouth!" she laughed. "He was always making fun or doing impressions, and I think it was to keep his energy up. He just rattled on with crazy phrases and I don't know if he did the "Do it for Arthur!" impression, but I remember it said with an accent. He would imitate us and our dialogue and some of it was very funny. Some of it was interfering but that was how he burned off steam."

A film set does become a sort of family. It's an intense period of time, whether a few weeks or months, emotions and passions run hard and all are tested by the crew that is there to create the film and support the actors.

Korzen affirmed this, believing film sets are family affairs. It's an instant family and it disbands as quickly as it forms.

2023 Miser Bros. Press/Rick Goldschmidt

Keats was remembered by both Joan Van Ark and Korzen as a pleasure to work with. "I don't remember anything bad about working with Steven," Benni revealed. "The answer is I remember nothing negative. This is really where actors are far more in tune with things like this than a movie crew. In my role as an associate producer, it was my responsibility to ensure that everyone was fulfilling their assigned duties. This involved keeping a close eye on the progress of the project to ensure that everything was going smoothly. Despite feeling anxious about the possibility of Richard being unable to perform his role, I was relieved to discover that everything went according to plan, and the project was a success."

Benni Korzen believes if there were any issues, they were handled in-house between the actors so that it did not impact the crew or production. "Actors are on another planet."

2023 Miser Bros. Press/Rick Goldschmidt

2023 Miser Bros. Press/Rick Goldschmidt

2023 Miser Bros. Press/Rick Goldschmidt

A TALE OF TWO DIRECTORS

The Last Dinosaur has two directors credited to its production. It's been hard to get clear answers on the lines drawn between the American, Oscar-winning director, Alexander Grasshoff and Japanese director Tsugunobu "Tom" Kotani, who spoke not a word of English.

Here are the scenarios I tried to clarify for the writing of this book.

1. Alexander Grasshoff was hired but was soon found to be in over his head and relieved of his duties and left the production.
2. Grasshoff directed the live-action actors on location and Kotani directed the special effects scenes both on location and then in the studio with **Tsuburaya Productions.**
3. Grasshoff and Kotani split directing duties with both being on set the entire time with Kotani possibly directing Grasshoff.

Before I get into addressing these three scenarios (all of which could be wrong) a little background on American director, Alexander Grasshoff.

Joan Van Ark was amazed to find out on set that she and Grasshoff were virtually neighbors back in Los Angeles. "It's like he lived inches from me above us on Mulholland Drive all that time!" she exclaimed. "I never knew that until we were shooting *Dinosaur.*"

Alexander Grasshoff came from the world of documentary filmmaking—reality. Well, as real as documentaries can be, but not from fictional or narrative filmmaking roots.

Grasshoff won the 1969 Academy Award for Best Feature Documentary for his film *Young Americans*. He wrote and directed.

Los Angeles Times, 1969

Alex Grasshoff holds his Oscar (left), 1969.

"We slept with the Oscar the first night," his wife laughed in interviews. "It was very exciting."

Just a few weeks after receiving the award, Grasshoff was forced to return it.

The reason for Grasshoff's disqualification and subsequent return of the Oscar was due to the fact that *Young Americans* showed in a theater in 1967 prior to its 1968 theatrical release. This violated the Academy's rules, which stated that a film must have a theatrical run in Los Angeles County for at least seven consecutive days in order to be eligible for an Oscar.

When the Academy discovered the violation, they launched an investigation, which ultimately led to Grasshoff's disqualification and the rescinding of his award. Grasshoff, who had no involvement in the decision to air the film on television before its theatrical release, was understandably disappointed by the turn of events.

Disappointed is an understatement. Joan Van Ark was unaware of this during *The Last Dinosaur*. Again, while there was press back in the day, it was not saturated like it is now with *Google* Alerts and constant immersion in data.

"That leaves scar tissue," she said in shock. She had to take several pauses when I revealed Grasshoff's Oscar heartbreak to her. "It explains a lot," she finally said and you could tell she felt for the director.

"It's just awful. I don't go on The Internet. I have a website but it's a Joan Van Ark site and it's just general. I don't tend to it or have anyone tending to it like some celebrities have. The Internet is so… dangerous and often toxic. I don't look at all of that. My husband does it for me. If I see anything in print, I never forget it."

She connected this scarring from online nastiness back to Grasshoff and losing his Oscar. "That's deep and that doesn't go away. I don't care what you say. To earn something and then have it taken away with the recognition for it…that's a hard thing to live with the rest of your creative life. Creativity is delicate. It takes so many layers of confidence and choice and caring and all those things that mix up in trying to deliver your A-game."

She felt that this all explained Grasshoff's directing style and his way of taking shortcuts and often not the best possible way of doing things. "Less than best," she said. "Because it was overwhelming."

While it is possible Van Ark talked the script with Grasshoff she has no recollection because of the whirlwind and challenging production. "This is thousands of years ago and thousands of projects ago that I don't know how to best answer that. I don't recall details or significant things before we started working."

Was Grasshoff fired and removed from the set I asked Joan. She said no. She does not remember the director leaving the set. "If they fired him it might've been after we wrapped but no, I don't remember that happening at all."

Actress Masumi Sekiya who played cavewoman, "Hazel" had difficulty remembering Grasshoff. She recalled her audition but found it hard to recall many specifics. "The main actors in the movie were already prominent, so I remember who else was there and what kind of audition was held. I remember it well. It was about 180 people, I think." [23]

2023 Miser Bros. Press/Rick Goldschmidt

Sekiya was told to think of the role as a sort of "Female Tarzan." "When I went to the audition venue, there were a lot of girls around the same age as me who were doing youth dramas at the time. The teacher and my friends had a lot of connections, so whenever we went to auditions, we were usually with the same people. Among the conditions was the requirement to bring a swimsuit photo, and on the day of the shoot, we were also required to wear swimsuits."

She recalled that the directive did not come from either Grasshoff or Kotani.

---

23   The Last Dinosaur, Special Edition DVD. Commentary by Masumi Sekiya, Tom Kotani. 2009. Toho Video.

"There were no lines, so I had to act as if I was peeking through a gap or something, looking nervously. We were made to act as if we were peeking. I think that was the second-to-last round, and the number of people kept decreasing. After that audition, eight people were chosen." [24]

2023 Miser Bros. Press/Rick Goldschmidt

24 The Last Dinosaur, Special Edition DVD. Commentary by Masumi Sekiya, Tom Kotani. 2009. Toho Video.

There were no lines as Luther Rackley would discover for his character, Bunta.

"We seemed to be able to act, but even after reading the script, I still didn't understand it very well, and until I went to the shooting location, I thought of myself as a female Tarzan. However, I was told to go to the dentist, and was told to come back with a reflexive tooth. So, I got one and was like, "What should I do with this?"

Sekiya referred to the fake teeth used to make a more primitive look for her character. [25]

As for Grasshoff, she likened but did not say definitively that his direction for her "cave walk" was akin to bullying.

"He told me to watch him walk and imitate him. So the director walked by spreading his legs and bending forward with his hands hanging down like a primitive man's walk. That's right, so I walked a little like that, and he looked at me with that face and said, "You're walking like a woman, aren't you?

He made me walk like that a few more times until I wasn't embarrassed anymore, and then he said, "From now on, we'll shoot everything with that walk." [26]

Tom Kotani watched Grasshoff direct the American actors as Kotani spoke no English.

"It's almost like an English play," Kotani remembered. So, it's necessary to direct the native English speakers with that language. But as you may already know, Alex was one of the directors of the documentary film about the 1972 Munich Olympics. He was also involved in making films with famous Japanese directors in different countries. He was more skilled in making documentaries and

---

25   Ibid.
26   Ibid.

recording such events. He had never made a special effects film before, so it was difficult to communicate with the staff. Although the producers were considering the work division, it was challenging to coordinate between multiple co-directors."

He felt Grasshoff was aloof, maybe nervous or even worried and unsure about the scope and type of narrative *The Last Dinosaur* was shaping up to be. [27]

Photo Courtesy of Brett Homenick

"I had to take on a more significant role in managing the production team and communicating with them. I talked to Alex about it many times, but he returned to America after completing the film's shooting, and left most of the work to me for post production. I had to communicate with foreign actors in English, which is where I struggled since I am not proficient in the language. But I managed to get through it." [28]

It appears Grasshoff felt his direction was for the human action and actors and once that was completed, he was gone to leave

27 Ibid.
28 Ibid.

Kotani to do the visual and practical effects work that still involved the American actors.

Joan Van Ark wondered why the producers hired a documentarian for a big monster adventure movie. "What was he doing there directing actors?" Joan wondered aloud. "God bless him, but what was he even doing there?"

Her question was connected to her belief that two directors with this kind of background wasn't good for the synergy of the film, even if there were moments in the movie that worked.

There is a similar debate on the making of 1982's *Poltergeist* where camps are divided on who really directed the film. While horror legend Tobe Hooper (1974's *The Texas Chainsaw Massacre*) is given official director billing, a number of cast and crew have said it was really Steven Spielberg who directed the hit film.

There are swirls of rumors, because again, this was a time when *CNN* was brand new, 24 hours news was just getting on its feet and the only real outlet for entertainment news was *Entertainment Tonight*.

There weren't "leaks" from sets like we know them today. The term "spoilers" or even the concept of a spoiler was non-existent save for some gossip column revelations. There was nowhere for legions of fans to congregate in forums to pick over every tiny detail of a film.

A big spoiler popped up once in a famous gossip columnist's newspaper piece that revealed a photo of the scarred and burned shark from *Jaws 2* before the movie released. *Universal* was pissed as they wanted that to be a surprise for the audiences. That might be the first time I ever got what would one day be called a "spoiler."

People Magazine, Star, National Enquirer, Rolling Stone and a handful of movie industry magazines like *Premiere* and *American Film* were where you got your entertainment news.

The rumor mill to this day says Hooper suffered a nervous breakdown or had some kind of substance issues that left him unable to handle most of the directing chores. Spielberg either directed the thing himself or directed behind Hooper and over his shoulder, guiding him the whole way.

One of the primary arguments used to support this theory is the fact that *Poltergeist* shares many similarities in style and tone with other Spielberg-directed films, such as *E.T. the Extra-Terrestrial* and *Close Encounters of the Third Kind*. Additionally, several of the film's stars have made comments over the years that suggest Spielberg was heavily involved in the film's direction, with some even claiming that they were directed more by Spielberg than by Hooper.

However, there are also those who dispute these claims, with some arguing that the similarities between *Poltergeist* and Spielberg's other films are simply the result of his involvement as a writer and producer. In addition, there are accounts from crew members who worked on the film who have stated that Hooper was, in fact, the film's director and was actively involved in the filmmaking process. One account is that Spielberg legally could not direct Poltergeist because he was under contract with *ET: The Extraterrestrial* and was prohibited from directing *Poltergeist* even if he wanted to.

Despite the ongoing debate, both Spielberg and Hooper remained largely silent on the issue. Spielberg occasionally made comments suggesting that he was heavily involved in the making of *Poltergeist*, but has never explicitly claimed to have directed the film. Hooper, on the other hand, maintained that he was the film's director and has dismissed the rumors as baseless.

Hooper himself admitted he and Spielberg worked closely, with the legendary director contributing to major plot points, script revisions and storyboards. He did affirm that Spielberg was on set almost every day and expressed dismay that the public perceived this as his film being hijacked. The debate continues long after Hooper's death.

Benni Korzen said this about the Grasshoff-Kotani situation on the set of *The Last Dinosaur.* "Having two directors didn't work. The two credits there — that had more to do with lawyers and stuff like that. Basically, it was an experiment, and it did not work out. Very shortly after the shooting started, Arthur brought in Kotani, who kind of took over. So, basically, the film was made by Kotani; it was directed by Kotani. It was not that Grasshoff was a bad direc-tor, but he did not have any experience working outside the United States. I don't remember how Arthur and Jules found him or started with him. So that's my recollection." [29]

I threw all three all three of my scenarios at Benni Korzen on the Grasshoff-Kotani controversy.

"Okay," he started. "There is a merger between two of the things you just mentioned. My recollection is that Grasshoff was not a very, let's say, "effective" director. The issue at that time was Kotani didn't speak English. Not a word. He was well known to Arthur because of Arthur's deep relationships in Japan. Picking Grasshoff functioning outside the United States was a decidedly bad idea. He was not the kind of person who could easily adapt—not to food or anything. We had some issues and I believe that part of the ongoing Tom Kotani situation started on *The Last Dinosaur.* We realized in order for us

---

29 Homenick, Brett. On the trail of The Last Dinosaur. A Candid Conversation with Rankin/Bass Associate Producer Benni Korzen. Vantage Point Interviews. June, 2022. https://vantagepointinterviews.com/2022/06/13/on-the-trail-of-the-last-dinosaur-a-candid-conversation-with-Rankin/Bass-associate-produc-er-benni-korzen/

to continue working on subsequent projects with Kotani, required translators and translation which we figured out."

Kotani did not replace Grasshoff and Joan Van Ark's memory was correct; the American director was not dismissed from the production and stayed right through to the end.

Did Boone and Grasshoff lock horns like the T-Rex and Triceratops? Sometimes, Korzen admitted. He felt that Grasshoff was not particularly skilled in action scenes and his setups were often flawed, and that created problems in the editing room.

The conflict of visual style and tone became a major issue between the diametrically opposed directors. This is where my previous chapters on the importance of surrealism vs. realism come into play through Western and Eastern perspectives.

Grasshoff hailed from the world of realism in the documentary world. His approach to the film was one of a realistic adventure film with the action grounded in reality. This meant if his actors were going to act real, they had to play off a realistic looking antagonist with their eponymous dinosaur.

Kotani's world was of surrealism with the aforementioned influence of Bunraku and Shintoism shading his perceptions and thus the results of the visual effects. This would be later seen in the American 1998 *Godzilla's* Japanese reception. Americans want realism, the Japanese want artistic expression. It was less a *Reese's Cup* than a Yin and Yang.

The few stories out there of Grasshoff's direction put him in conflict with Richard Boone. Tom Kotani on the other hand found Boone a delight to work with and had no complaints and up until Kotani's recent death, said how much he missed and respected the actor.

Stories exist of Boone having issues with the script and Grasshoff's direction. Others have him frustrated with wardrobe choices (one account had him feeling the safari hat was not the right style and demanded a new one. The demand was rejected as footage was in the can with the one he had) as well as the script and its dialogue. I couldn't find specifics, but Benni Korzen confirmed there was truth to these issues.

Did Boone flip out or cause a scene? No. He did bring his concerns to Grasshoff who seemed unable to address these things; giving off the aura he was unsure about his own directorial footing on the production.

Kotani's direction was less character-oriented and more on action that would dovetail with the visual effects work. Boone is alleged to have expressed frustration here in this specific area with Kotani because he was not accustomed to studio visual effects work.

"This was back before modern computers and their effects," Korzen reminded me. "The effects work we were using on *Dinosaur* was primitive at best."

Richard came from a world of TV rear projection where I described earlier the process of an actor standing in front of a blank screen and the back projected behind the actor and screen to give the illusion of being on that location in a soundstage.

Boone was then put into the world of feature blue screen projection and forced perspective and this caused the friction between Grasshoff on the practical, real location and then later under Kotani's supervision in the studio.

While I will go into greater detail of how the live action was shot on location, I will stick with the directing styles between the two directors. Kotani's focus was on action scenes while on location, putting Boone through some rigorous physical work and the actor was not in the greatest of shape to perform.

When it came time for the blue-screen process it's not hard to imagine Richard feeling like a dinosaur against what was revolutionary technology at the time. The concept of blue screen and rotoscoping became more common place in American understanding after the special effects extravaganza of *Star Wars* and then *Superman The Movie.*

Boone allegedly grew frustrated with reacting to nothing on location for the dinosaur action scenes and then to "ping pong balls" in front of the blue screen when on the sound stage. Likely he referred to ping pong balls attached to filaments to give him a line of sight and point of focus. He would be shot in the foreground, turned into a matte while the dinosaur effects scenes would be superimposed into the scene later.

"Throughout our collaborations in Japan, we relied on a translator as Kotani did not speak a word of English. Despite this linguistic barrier, he refused to give up on any challenge presented on set, earning him the role of director for all of our subsequent projects. While his work ethic was unparalleled, his difficulty sleeping posed a slight inconvenience.

To remedy this, he required sleeping pills, which occasionally necessitated our assistance in getting him to the set. Nonetheless, his tireless commitment to his craft earned him a reputation as a workaholic, making him a valuable asset to Arthur and Jules for all their film ventures in Japan." That was Benni Korzen's assessment of Kotani.

Despite frustrations with both directors Boone showed affection for Kotani and wanted to be of help. He would translate Kotani's direction to the cast and crew when he could. Boone's assistance left a lasting impression on Kotani. With his extensive experience in front of the camera, Boone had acquired valuable knowledge that he shared generously. Considering Kotani was still relatively young at the time, it is understandable that he would recall the encounter in such a favorable light.

Little exists of post-release comments from Alexander Grasshoff on his time with *The Last Dinosaur*. He continued to work and went on to direct the 1981 adaptation of *The Wave*, a teen thriller and modern-day Nazi allegory. This seems to fit more with Grasshoff's documentary background with young adults as well as his proclivity for realism.

Gen X'rs will remember *The Wave* as a staple of history and/or English classes, especially after the advent of VCRs in the classroom. I saw it throughout my high school years and never made the connection that the guy who did *The Last Dinosaur* brought this very different movie to my attention.

Kotani would continue a very fruitful relationship with *Rankin/Bass* who continued their reputation for finding good people and hanging on to them. He would go on to helm the *Rankin/Bass* features, *The Bermuda Depths, The Ivory Ape* and *The Bushido Blade*.

Joan Van Ark seems to have an objective and clear description of the set under either director: "They yelled action and you did your thing and you did it to the best of your ability. There was little time for anything else."

Korzen believed the two areas most accurate for the director issue were Grasshoff and Kotani shared location directing chores with Kotani likely shouldering most of it as Grasshoff proved ineffective for the location and the challenges they presented. They both shared directing credit and did contribute to the picture in their respective ways.

The fallout in my estimation is the film suffered from a unified vision. There are two kinds of films going on here. We have a *Land That Time Forgot* action-adventure and we also have a giant monster Kaiju film and at its center a human story that is torn between the two.

Because of this polarity in vision, Richard Boone's great work in this movie is diminished when the lesser than special effects come into play. Direction is also responsible for major lapses of reason.

Either director should have caught a number glaring issues that may play out as modern-day tropes, but a few stand out to me as, as a director myself, as glaring story issues. The biggest might be Boone's tossing of his rifle.

I am not a hunter, but even as a kid I knew a deer rifle when I saw one and when Masten reveals the weapon he's brought, I wondered why he didn't have an elephant gun as minimal firepower.

I knew rhinos have thick skin and many high caliber bullets barely penetrate their fleshy armor. I also knew the same applied to bears from my father's hunting stories. A .22 bullet will do nothing to halt a 400 pound black bear.

When Boone has his chance at the dinosaur when it sneaks up on Bunta in the tree, he has trouble getting a bead on the animal. "Stand still!" he screams at it, and there is indeed a shot of the purple dinosaur doing a light dance to the left and dodge to the right, but really, you can't hit something the size of an apartment building?

This is Masten Thrust, the world's greatest big game hunter who has downed animals far smaller than this, and it's giving him trouble as a target?

When he gets off a shot, the gun jams. Why he isn't able to clear it fast is beyond me, but then he decides the best course of action is to toss the weapon into the stream (we are told it's a river) and leave it behind.

Either director should have caught this and not allowed it. It makes zero sense, especially later when Masten goes through the trouble to fashion a pretty damned good crossbow out of broken tents and equipment. Wouldn't it have been easier to just fix the jammed gun and clear it?

If one director favored realism, the idea of creating a catapult to kill the dinosaur pushes those boundaries. That starts with the script, however it's the execution of this scene that also makes it into pretty much every review both text and video.

Masten and the team somehow created this intricately designed medieval weapon without any mention of tools or design. It has interlocking gears hewn from massive trees. They did all this with Bunta's machete?

That's just picking the fly shit out of pepper. The problem was the directorial choice of the assault on the dinosaur when a boulder was launched into the air to kill it. The whole scene from launch to impact was shot in slow motion.

This was a terrible directorial choice. If Grasshoff chose it, I can't imagine he thought this looked more real in slow motion than regular. The slowed down speed and bad editing showed the limitations of the mechanism and the boulder clearly dropped out of the scoop and arm before the next edit shows it hurtling through the air.

It's the following image—the direct hit on the dinosaur's noggin that creates the biggest directorial mistake for this scene. The slow motion shows the rock hitting the dinosaur above and between its eyes. The skull dents in. Now we know there is no skull because it's a man in a suit. However, realism on Grasshoff's side would show the skull was crushed and whatever brain that thing had was smashed.

Toho Video, 2009

This would kill that dinosaur no matter how big it was.

Instead the slow motion turns what should've been a climactic moment into an unintentionally funny one and also one that draws us out of the scene and focused on the imperfections of the special effects. This would be an insult to Kotani if he were directing this scene because even a love for the surreal and artistic doesn't make up the fact that this is just a terrible shot and it's laughable. Had the scene been played at regular speed, the massive divot in the dino's cranium would have been far less noticeable.

No matter who was in the editing room, this should have been removed or re-shot.

Strong direction would have avoided the strong female paradox. I will use the scene with the charging four-legged dinosaur that almost ran down Joan Van Ark.

Francesca shows no fear as she moves right into the path of the charging giant beast. She ignores all calls by Masten to get out of the monster's way. She keeps on shooting and Masten rushes into harm's way to tackle Francesca and save her life as she would have been trampled to death.

The scene on paper and onscreen shows us the woman we've been told is bold, courageous and willing to risk her life for the shot. Fair enough.

Maybe 15 minutes later Francesca finds she unknowingly walked out onto the back of a giant turtle (Joan has stories about this coming up) and freaks out when the slow, docile beast starts to wiggle and move, drifting out into the lake with her standing atop of it.

It takes Steven Keats's Chuck Wade to rush to her rescue. The woman who had no compunction to stand in front of a charging prehistoric beast is spooked into frightened screeches by…a turtle.

This was a major story issue that is the responsibility of the director to resolve before a single frame is shot. Either it was ignored or overlooked. Maybe it was interpreted differently, or perhaps it was Kotani who directed and his inability to speak or comprehend English didn't make him aware of previous character development. Either way it creates a major narrative problem.

"Ding dong!" should never have been allowed. It makes Masten look foolish. Benni Korzen said that everything Richard did on a set was "big." When he yelled it was big, when he swore it was big. He could be intimidating but in reality it was just how he carried himself.

This is why "ding dong" resonates. Coming from one of the other actors, the impact might not have been so potent. With Boone saying it, it stood out.

Richard Boone also towered over much of the Japanese crew who were remarkably short. With all of this emphasis on big, fearsome, why allow such silly dialogue, sure to induce unintentional laughter to get through? "You ding dong!" Really?

We could allow for Kotani's lack of English to let this slip through. This would not translate to anything for Kotani to have context, but surely Grasshoff knew it was a bad line? It should have been changed when the director gets a first read through.

There is also the thing called a "director's pass" where the director themselves get a chance to make written changes to the script to fit more to their vision for the film. This must have been skipped because it was a major red flag.

Why the big deal? Because…as I said, it diminishes Richard's performance and this in turn gives credence to alleged accounts of him having conflicts with Grasshoff on the set over the script and specifically dialogue. If you remember earlier, that's what brought Richard into the world of acting. He searched out live theater actors to get their input on improving the dialogue in his own stories.

This does make a lot of sense and the circumstantial evidence is strong in supporting Richard's legitimate gripes during the production.

Boone had an instinct for smelling insecurity or inability. While some have attributed his walk out on a previous film that left the production forced to record someone else's voice for his dialogue, others say if he knew a director was not up to snuff, he would fill the vacuum because he did not want to look foolish.

Why did Boone let "ding dong" get recorded? After that first take (if it was the first take) he should've said, "We're doing another. That's awful." Maybe he did and Grasshoff used it anyway.

Maybe Grasshoff didn't care when the film got to post? Maybe he was also disillusioned with the experience and let it go through, knowing it was a silly line and would embarrass Boone? Who knows? Alexander Grasshoff, Tom Kotani and Richard Boone are no longer here to set the record straight. It's all speculation but it does present good questions.

As a director of over ten feature films at the time of this writing, with a variety of movie stars, I am always sensitive to dialogue: how it's written and how it's delivered. I can't believe no one on that set broke out into laughter or maybe the Japanese crew didn't understand and that's how it got through?

The final thought is: Maybe Richard, by the time they filmed that scene, just didn't care.

I have no idea. As Benni Korzen said during my interview, "There is a mix of truths."

What I do know is that the film has its faults for sure, and we will get into all of those, but it does seem that the central fault lies in its direction and lack of consistency in vision and style that was both a personal and cultural roadblock.

★★★★★ YOU DING DONG!

Reviewed in the United States 🇰🇷 on November 19, 2021

Verified Purchase

A fun Rankin and Bass film about the last T-REX and the dinosaur that wants to put him on a trophy wall! A fun romp through a pre-historic land filled with beasties, cavemen, and the titular target of Richard Boone's hunt. Boone's Masten Thrust (what a last name) gravely voiced and gruff, is going to get that beast if its the last thing he dose! Special effects are 1970's TV movie quality....but what can you do...it was made in the 1970's! Sit back and enjoy!

STORIES FROM JURASSIC SET

The Last Dinosaur is a testosterone-driven movie fueled with "toxic masculinity" (Masten Thrust is a perfect porn actor name) and starring men (even the dinosaur is male), made by men and conceived by men.

Joan Van Ark was the only female American star and it's best to start with her accounts of making the film and her experiences.

Imagine Joan in 1976…young, blonde, beautiful and up for just about anything. She is a professional actress, always looking for a challenge. She uses the word "diva" to describe herself and after her impressive resume is deserving of the title.

She gets this script about a dinosaur and pitched as action, adventure, romance and she gets to work with her father's idol and play a strong, independent woman (a character type not so common in those days). Add two free tickets to an exotic locale and she gets to bring her husband to boot.

Not a bad deal.

Now picture Joan going to The Hollywood Agent at *William Morris* and inquiring about the basic amenities of the trip. Will she have makeup and hair? What kind of set support will be in place?

The Hollywood Agent assures her it will be great. She will have everything she needs and it will be a fun gig. You can see some guy in suit and tie, white teeth relaxed behind a big desk overlooking the town, mansplaining to this beautiful, nervous blonde actress that she just needs to relax. "Joan…baby, doll…it's all going to be great!"

Cut to Joan and her husband flying first class across the Pacific, the *Indiana Jones* red line traversing a map, touching down in Tokyo.

All seems as promised. A beautiful hotel, perhaps the nicest in the entire city, with all the perks befitting a top American actress. The arrival goes off without a hitch.

Fade to black.

Fade in to our adventuresome blonde babe shuttling out from the luxurious metropolitan Tokyo hotel to the Japanese Alps. The van takes our heroine to the Kamikochi Prefect.

Rugged, volcanic terrain dotted with stripped dead trees jutting from a giant, dark lake. Mountains loom over a wooden and barren landscape with bleached lake shores and flat dead lands bordered by a mantle of evergreen forests.

2023 Miser Bros. Press/Rick Goldschmidt

It's not the bright, sunny, warm tropical climes of the Canary Islands or Spain where other big dinosaur movies had been shot. This is a haunting location and the location manager scored a production bulls eye with finding this eerie place.

Cue the rains. It's monsoon season and steel grey skies have become the backdrop and lighting. It's cold. It's miserable.

Our blonde diva takes her shuttle to a hotel that just might be the only lodging for hundreds of miles.

"It was that remote," she said. It was nothing close in comparison to the luxury palace they left behind in Tokyo. "We were lodged in one of the most opulent hotels that were available at the time. Then we went to a place where taking a shower was an entirely different experience, as you had to use cold water. It involved spraying yourself, soaping, spraying again. It was undoubtedly a Japanese approach, but as a diva, I required a *staff* to cater to my every whim and fancy while working. At least that's what I had hoped for," she joked. I needed someone to peel grapes for me!"

The adventure was just beginning.

Masumi Sekiya remembered footwear for the long, wet periods of the rainy weather. "The staff had long boots that went up to their chest, and they were wearing them while the lighting people were constantly going in and out, right? That was it. For me, it was just a moment of running, so it was fine, but if the staff were outside for a long time, I think it must have been cold for them." [30]

Tom Kotani went on location scouts ahead of production. "I went on location hunting with Mr. Sagawa, and we went together to the main shooting locations like Kamikochi. It wasn't a national

---

30   The Last Dinosaur, Special Edition DVD. Commentary by Masumi Sekiya, Tom Kotani. 2009. Toho Video.

park back then. It was difficult, but we discussed things like "place the actor in the foreground like this," "use this Nikon function from the afternoon," and so on. We had many meetings on set." [31]

"Our crew was Japanese and almost all men," Benni Korzen started out. "A blonde whether male or female was a rarity and something of a commodity. When Joan arrived on set, the men could not take their eyes off of her. That bright, golden blonde hair…not to mention she was a beauty."

"When I arrived, I noticed the men would make this sucking sound, like a deep inhaling or gasp. It was from seeing a blonde, which is considered uncommon to them. We blondes stand out, I guess," said Joan.

Joan went on with the blonde point to add, "Just prior to or following the commencement of production in Tokyo. My passion for jogging led me to traverse the grounds of the Imperial Palace there in Tokyo. I don't remember if this was before but probably after the on location work.

If we consider it leisure time, it was not while the filming was in progress. There was no down time with the weather challenges and everything else. It was like we were shooting 24 hours a day.

It was either before or after the shoot. I would go for a jog and a run. As I ran around the Imperial Palace, I noticed men running towards me. I greeted them with a hello, and we made eye contact. "Hai" translates to "yes" in Japanese. So here was this blonde running around the Imperial Palace, saying "yes" to all the men! You can imagine how mistaken-hooker Joan I came across with that."

If you remember, bananas and honey were Joan's "go to" food on *Knot's Landing* and other jobs. The *Fuji Apples*, were now the better

---

31 Ibid.

option. "I ended up bringing them to the set as the food they provided was somewhat unusual, such as eel and octopus, which did not appeal to me. Although, as I told you, I had sushi for the first time with *The Last Dinosaur* at the wrap party."

I would stick to salads if they were available and eat the giant apples for the most part. Even after returning home to Los Angeles, I continued to eat them. They are incredibly delicious and nearly as large as a grapefruit. The hotels were adequate, but if you're looking for something of a higher standard, this place wasn't it."

Bernie Korzen also had his tales of food. "We all stayed in that one hotel and where I heard the most complaints was in the food department. The breakfast was not typically Japanese which could seem like to most Americans as something from another planet. The guy from the kitchen would bring in the same breakfast every day—fried eggs. We had it every day we were there. I think at some point it was either Richard Boone or his wife said something to effect of, "Well, we may die from food poisoning after all." However Richard could fall back on his bottle of diluted vodka. I was always impressed with what I saw in that regard."

Joan Van Ark took a look at her makeup and hair "staff" on the first day. "The crew! The makeup and hair people were all TWELVE YEAR OLDS who didn't understand English! So I was trying to communicate with what I call my "pit crew." My makeup help, my wardrobe help…with people who didn't speak English! That was one of the shocks and challenges of all time--to have my pit crew not understand English and just try to make it work."

She needed makeup and hair advice to look realistic. "I am much more aware as I've done some directing since then and I've done things since that makes me think with not just an actress mind which is all I was at the time on *Dinosaur*. Nowadays I see things on different levels. I would have tried to do that on *Dinosaur* if I had an advice person who spoke English, and told me the truth to modify what I did."

Masumi Sekiya had similar makeup stories. "On the first day of filming, the makeup artist had already done my makeup perfectly, and while sighing like 'Ah, this is difficult', she drew my eyebrows like 'Sorry, honey, I have to do this to you.' I was like, 'What's wrong with me?' When I went to the filming location, the director told the makeup artist to do the whole thing like a musical. So she kept drawing on my face. And then my eyebrows got stuck together. So they stuck my eyebrows together. They had a black line here and let it out by the side of the mouth, and of course they put cotton in it, and then they make you apply black teeth paint. When you see yourself in the mirror after that, you feel like crying." [32]

I got the impression between Joan and Benni that the actors were kind of on their own. Skeiya also reflected this. The anecdotal data paints a picture of one director aloof and out of his depth and another who was limited by the language barrier and depended more on visual cues.

Joan described, just as Benni, that it was a call of "Action!" They launched into their roles with how they developed their characters and interactions and performed their best until "Cut!" was called.

Benni recalled much of the same lack of director-actor interaction. While he emphasized, just like Joan Van Ark, that the set was overall pleasant and the actors all got along with no on set issues (unlike what modern reviewers want to hear) there seemed little to no recall of interaction with Alexander Grasshoff and in similar ways with Kotani.

---

32   The Last Dinosaur, Special Edition DVD. Commentary by Masumi Sekiya, Tom Kotani. 2009. Toho Video.

Benni did allude to the idea that the production was not happy with Grasshoff and it's likely he picked up on it, and if he was also not happy with his time there it likely showed with his direction of the actors.

To give Grasshoff the benefit of the doubt and not having a language barrier to overcome, it is also possible that coming from the documentary world, he directed with a lighter hand. His goal would be realism and in a documentary you want your characters to be as real as possible. No human being will act or speak with absolute inhibition knowing they are being recorded.

It would make sense that Grasshoff, as a documentary filmmaker, stood back and kind of "let things happen." He might've given them basic direction, to follow the script and then stepped back to see what his actors would do. Out of that kind of "free range directing" he would see what kind of results he got and take the best of what his actors gave him.

Joan herself described Grasshoff as "easy."

"He was very nice. He was understanding and patient. I found him to be funny. I

have worked with some very off-putting directors but Alex was a great, go-with-the-flow kind of guy."

This would make sense in the context of a documentary director. It's in the best interest of the production to direct from afar, to allow things to happen as they unfold. What Joan Van Ark remembers about Grasshoff gives some credence to this conjecture.

"We did the first part of the film, which was hotel-wise once we got back to Tokyo. The prime effort was the outdoor Kamikochi outdoor work, the principal of the film was done first. The last was back in Tokyo for all of the beginning of the film."

The post wilderness shots were all real locations. She had no recollection of her first scene with Richard Boone. "That can be a norm," she told me. "I did a movie with Patty Duke and David Burney and my first scene was in bed with David. The schedule is done with not what's best for the actors, but rather economically."

She did recall "the mud scene" where she and Boone flirted after almost trampled to death by the giant Joan tried to photograph. There wasn't a lot to tell except for continuity. They had to get the scene in a few takes because of the way the mud covered them. Every time you move it creates changes in the mud patterns on the clothing and actors. That makes for an editing nightmare in post production.

"To do a retake of that, folks, you gotta start all over," Joan told me. "Start over with wardrobe. Start over with makeup. Two actors who have done a few things like us knew, you have to get it right the first time. You saw two actors in the mud, and I was in a white outfit in the mud…that's the print. That was it. One take and done."

She followed this up with a *Knot's Landing* story that showed the importance of getting it right with continuity. "I wake up as a hooker. It was one of Valene's best storylines. I woke up as a hooker trying to be more like Abby (Donna Mills). She goes to this bar and gets drunk with all these guys. She goes back to her motel in Nashville. She wakes up and goes to the bathroom and ends up scrubbing her face, this tear stained mascara ridden face—the lipstick's all smeared and she's a mess.

She looks in the mirror and thinks "My God." I look in the mirror then turn on the water full force and wash my entire face of absolutely no makeup. For Joan Van Ark this is a big step all in and of itself. Scrub it all off and start all over make myself up as a goody-two-shoes.

Then I had this long monologue saying you're gonna go (she did her Southern accent for this here) and you're gonna get your accent back (the producers didn't want Valene talking with that accent for 14 years) so I washed my face and did this monologue and ended up with goody-two-shoes with what I call pink and white makeup, meaning it was soft, youthful, fragile, lovely, whatever.

Before we started the scene, I said to the cameramen, "If something goes wrong, stop me immediately before I wash my face. Because if this didn't work, and we have to start over, and do a new hooker-heavy makeup on me, it will take us the rest of the day to start over," I joked.

There was one false start but the second one went all the way, straight through in one clip. When it was over it was like the set of the last episode of *The Mary Tyler Moore Show*. We all held each other--hair, makeup, camera operator, director in a circle, in a group hug. It gets me all verklempt, even now to think about the synergy, the pinnacle of doing something that was a team effort. I have never, ever been so proud and as happy as I was for that particular scene. It's my proudest piece of work. Synergy."

The Last Dinosaur didn't have those moments. Because it was either so freezing cold or raining so hard or one endless row of challenges that kept us from doing a lot of high fives and a whole lot of "hugger mugger."

Joan referred to that term from a director who called emotional moments on set between actors "Hugger mugger" moments.

"There wasn't a lot of "hugger mugger." It was keep your eye on the prize, and when they say action, give it everything you got. Because the first take is really the only chance you're gonna get."

Everything Joan spoke of called attention to getting things consistent between shots. It's called "continuity," the process of making sure shots match, especially if done over a period of days. Hair, makeup, jewelry, wardrobe, lighting…it all has to match. Continuity errors end up on the blooper reel these days."

Some directors like famous filmmaker John Cassavettes couldn't care less about it. He felt that actors should act with long, unbroken edits for a more streaming continuity in the flow of the pictures. He would not get hung up on whether the hair was in the same place between shots or small things like that.

Cassavettes felt that if an audience focuses on those small things, they were never invested in the film's story in the first place.

Perhaps Grasshoff felt similarly and for all we know could've admired Cassavettes as the timing would be right for both men in the industry as Cassavettes was about at the height of his popularity. Again, we will never know.

There are numerous continuity issues in *The Last Dinosaur* including one that hints of a deleted scene. I asked Benni Korzen about this as well as Joan Van Ark but neither could remember if there was anything that got shot but not used.

The scene must have come between the time the group sets out in search of the dinosaur, leaving Dr. Kawamoto behind at base camp and returning to find the good doctor dead and the Polar Borer gone.

Their clothes are ripped, their faces and appendages dirty. What happened? We never see a scene explaining these issues which creates a rather large story gap.

"The turtles!" Joan exclaimed on our call. "That scene with the turtle!" She's was talking of the scene where the troupe moves through the forest on the trail of the T-Rex when Joan's Francesca steps out onto what she thinks is a rock to get a better shot of something.

The rock moves from under her to reveal it's not a large stone but rather she is standing atop a massive prehistoric turtle. The turtle's head bobbles, the body trembles as it sets sail with Joan riding along on top! She's rescued by Steven Keats (again falling down in the mud where flirtatious hijinks ensue).

"I remember a vision of a bunch of turtles--which was of the shortest male members on the crew. They wanted to save money of course, and these short guys were underneath the turtle tops, which was the curved back of the turtle shell with a little nose and big head."

She laughed while telling me all about this, but intrigued me over the idea that there could have been several of the creatures (there actually three or four), but only one made it into the final cut.

"These guys would trundle under the water, under the fake shell, they could only do short takes. They were little Japanese crew members or maybe they hired extras to do it. But they would hold their breath as long as they could downstream, doop, doop, doop…splash."

She made the sound of these crew making trotting sounds underneath this shell, submerged with breath held. Her account was in between girlish laughter as she fondly remembered this silly scenario. You could feel this was fun to shoot.

"That was one of those hysterical days. It was a little dicey to keep your balance when there's this little guy underneath making it move. You couldn't find a turtle that big and make it move, you had to have a guy do it. And that was it."

She had to stop a moment to let the last laughs out and then, drawing a breath that said "Okay, seriously" she said: "I mean, come on! I have no idea why this movie was never nominated for an Academy Award. I have no idea. Yeah, right!"

Her sense of humor and good nature about making a movie she found not her finest, was a self-effacing delight.

There are set stories of the actors in *Jurassic Park* running from crew holding giant cardboard dinosaur heads on poles, chasing them through the forest. The dinosaurs were not there, as they would be added in later through the magic of CGI and rotoscoping. Your actors still need to know where to look: proper distance, height, eye tracking…it's a complicated thing.

"We were always running from nothing on set! Nothing!" Joan said, clearly amused. "Oh my God! It was a crew member or Alex telling us to run here! Go there! It's over there! Look up!"

Richard Boone experienced frustration with this process. His character had to hunt an invisible prey. Benni Korzen recounts Boone grumbled loudly. "He had a big voice. Everything about him was big--his voice, his profanity…"

Boone was directed in one scene to crawl through a dense, tight spot, fleeing the dinosaur. Benni Korzen wants to say it was a ditch or something like that and it was clogged with brush and vegetation. Boone was a big man, he was older, and he was tired and likely working on a "liquid breakfast."

"I was surprised that he only drank large amounts of alcohol. Vodka was overlapping." Tom Kotani admitted he liked to drink with Boone.

"I bring it and we usually drink it until lunchtime." He admitted they drank on set and got drunk together. "Of course, we did. Well, we could tell just by his size and lines what he was thinking. He (Boone) wasn't really fond of rehearsals, he acted that it was a live broadcast, and he didn't come just before the performance. It was just right for him to play this role at his age, and he himself likes this kind of Western-like dressing or roles that suit him. It was a role that he really liked." [33]

---

33 The Last Dinosaur, Special Edition DVD. Commentary by Masumi Sekiya, Tom Kotani. 2009. Toho Video.

Did Alex Grasshoff drink?

"Yes, he did drink a lot." Tom Kotani revealed and it looks like Grasshoff drank with Boone as well. "They really started drinking and drank a lot. I went to eat with the American staff and cast, and then to the large hall on this side with the Japanese staff and cast, and came back and forth to the cafeteria here.

So, I drank about twice as much as I should have, but I had to write a storyboard for the special effects and discuss it with them, so I had to return to my room in moderation, but sometimes I was too drunk to wake up in the morning, thinking that it would be okay. That's what it was, he loved to drink." [34]

"It was wet and cold or it was hot and dry," Korzen remembered of Kamikochi. The day Boone reached his end with the numerous takes of going through this on set boot camp. He finally let loose with a string of profanity and yelled that he wanted this over with.

2023 Miser Bros. Press/Rick Goldschmidt

"He was gentle and kind," Masumi Sekiya said of Richard Boone. She reflected on the scene where she had to crawl "into bed" with him. He yells at her, driving her from the cave and his bed. Boone's Thrust rails about how bad the cave girl smells, but she saw him as an alpha male and was attracted. A little foreshadowing for the ending.

---

34 Ibid.

Sekiya felt his actions in that scene were opposite of the kindness and quiet dignity Boone showed to her and the cast and crew on set. [35]

"When I was running away, I tripped there. I really hurt my foot. It swelled up a lot and there was even blood. It was painful. This cannot be called a bed scene." Sekiya said.

This punches more holes in the "difficult and drunken Richard Boone" narrative propagated by so many online reviewers. It appears many took the fact that Boone did drink and sometimes heavily (It doesn't seem anyone with the production tried to keep a secret) and just filled in the dino DNA with their own code to get the narrative they needed to get people to read their reviews.

While it's unknown whether this was Grasshoff or Kotani at the helm with Richard's grievances, Korzen repeated that Richard's complaints were always well-founded. "He'd had enough," he said of the ditch scene.

When I heard this, it took me to the mystery deleted scene I mentioned earlier. There is no such "crawling through a ditch" scene like this in the final film, so it gives support to the idea that some chase scene or dinosaur confrontation took place and for whatever reason, wasn't used. This would explain why the group's clothing is a mess and they are dirty as if going through combat when originally we saw them doing a simple tracking with no dangerous scenario before they return to base camp.

I took Joan back to the scene where she and Sekiya are by the water. Joan is teaching her proper grooming techniques and maybe we get a little insight into what she went through trying to talk to her own makeup crew of non-English speaking kids. In the meantime, Joan drafted her husband to be her sort-of-assistant while he was there.

---

35 Ibid.

While the two women bond by the side of the river (it was really a creek and couldn't have been more than two feet deep all the way across) the dinosaur does its stealth move and somehow sneaks up behind them without as much of a twig snapping.

Hazel sees the beast's reflection in the pan of water Joan holds, looks up and let's out the big monster movie scream.

The T-Rex roars back as if yelling: "Surprise!" The two women panic.

Both had to look up at nothing. They were directed to look up, react and then run. Run to where?

2023 Miser Bros. Press/Rick Goldschmidt

Kotani remembered they tried to get the image of the dinosaur for both women to see. There was some practical effect in the pan of water. They were to look up to see a crew member giving them their focal points.

While Hazel made the smart move and ran through the water to the cover of the forest, Joan ran…right toward the dinosaur and between its legs (?!).

"They would yell things like, "Joan! There's the dinosaur!" Yes, yes, that's exactly what they did and they still do it today. They do this with the action and Marvel films. They talked us through it.

2023 Miser Bros. Press/Rick Goldschmidt

We had nothing there. Absolutely nothing. We had to look at a spot predetermined before the cameras rolled. You heard "action" and then you…well…you pulled it out of somewhere to get it right. You do an "As if." "

I told her how the actors had to react to the imaginary dinosaurs in *Jurassic Park* and she exclaimed that nothing had changed. It was just what they did on set of her dinosaur movie.

"They did everything in post," she confirmed. "I never saw the dinosaur once while on set."

Richard wanted isolation on set. Joan did as well. The physical demands of the movie were draining and mentally exhausting. She described how it started with boots on the ground in the early morning and many times Benni Korzen would come to them and ask them to keep going. What should be an 8-10 hour day sometimes became

18-20 hours. Mud, rain, running, falling, injuries from the terrain, heat exhaustion…it was more a trial by fire than it was a movie set.

"Do it for Arthurrrrr," Joan imitated Benni again. She was mixing his real accent with the Steven Keats impression. "He would come to us and urge us to give everything we had. We WERE giving everything we had, but you know, you just give more. You want it right. You want to do your best."

She didn't do it for Arthur, she did it for Joan. Richard did it for Richard.

2023 Miser Bros. Press/Rick Goldschmidt

2023 Miser Bros. Press/Rick Goldschmidt

ABOVE: A behind the stills shot reveals the boom mike onset.

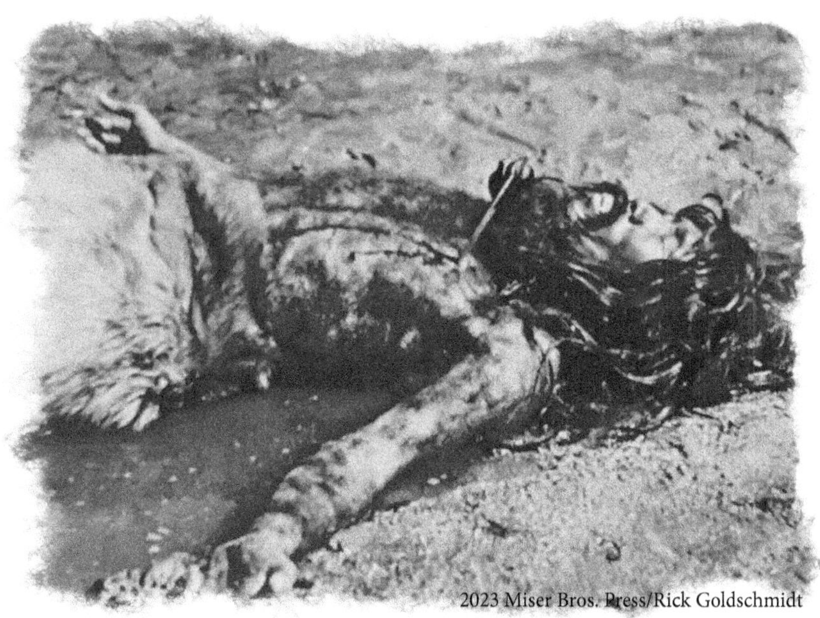

2023 Miser Bros. Press/Rick Goldschmidt

2023 Miser Bros. Press/Rick Goldschmidt

2023 Miser Bros. Press/Rick Goldschmidt

2023 Miser Bros. Press/Rick Goldschmidt

2023 Miser Bros. Press/Rick Goldschmidt

2023 Miser Bros. Press/Rick Goldschmidt

2023 Miser Bros. Press/Rick Goldschmidt

2023 Miser Bros. Press/Rick Goldschmidt

"We were on location in the Japanese Alps for about two fat weeks." By "fat" Joan meant a little over two weeks. Could be a day or several days but just under three.

"My husband was only there for maybe a week, ten days tops."

She did not remember Richard participating much with the cast and crew between scenes. Joan never took this to be offensive, but this shows how the unsubstantiated accounts of him being "rude" or even "condescending" to Joan could be exaggerated over half a century.

"I never got that," Joan insisted. She knew she needed her own space but she also knew Richard carried a lot of baggage with him. He also was dedicated to the character of Masten. She recounted how she's worked on projects where actors will stay in character all during the shooting day. They didn't want to be taken out of the mindset that would hamper their performance.

"The crabbiness would come out of him in that in-between time. Maybe it was because he just wanted to get a shot over with?" That made me think of Korzen's account of Richard reaching his patience threshold with the ditch scene.

"Who knows what the reasons are, but I understood." Joan made her affections for Richard clear.

I replied to her that maybe Richard's taciturn nature and being isolated stemmed from him coming to this film with a certain expectation and finding it was going to fall short.

That's when Joan came really alive. "Didn't we all?!" She exclaimed over my speaker. She sounded almost indignant. "Hold off! Didn't we all? Didn't WE ALL?! All of us did! For sure!"

"Maybe Richard coped his own way with the challenges we faced. All I had were big apples. He coped with it with his "liquid" there. All of us dealt as best we could. Given the challenges, that no one, the viewer, would never see or know, that's what we had to deal with in between. Incredible obstacles."

"When I put forth my supposition that Richard identified with Masten and saw himself in real-life as a last dinosaur, Joan replied, "You're giving me chills. That is exactly what I saw watching that film last night. That's who he was."

That's when we talked of his final three words in the film.

"God bless you for bringing it up." Joan thanked me. "That was the most honest piece of dialogue and delivery on his and our part. It grabbed me like crazy last night. He said those three words with both heart and soul and I thought, "Goddamn!" Standing ovation, Richard! Standing ovation! He gave it that and it was brilliant. It just was brilliant."

Her emotion was palpable over my phone. She was there again, looking into his eyes and hearing his sad reply over a gulf of fifty years.

"That's who he was. That was his way of coping."

2023 Miser Bros. Press/Rick Goldschmidt

I went further and said that my research on the limited accounts by Richard Boone on the film led me to believe that when it came time to do the effects part of the production he was greatly disappointed.

When he got a look at the dinosaur suit, maybe when he saw the sound stage mock ups of the real life locations, he saw where this was going and his heart fell. There was still the whole beginning of the film to shoot when they got back to Tokyo and by that time Richard would have been exposed to the visual effects work.

He would have had to have seen the dinosaur whether in dailies, in test shots to give him an idea of what he would be looking at when doing blue screen work. Perhaps when he saw the surrealistic Japanese Kaiju look, it went against what he envisioned and all he put into his performance. There's part of me that thinks he saw *The*

Last Dinosaur as his swan song film, the last film that would truly define who he was as a man and an artist.

"The effects, yes," Joan agreed. "The effects were just…awful. That's where the kitsch comes in and the criticism completely justified."

I reminded her of the dueling styles between two directors. I gave the example of terrific, live dramatic scenes with Masten, like the one she just saw the night before, then the dinosaur shows up and it all gets silly.

She grumbled over the last name, "Thrust" as it came back to her. "My God, that's a joke."

When I revealed to Joan that the script came from a comic strip writer, she stopped me. "See? You're describing the two directors— if one is a documentarian what is he doing there directing three actors in a script? What was he even doing there?"

It doesn't make for a synergy that's gonna look great on the screen. It's a miracle that it came out as good as it did, actor-wise, that it did. There were moments that worked."

I agreed.

I walked her through the mixed quality of the effects work, with the innovative use of real, existing daylight on certain scenes that did bring a higher level of quality and realism to the film. The blue screen effect was substandard and didn't work.

"The look of the monster…that monster is a sight gag. Right away. It's goofy. The eyes. Oh my God. It heightens even more that Richard was the last dinosaur. That's the irony of the whole piece. That creature I am looking at right here in front of me (she had the artwork for the cover of this book) the eyes, the teeth…it's a joke!"

I told her that to the Japanese and especially Tom Kotani, it wasn't a joke.

2023 Miser Bros. Press/Rick Goldschmidt

She agreed. "No it isn't! Especially 50 years ago when that was the appetite. Right now the appetite is no makeup, very real, no fabulous glamour lighting, relatable, feet on the ground and cheaper. I haven't seen product or any nominated films. At that time, when *The Last Dinosaur* was made, all those films out of Japan were like *The Last Dinosaur*. That's what they wanted. That was the appetite. That's what the studios there delivered. Now it couldn't be more opposite. More different."

Once again I agreed with her. I stated my belief there was a force of wills going on between the directors during the production. "You're looking at it with the view of a director," Joan pointed out. "I was looking to see about the work, but I think you're right. Other than people giggling and making fun of it very often and very rightly so, it's not complicated but it is a choice tidbit for anyone to take this film apart."

Kotani was open about the pull between directors for the vision of the film.

"For shooting, lighting, sound recording, and art, there's a lot of communication with the staff, and you have to make sure everything is going smoothly. The producer had thought about dividing up the work, but as I've experienced myself and heard from senior directors, it's not easy to work as co-directors.

Since I was on the set and had to deal with things like speed all day long and discuss special effects, I ended up becoming the center of attention.

2023 Miser Bros. Press/Rick Goldschmidt

Well, I talked with Alex many times about this, and he stayed in Japan until all the [location] filming was done. But after shooting in Takayama was finished, I had to work with foreign actors in places like Jōgashima, and I also directed the acting." [36]

When I offered nostalgia as a part of the film's endurance and continuing popularity, Joan countered. "I don't know so much about

---

36 The Last Dinosaur, Special Edition DVD. Commentary by Masumi Sekiya, Tom Kotani. 2009. Toho Video.

nostalgia. When you see a monster like that…clump, clump, clump-ing through pre-done shots of landscape and trees and things, and try to mix them (she did some doofy monster walking sounds) with this clunky monster that looks ridiculous, it's very hard to stay in it and not say "Oh my God, this could be funny" or whatever. I think you lose the audience. But maybe not if you're looking for a giggle."

She clarified that there was no market for this kind of movie anymore. Maybe with movies like *Sharknado* and other giant, mega animal movies, but none of them were meant to be taken seriously. I think Joan was saying that they all thought this would be something far more serious than what they got.

Her final thoughts on Alexander Grasshoff gave support to some of my conjecture on the director. "I think he came off as someone who was there to just get it done. I didn't seem to feel that he reached or asked us to reach for something deeper than that. It was get it on film and move on. I never felt aware of the finer "dot the i's" and cross the "t's." I don't recall that. It wasn't conveyer belt but rather if it was decent that was good enough."

Good enough…

She thought about all of this further. "I think the three actors that were involved…we realized this, and knew whatever we had to do between takes, we had to find before the cameras rolled. It was usually moment to moment, fast and do it. Especially with the weather situ-ation. Kamikochi has a spot in Japan, where it's epic, with the heavy rains and trees falling. It was dangerous. It was done as economically and quickly in Kamikochi as we could, between rain squalls."

Two "fat" weeks of movie boot camp and then they brought the actors back to Tokyo-- back to the beginning act, and the special effects work.

They arrived with excitement and anticipation.

They left tired, worn and wondering just what this would all turn out to be.

Tom Kotani reflected on his last moments onset with Alex Grasshoff. "When the filming was over and I said goodbye to Alex, we were staying at the old Tokyo Hilton. I don't remember exactly what we said. At that time, we made origami and drank Japanese sake, and he said that he had a good experience. We talked about saying goodbye while drinking sake and beer."

Kotani implied there was a dust up over directing credit with the Director's Guild of America. "It was regrettable, but he was a member of the Directors Guild of America. He said he would report his experience and do something like that in the future, so if there were any regulations in the future, I would collaborate next time. It was the last day we parted." [37]

They would never work together again.

"I have watched the film recently," Sekiya said when asked by an interviewer. What were her thoughts? "It's nostalgic. If I could go back, I would have done things a little better, I think. I may be more interested in reflection. But sometimes I see all of those things and watch Tokuyama, and our spirits are DVDs, and we say things like, 'If only we had done it a little differently, we would have understood,' and laughed." [38]

Fade to black.

37　The Last Dinosaur, Special Edition DVD. Commentary by Masumi Sekiya, Tom Kotani. 2009. Toho Video.

38　Ibid.

The full Japanese press book for the film, 1977.

●未知の世界を探る──

それは人類の果しない夢

（映画評論家）　後藤　敏

この映画を観ながら，ふと小学生の頃，夢中になってみた映画を想い出した。確か「海底下の科学戦」と覚えているが，一口でいうなら未来戦争を扱ったもので，大西洋に沈んだ大陸が，善悪二ヵ国に分れて戦争をしている。そこへ迷い込んだのが，アメリカの潜水艦と乗組員たち。彼らが善玉国へ味方して，遂に悪玉国を滅ぼすまでのお話で，前後編になっていた娯楽大作だった。

　今，何もその映画について語ろうとする訳ではないが，ＳＦものの楽しさを思い出したからである。第二次大戦で活躍したロケット弾，ドイツのＶ２号，さらに今でいうミサイル弾などが，すでにその映画で登場していた。果てしない科学の力，それにも増して，想像力のたくましさが，映画をどれだけ楽しくおもしろくさせていたことか。

　はからずも，その昔，胸を躍らせた映画を思い出したのだった。

　そうした楽しさを，この映画は持っている。ＳＦアドベンチャーの魅力である。極底探険船で，まったく想像もつかない未知の世界を探り，挑む。巧みなトリ

2023 Miser Bros. Press/Rick Goldschmidt

ックの世界が，それに酔わしてくれる。

すべてが作りことと分っていながら，さながら現実社会に実存するように，巧妙に観客に迫ってくるおもしろさ。

また，架空の世界でありながら，さもそれらしく思わせる程の巧みな描き方で，観客を巧みに酔わせてしまうおもしろさ。

いずれも，"ＳＦもの"と称される映画を定義づけたいい方である。

前者でいうなら，さしづめ「キングコング」などがその部類に入り，後者では「ミクロの決死圏」などがいえるだろう。

ミュージカル「失なわれた地平線」も前者で，大ヒット作「猿の惑星」シリーズは後者である。

また，それらをミックスしたＳＦものも数多い。完全に，すべてが想像の世界の魅力にあふれている。いいかえるなら，それが，ＳＦものの楽しさである。

未知の世界を探る，それは人類が果てしなく抱く"夢"である。成功の確率の低い，冒険家，探険家が常に絶え

ないのも，"夢"を征服したという願望の表われである。

×　　　　　×

ポーラーボーラは，レーザー光線で地中の石油を探掘する円筒形のタンクである。先頭部が回転して進む。北極海の海底を探査中に，ポーラーボーラが急に浮上したところは，全く別天地。前世紀の世界だった。恐竜と原始人が棲む大自然そのままの姿。

濃い霧がたちこめる湖，わがもの顔に飛び交う翼竜。遠く氷壁が望めながら気温は華氏90度。おあつらえ向きの舞台である。

そこに棲む恐竜，ティラノザウルスと二本ツノのトリケラトプスに立ち向う探険隊との闘争。その中心は，世界的なハンターとして知られるマステン，リチャード・ブーンで，ハンターの面目にかけてただ一人残ってでも，ティラノザウルスを仕止めようとする最地の見せ方である。特別に新しい武器を使うわけでもなく，ごくありふれたハンターの装備で単身，向って行く。人間の持つ闘争本能が，獲物を求めて原始的に爆発する。人の心をくすぐるような，素朴な楽しさが，そこにある。

●ティラノザウルス

白亜紀に栄えた最も強大な恐竜で、一般には "しし竜" と呼ばれる。竜盤類に属し、肉食、陸上生活をする。体型の特徴としては、頭蓋部は深く、幅は狭い。大きなあご全てに鋭い歯があり、肉食性の恐竜としては、極端に進化したものである。体長15m、体重7トン余、皮フ甲でおおわれ、立ち上がった時の体高は6－7mにも達する。

すでに北アメリカの白亜紀層から、化石も発見されている。

巨大な恐竜の時代は、この白亜紀をもって終了する。すなわち、ティラノザウルスは最も進化した、強大な、"最後の恐竜" であった。食物は主に、草食性の恐竜であり、両者の間にはすさまじい闘争がくり広げられた。

●プロントテリウム

恐竜の中では比較的おとなしい、肉食、陸上生活の恐竜である。鳥盤類に属し、頭部から上顎にかけて、並列した6本の角が特徴である。背だけは2.5mと低いが、重さが4－6トンと横幅のある体型だ。白亜紀を境にして絶滅した。

●プテラノドン

　一般に翼竜と呼ばれる飛恐竜は，白亜紀の前，ジュラ紀から出現した。
このプテラノドンは，白亜紀の代表的翼竜で，翼幅は7－8mにも及んだ。
空中から湖沼の魚を捕えて常食としており，肉食である。

●トリケラトプス

　白亜紀後期に現われ，角竜では最後の種類のものである。鼻の上と，両眼の上に三本の大きな角を持つところから"三奇竜""三角竜"とも呼ばれる。鳥盤類に属し，草食，陸上生活をする。現在のサイの遠い祖先とも言われ，乾いた土地に生息し角を武器として敵と戦った。全長6－9m，体重8.5トン。特徴としては，口の前方には歯がなく，手足のツメは平ツメかひづめであった。皮フは，よろいのような甲らでおおわれていた。

この映画に描かれた恐竜時代とは———

巨大な恐竜が生息していたのは、今からおよそ1億3500万年から6500万年前の間で、中世代白亜紀と呼ばれる時代である。この白亜紀の時代には、植物はようやく花の咲く木が栄えた頃で、草花はまだなかった。そして生物は、巨大な恐竜がその進化を最も深め、同時に絶滅へとたどる最盛期であり、最後の時代でもあった。

人類の祖先とも言うべき、ジンジャントロプス、アウストラロピテクスが出現したのが、第4紀と呼ばれる今からおよそ200万年前、原人と呼ばれるシナントロプス、ピテカントロプスが大体50万年前である。いかに太古の恐竜の世界が遠く、想像もつかない時代であったかがわかる。しかし、今日に至っても太古の生物が現存し、数多くの化石も発見され、さらにはネッシー（プレシオザウルス？）と思われる恐竜の死骸が発見されるなど、決して夢ではない身近かな世界となった。

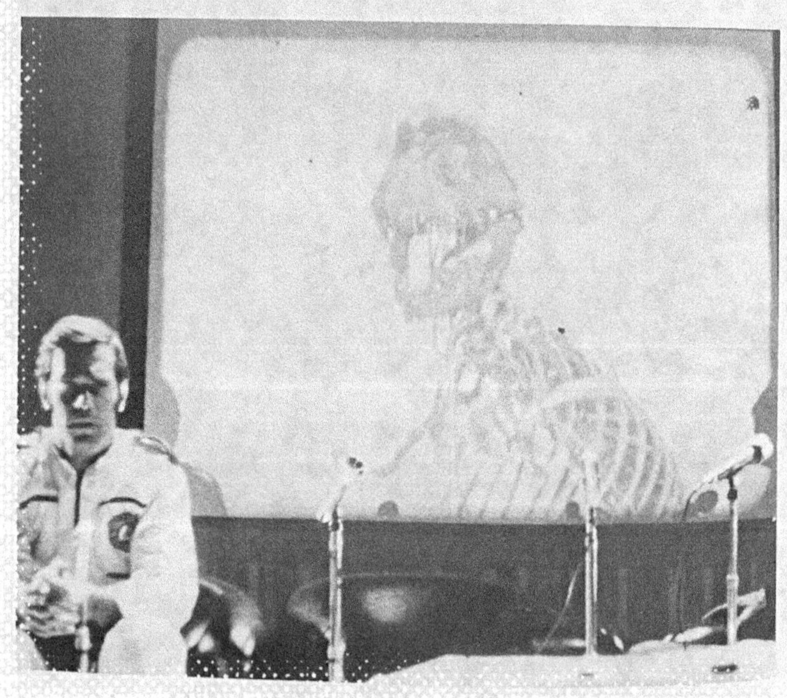

2023 Miser Bros. Press/Rick Goldschmidt

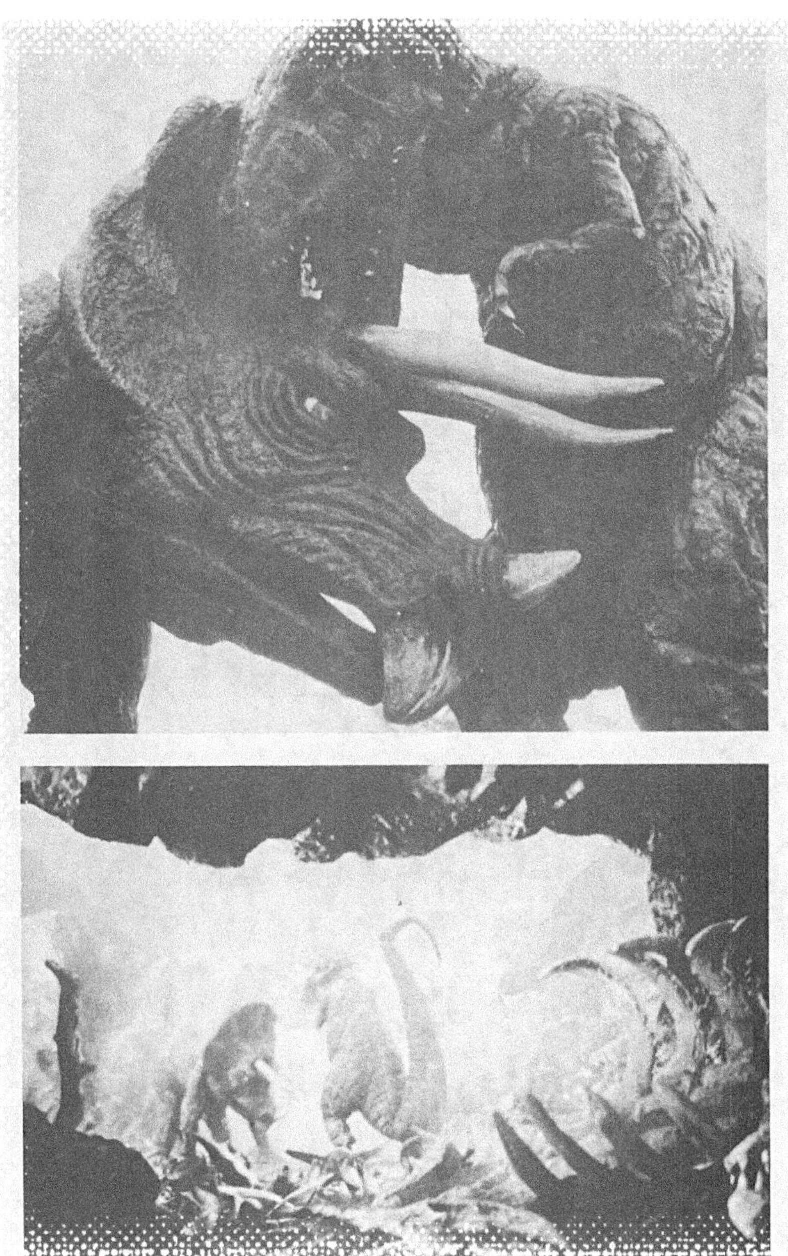

2023 Miser Bros. Press/Rick Goldschmidt

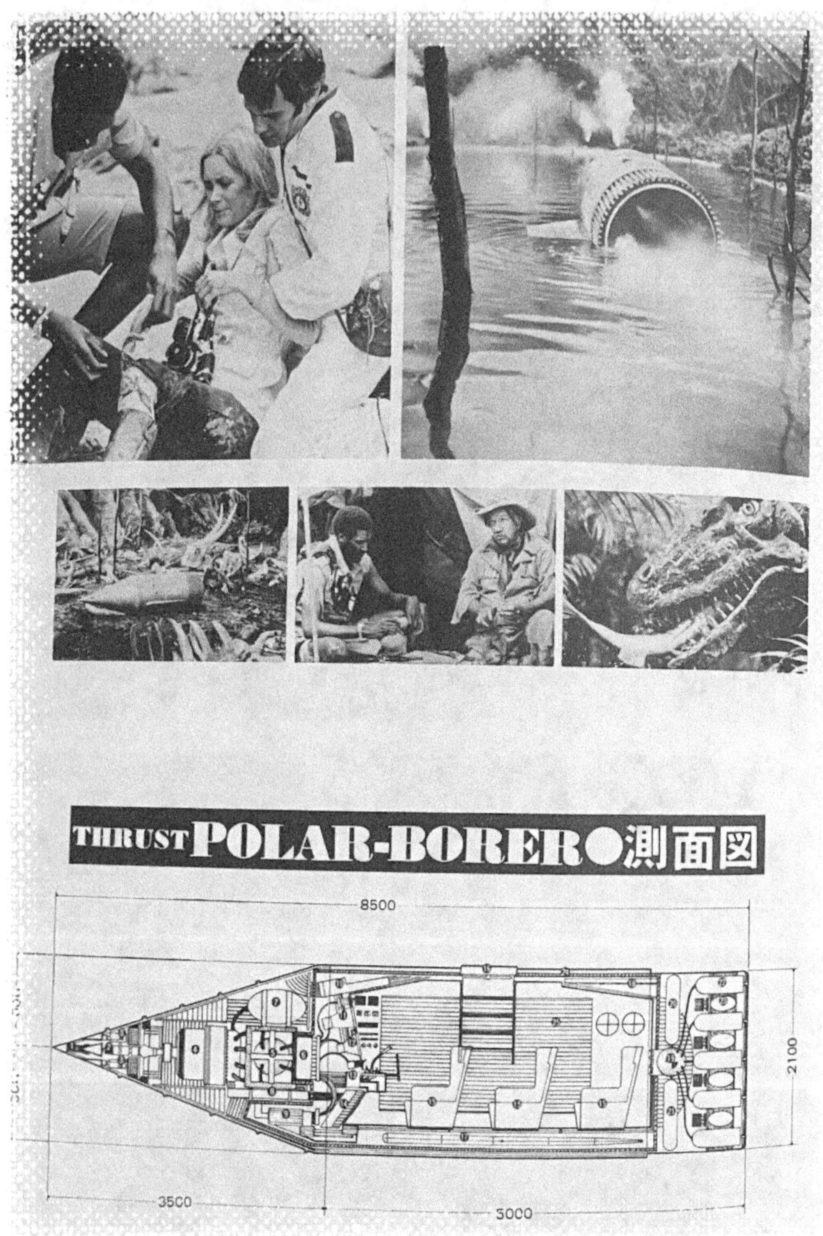

2023 Miser Bros. Press/Rick Goldschmidt

ボディ●マグネシウム鋼板／電気系統●3000VDC
モーター出力●250HP　3000VDC
原子炉●ブルトニウム0.5メガトンPC
速度●空中マッハ1.5／海中67ノット／地底30km H

①レーザービーム
②高波砲
③ＴＶカメラ
④モーター
⑤ブルトニウム原子炉
⑥制御板
⑦重水素
⑧電気制御板
⑨動力コンピューター
⑩無線機
⑪手向器
⑫ＴＶ＆レーダー
⑬操舵機
⑭配線コンピューター
⑮椅子
⑯ハッチ
⑰可変翼
⑱推進制御板
⑲燃料混合機
⑳重水素タンク
㉑圧縮酸素
㉒ロケット・ブースター
㉓冷化アンモニウム
㉔放射能遮断板
㉕生命維持機（気圧・空調機）

2023 Miser Bros. Press/Rick Goldschmidt

ーゲットは，太古の恐竜ティラノザウルスぐらいなものだ。

　マステン石油会社の極東工場で，社長自身がキャッチした奇怪な事件——，それはポーラーポーラに起った緊急異常事態であった。地下の石油をレーザー光線で探掘する地底タンクでもあるポーラーポーラで，地質学担当員のチャックが北極油の海底を潜航中，突然昇も知らぬ火口湖に急浮上してしまったのだ。そしてそこでチャックが目撃した光景——，それは絶滅した筈の恐竜たちが棲む有史以前の不思議な世界だった。

　マステンは直ちに人類史上最大のハンティングとして，恐竜狩りを計画し，これを実行した。マステンを隊長とする一行は，案内役のチャック，ノーベル賞学者川本博士，マスコミ代表の女性記者バンクス，それにマステンの従者ブンタの6名。彼等はポーラーポーラに搭乗し，日本から一路北極へ，そして目的地の火口湖に到着した。チャックの報告通り，湖畔にはプレシオサウルス，空には翼竜が飛びかい，まさしくそこは驚異の世界。やがてマステンたちは，ジャングルに踏みこむと，巨大な恐竜の足跡と出会った。これこそ地球上に存在した動物の中で最大の陸棲肉食竜ティラノザウルス。足跡を追うマステンの一行の目の前に，遂に姿を現わしたこの恐竜は，想像を絶するほど大きく，かつ強力だった。マステンは夢中でライフルを連射したが，途中で銃が壊れ，ティラノザウルスを倒すことができなかった。

　極底探険船ポーラーポーラによる恐竜ハンティングは，なかなか成功までは到達しなかった。それに女性記者バンクスは，動物保護論者の立場から，マステンの殺戮にも心痛む殺戮戦を批判，2人の間で激烈な議論が闘わされた。だがマステンは恐竜を殺すことを絶対あきらめず再度のアタック。この間，恐竜はキャンプに1人残っていた川本博士を襲撃し，さらに湖面に浮いていたポーラーポーラをくわえこむと，それを恐竜の縄張まで運んでいってしまった。その不気味な葦場で出会ったティラノザウルスとトリケラトプス。やがてこの二つの巨大な恐竜は，凄惨きわまりない血闘をくりひろげて，大地を揺るがし，挑え，のたうちまわった。

　一方，極底探険船ポーラーポーラを失った本国の田舎基地では，6人の乗組員の安否を気づかって，一大救出作戦が開始されようとしていた……………。

〈かいせつ〉

77年から78年にかけて，いよいよ世界を席捲しはじめたSF映画ブーム。いまアメリカでは，「スター・ウォーズ」の大ヒット，つづいて「未知との遭遇」をひかえ，文字通り映画界は完全にフューチャー・ロマンを志向，その魅力開発に，多くの優れた才能を投じている。そうした世界的な動きのなかで，アメリカのランキン＝バス・プロダクションが，SF異色アドベンチャーの新作を企画し，しかも日本の最高SF技術の持主としてあまりにも有名な円谷プロダクションを招いて，堂々と完成させたのが，この素晴らしい異色のSFドラマ。アメリカ映画の壮大な構

2023 Miser Bros. Press/Rick Goldschmidt

想，破格の巨費と，日本の優秀な特撮技術が見事にジョイントされた話題作として，いま全米で大ヒットの娯楽大作である。

未来を先取りする世界最高の科学者グループが遂に完成させた極底探険船ポーラーポーラ。このスーパーSFマシンは，切迫した石油危機に対処してつくられた特別石油探掘艇であり，また一方では海底から極底へ突き進むパワフルなニュー・アドベンチャー・メカとして充分にその機能を発揮するというもの。映画はこのポーラーポーラ号が，北極探険の途中，ある日突然，異常な海底変化に遭遇し，見知らぬ火口湖へ浮上。そこでまさしく太古の恐竜世界に呑みこまれるというショッキングなオープニングで始まる。やがて火ぶたを切る極底探険船と巨大な恐竜ティラノザウルス。全く絶滅した筈の太古の恐竜に，ポーラーポーラ号の乗組員たちが対決して行くというユニークな発想と，大スケールの特殊撮影で見せる緊迫のストーリー展開。そして想像を絶するクライマックス，人類史上最大のSFハンティングが硯る者を圧倒する待望のフューチャー・アドベンチャー映画である。

監督はアメリカ側から新鋭アレックス・グラスホフ，日本側からは「若大将シリーズ」などでおなじみのベテラン小谷承晴監督が担当。これに日本世界に誇る，佐川和夫特撮監督以下円谷プロ特撮スタッフ陣が全面参加ています。

主演は「地獄の戦場」「アレンジメント」などの，ベテラン俳優リチャード・ブーン，それに女性記者に扮するジョン・バン・アークなど，多数の若手ハリウッド・スターが出演している。また日本側からも，180人の応募者の中から厳選され，早くも来年のホープとされている関谷ますみが特別参加。して楽しいテーマ曲をナンシー・ウイルソンが歌い，この映画に花を添えています。（ビスタサイズ／上映時間1時間46分）

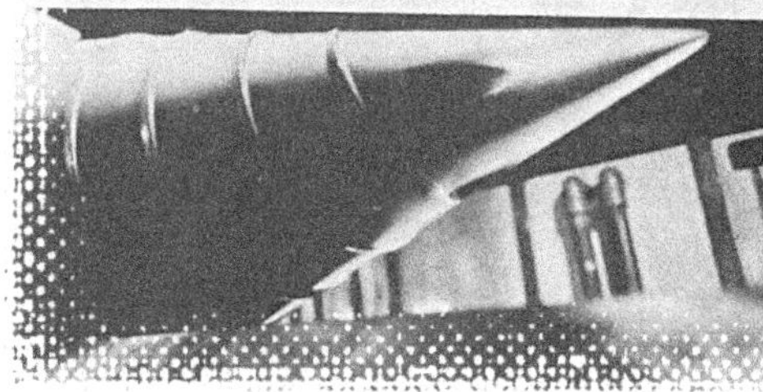

2023 Miser Bros. Press/Rick Goldschmidt

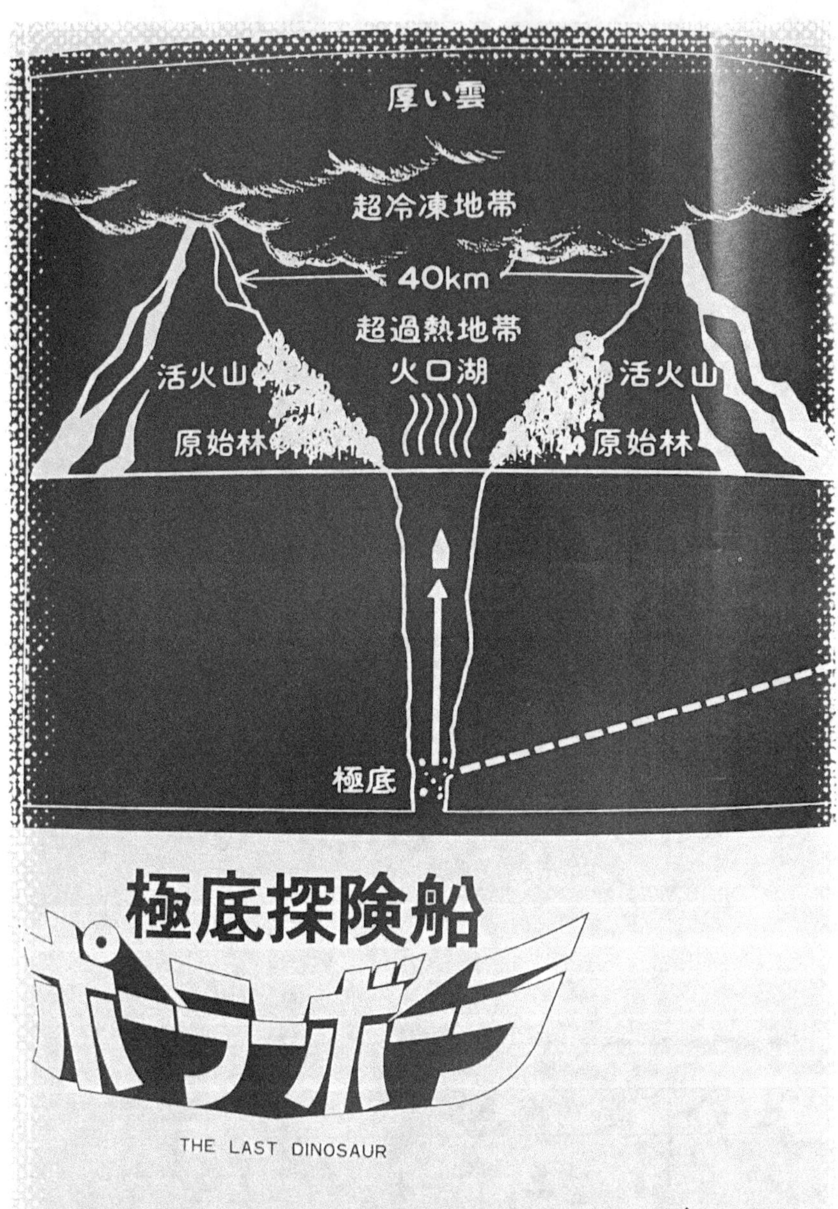

2023 Miser Bros. Press/Rick Goldschmidt

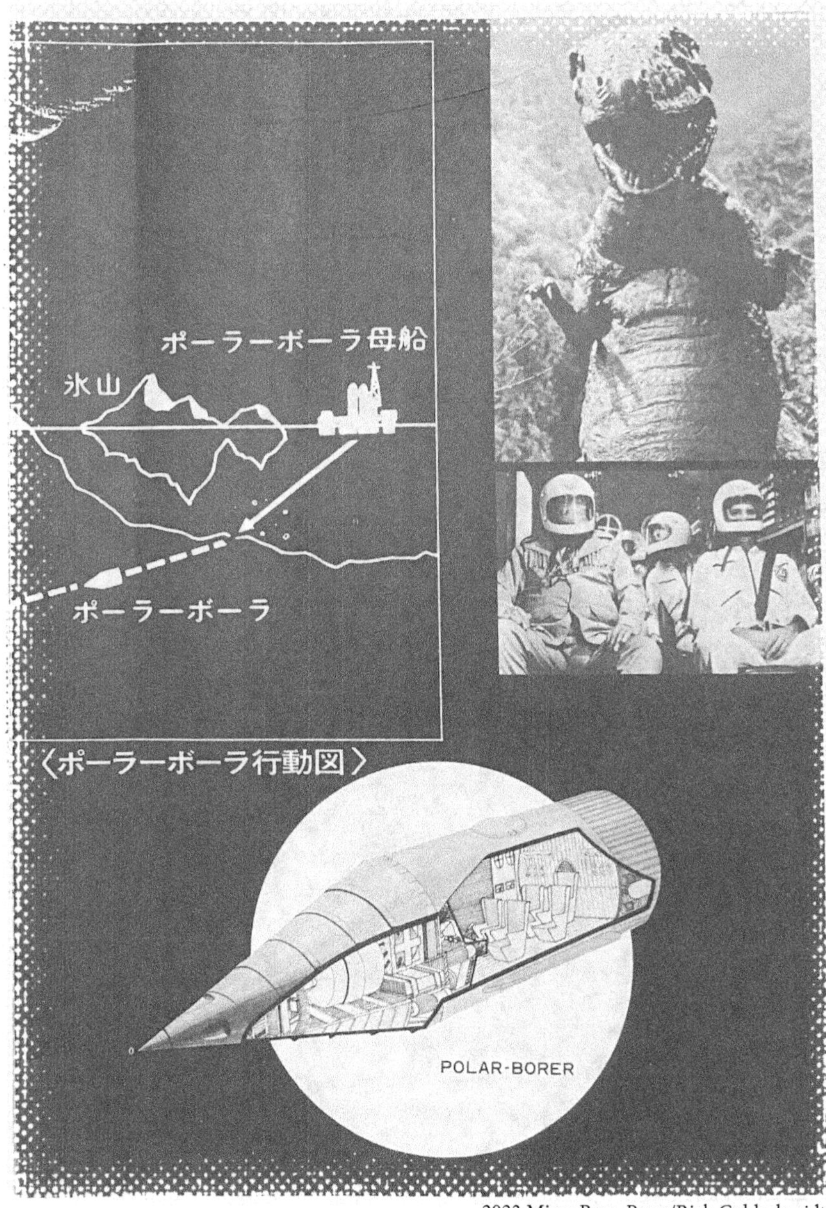
ポーラーボーラ母船
氷山
ポーラーボーラ
〈ポーラーボーラ行動図〉
POLAR-BORER

2023 Miser Bros. Press/Rick Goldschmidt

POST PRODUCTION: FORCED PERSPECTIVE

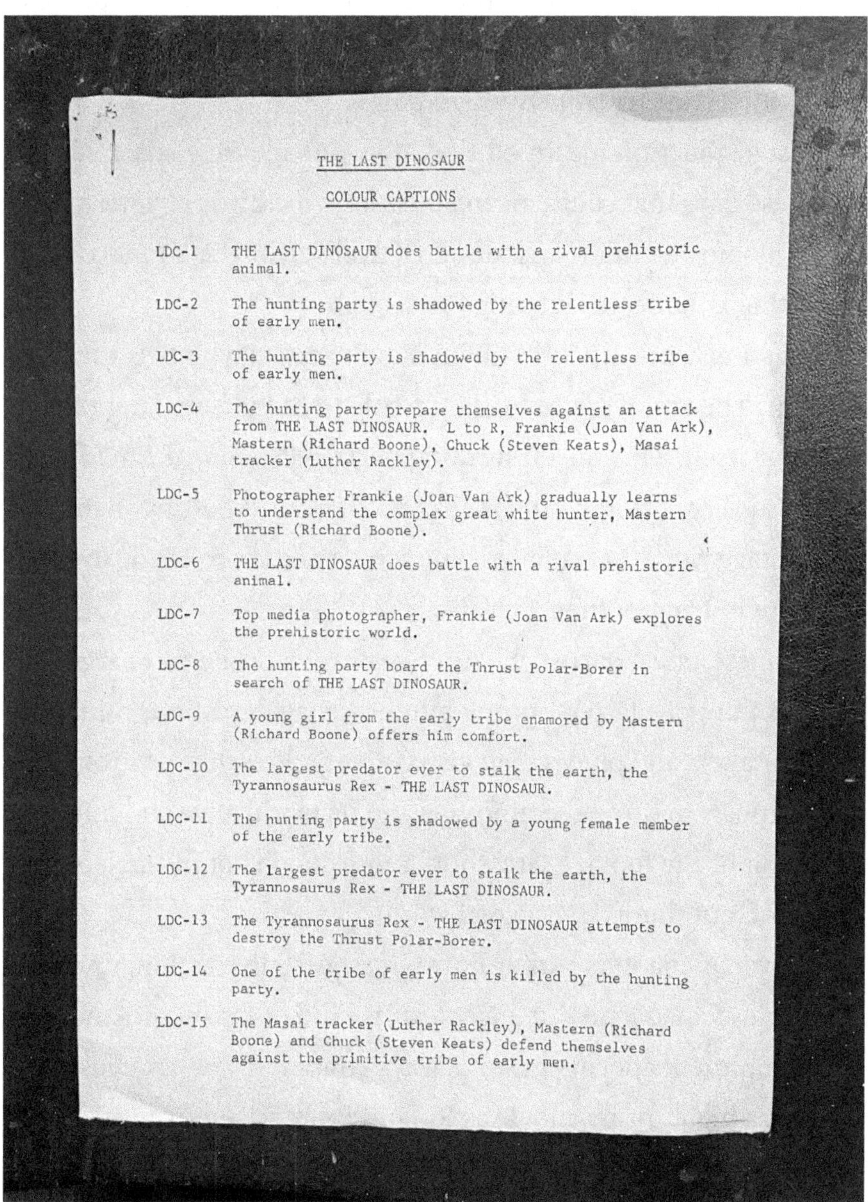

THE LAST DINOSAUR

COLOUR CAPTIONS

LDC-1   THE LAST DINOSAUR does battle with a rival prehistoric animal.

LDC-2   The hunting party is shadowed by the relentless tribe of early men.

LDC-3   The hunting party is shadowed by the relentless tribe of early men.

LDC-4   The hunting party prepare themselves against an attack from THE LAST DINOSAUR. L to R, Frankie (Joan Van Ark), Mastern (Richard Boone), Chuck (Steven Keats), Masai tracker (Luther Rackley).

LDC-5   Photographer Frankie (Joan Van Ark) gradually learns to understand the complex great white hunter, Mastern Thrust (Richard Boone).

LDC-6   THE LAST DINOSAUR does battle with a rival prehistoric animal.

LDC-7   Top media photographer, Frankie (Joan Van Ark) explores the prehistoric world.

LDC-8   The hunting party board the Thrust Polar-Borer in search of THE LAST DINOSAUR.

LDC-9   A young girl from the early tribe enamored by Mastern (Richard Boone) offers him comfort.

LDC-10 The largest predator ever to stalk the earth, the Tyrannosaurus Rex - THE LAST DINOSAUR.

LDC-11 The hunting party is shadowed by a young female member of the early tribe.

LDC-12 The largest predator ever to stalk the earth, the Tyrannosaurus Rex - THE LAST DINOSAUR.

LDC-13 The Tyrannosaurus Rex - THE LAST DINOSAUR attempts to destroy the Thrust Polar-Borer.

LDC-14 One of the tribe of early men is killed by the hunting party.

LDC-15 The Masai tracker (Luther Rackley), Mastern (Richard Boone) and Chuck (Steven Keats) defend themselves against the primitive tribe of early men.

The actual typed manifest from *Tsuburaya Enterprise* for the press package from Rankin/Bass.

"Wrapping" a location often means "it's over" for most of the cast. For me, my business partners and other crew, the work is just beginning. It comes time for "post."

Joan mentioned post earlier. You will hear a common joke among the crew and director on a set, "We'll fix it in post." The joke is you often can't fix something in post.

Post production means editing. It means special visual effects—and these days that could mean an entire two-thirds of your movie. It means music and sound design (layering in the sound effects, correcting volume, re-dubbing lines, etc.).

Location work with the main actors was maybe two-thirds of the film. The real work to bring the title to life was making the last dinosaur itself. This meant heading back to *Tsuburaya Productions* effects studios; bringing the main cast there and putting them into sound stage work that entailed blue screen and more acting to nothing there in front of them.

Japanese effects artist, Kazuo Sagawa would be in charge of a team of puppet masters, props builders, stage creation, miniature model makers and blue screen visual artists. This diverse group had one purpose: to bring the dinosaur and its world alive and interface it with all of the footage Grasshoff and Kotani shot in the Japanese Alps and "out there" in "the real world."

I covered chapters earlier how Grasshoff's live action, dramatic direction seemed a poor choice for this kind of Japanese-American collaboration. It appears in some ways Grasshoff was about as qualified for a big monster movie as Roland Emmerich was for *Godzilla* 1998. Emmerich's instinct was to make Godzilla, a mythical beast, a god-like thing into a real animal more akin to a dinosaur.

I suspect from everything I have researched, that Grasshoff felt that way. His world was documentary filmmaking and reality. He could have researched (and perhaps he did) *Toho* and *Tsuburaya Productions*, he might have seen *Ultraman*, but access, aside from American theaters and weekend TV, was limited.

Gigazine, 2011

Kotani admits he discussed effects with Grasshoff, especially while on set. Kotani got the feeling while shooting up in the mountains, that he inadvertently became "the center of attention" when he did his part of the co-direction, and moved the actors through the scenes that would require later effects work. He alluded to perhaps a professional jealousy or at the least tension from Grasshoff, who might've felt his work or presence as "the director" was undermined by a man who didn't speak a word of English.

Kotani had said, "I had to take on a more significant role in managing the production team and communicating with them. I talked to Alex about it many times, but he returned to Japan after completing the film's shooting and left most of the work to me. I had to communicate with foreign actors in English, which is where I struggled since I am not proficient in the language. But I managed to get through it." [39]

The suspected tension is hinted in Kotani's words here. "You're not that proficient. You're physically able. That's how it started and ended. When the filming was over and I said goodbye to Alex, they were staying at the old Tokyo Hilton. I don't remember exactly what we said." [40]

The two men left each other friendly enough but Benni Korzen also relayed there was some kind of title issue with the Director's Guild. "Kotani took charge soon after the shooting began, making him the director of the film in my view. Grasshoff wasn't necessarily a poor director, but his lack of international experience made him less suitable for the project."

Joan Van Ark referred to the look of the beast as a joke. The dinosaur does have a silly appearance, no argument there. It (or he) might be the pre-cursor to *Barney* with its purple-hued skin (depending on the light and rendering of the footage in post). Sometimes it's bluish, sometimes purple, sometimes a more charcoal grey.

The point is, by Western assessment, the dinosaur was silly, B-movie fare--hardly threatening and the epitome of kitsch and cheese.

---

39 *The Last Dinosaur, Special Edition DVD.* Commentary by Tom Kotani. 2009. Toho Video.

40 Ibid.

On the flipside (or eastern side) Sagawa was proud of his monster. It had a unique look, a fantastical style and design. Kotani, by the accounts I have found, felt in similar ways, approving the look of the dinosaur and its offbeat appearance.

2023 Miser Bros. Press/Rick Goldschmidt

The creature was comprised of two heavy, latex, foam and rubber suits that an actor slipped inside. The "zipper" ran up the back and the seam covered in bumps or small spines. The big joke in Godzilla movies for American viewers was that you could see "the zipper running up the back" on the monster outfits.

Studio artists found more clever ways to hide the point of entry into the suits and they usually were not literal zippers, but rather seams that were sealed together by other means.

Toho Video, 2009

"When you look at it, dinosaur suits seem quite easy to move around in. The one without a mechanical component, basically just the parts where the mechanical component isn't for ease of movement. Afterwards, it's a drinking party." [41]

Wearing the suit is a physical workout. *Gojira* suit actor, Haruo Nakajima said the original monster outfit weighed over 200 pounds. He lost considerable weight, sweating it out under the layers of foam and rubber while making the original 1954 film. The suit was so cumbersome and heavy that at one point he almost drowned when he fell over in one of the giant indoor pools and was electrocuted when water hit the wires that lit up Godzilla's spikes.

There were similar issues with *The Last Dinosaur*. "Even though [the actor] is wearing such a thick costume, there is no difference now, apparently, with water and everything. Among the days of filming, there are some that are one-day trips, so the most important thing is the actor endurance during the summer when it was filmed. The most important thing is that monsters, dinosaurs, or whatever, when they are healthy, they are healthy. If the monsters, even dinosaurs, are not feeling well, then humans cannot be too healthy either." [42]

Good point.

While it was one man inside a T-Rex suit, there were two types of suits made for the film. Sagawa relayed there was one suit that contained a mechanical apparatus and the other was just a less animated suit for walking, moving, chasing.

The mechanical part was a puppet design where the actor wore the suit but was more hunched to allow his hands up into the head

---

41 *The Last Dinosaur, Special Edition DVD.* Commentary by Kazuo Sagawa. 2009. *Toho Video.*

42 *The Last Dinosaur, Special Edition DVD.* Commentary by Kazuo Sagawa. 2009. *Toho Video.*

to operate the jaws. This allowed the beast to roar while walking or bite and attack as in the T-Rex and Triceratops battle.

There is a quick moment (at about 40 minutes into the film) when we see the dinosaur for the first time and the puppet-mouth procedure not working at its best. The dinosaur trudges toward Boone and Rackley and the bottom jaw flops comically.

Keep in mind that this was a time before remote control animatronics or even headsets for an actor to hear direction from the outside. Often the director has to yell the direction to the suit actor and make the moves according to the shouts.

The way the jaw flops like crazy seems to be a moment where the actor either lost control of the mechanical jaw controls or just over compensated to give the director what he wanted with possible shouts of "Faster!"

The dinosaur suits used in the film were designed to be as realistic as possible. They were created with movable limbs and animatronic features that allowed the dinosaurs to move and react in a lifelike manner. The suits were also detailed with realistic textures and colors to make them look like real dinosaurs. Movement, texturing the suit, or even the subtleties of footsteps all played into the process.

This harkens back to the artistry of Bunraku. "We watched a lot of dinosaurs," Sagawa laughed. "We watched the way they walked. When you see it, the dinosaur suit seems to be quite easy to move in. It's just that there's no "mecha" (mechanics) in it, so we put in easy-to-move parts and mecha. And then we had the drinking party..."

Sagawa loved to reference the fact that these suit actors worked and played hard afterwards. [43]

---

43 Ibid.

Toho Video, 2009

2023 Miser Bros. Press/Rick Goldschmidt

2023 Miser Bros. Press/Rick Goldschmidt

The effects artist acknowledged the difference in visual styles and audience acceptance. He admitted that they had to add elements of realism to the dinosaur suit because of Western demands for realism.

"Westerners still like Japanese monsters. They are descendants of the Kaiju and fans of Tanaka [producer of the Godzilla films]. They won't accept it [meaning "fake" or unrealistic effects]." [44]

He added that American audiences want lots of dinosaurs in their movies. Lots of monsters, which is what *Ultraman* often gave or films like *The Land That Time Forgot* and its *Amicus* sequels and siblings. Remember how disappointed I said I was in watching 1976's *King Kong* to find there were no other dinosaurs in the film except that big, rubber dopey snake? I'm still traumatized.

"So, the common denominator here is the need to have [many] animals. Of course, in the past, there were no CG images available. But, it's the closest we can get. These are all living creatures. It's just for reference. Everyone is tired, but it's in their heads. The reference is a metaphor, and the animal used as a metaphor is a dinosaur. I heard that it's the most carnivorous and vicious animal. That's what we struggled with the most. To make the creature look real." [45]

There it is. The struggle between East and West on this film is vocalized by the man that was responsible for rendering its imagery. He was torn. Sagawa is clear that this design is a *metaphor* which fits the Japanese love for art and surrealism. Yet, he knew he had to deliver an element of realism for American audiences because this was the primary demographic.

---

44 Ibid.

45 *The Last Dinosaur, Special Edition DVD.* Commentary by Kazuo Sagawa. 2009. *Toho Video.*

ABC, an American TV network was footing the bill for this co-production. They wanted this for their North American viewership. This is why the main cast was all recognizable US names, virtually unknown in Japan. Keep in mind, no Internet, no 24 hours news at this time and no outlets dedicated to the sole distribution of entertainment content.

Think of it this way--a number of US celebrities have and continue to do so, make commercials for Japanese audiences that never get seen here. You have to search them out online and are not common knowledge.

None of the American actors with *The Last Dinosaur* were all that well-known to their Japanese crew or Japanese movie goers or TV watchers.

Sagawa was torn between his instincts of what works at home versus a whole other perspective from a Western audience.

2023 Miser Bros. Press/Rick Goldschmidt

He talked of lots of discussion on the T-Rex and its design. "Underlying materials. In other words, there is a discussion about the material of this dinosaur from ancient times. The question is how to imagine this walking dinosaur with Japanese feet, whether it's 6 meters or 12 meters." [46]

Aside from actors running from nothing or general directions on set, and then doing almost the same thing on a sound stage, fighting an invisible enemy; the other issue with this kind of effects work is scale.

2023 Miser Bros. Press/Rick Goldschmidt

46   Ibid.

Something is lost in translation between the Western use of "feet" and the Eastern use of "meters" in measurement. Americans were supposed to switch over to a full metric system by 2000. To date we have not and when the pandemic hit, we saw all kinds of illustrations for social distancing measurements. Six feet was equal to "12 penguins" or recently as a meteor burning up in our atmosphere was headlined as the length of "six elephants."

Americans will do just about anything to avoid using the metric system.

Science tells us the real T-Rex was anywhere between 12-20 feet high and around 40 feet in length. Steven Keats confirms this in the opening of the film at the press conference scene. Richard Boone's Masten shows the press corps real museum footage of a T-Rex skeleton that matches those dimensions.

The problem was Keats's character's description to the press corps about seeing the monster for the first time. He said he saw something moving over the tree tops. They had to be smaller trees. The T-Rex is verbally described as a gigantic thing far larger than the dimensions were just told in Masten's exposition.

Jurassic Park went for realism. Science is changing our view of dinosaurs with the latest entry into the franchise giving us lizards with feathers. The scale of the creatures remains pretty consistent. They don't just suddenly go from 20 feet high to fifty or even a hundred feet high.

Thanks to better imaging control in the computer with precise measurements with both man and monster, scale issues have become far less of an issue in modern-day big monster films in the advent of the digital revolution.

1977 was a whole other beast.

Sagawa dismissed such a small height of six meters. "Probably not six meters. Anyway, it's about four times bigger. I don't think it's suitable for a person who is not oriented towards meters. The focus is always on people, and the emphasis is on how people will be in relation to the dinosaur, whether it's six meters or 10 meters. The most important thing is to make the Kaiju bigger than the human figures." [47]

Japanese and even Americans wanted their monsters BIG back then. Everything was bigger in the 70s. Dino DeLaurentiis said of his *King Kong* movie that it would be bigger in every way in comparison to *Jaws*. Even the death of his title character. The production and studio tried to imply the giant, mechanical ape used for those brief several seconds in the film was used throughout. Big! Big ! Big! Hai! Hai! Hai! (Joan would appreciate that).

How did it all work? Today computers and green screen tutorials allow anyone at home to make their own CGI effects and backdrops. Back then it was a different story.

One of the oldest visual effects tricks is "forced perspective." This is what is called an "in camera" effect because it really relies on the positioning of the camera rather than image manipulation afterward in a studio.

"Forced perspective" is a visual special effect used in filmmaking to create the illusion of depth and size by manipulating the scale of objects and people within the frame. It's often used in movies, especially in scenes involving giant monsters or otherworldly creatures. *The Last Dinosaur* uses it quite a bit, especially in its "Dino Stomp" scenes with the foot coming down at the camera to convey massive size.

In forced perspective shots, the filmmakers place objects or people at different distances from the camera, making them appear

---

47 Ibid.

to be closer or further away than they actually are. This creates the illusion of depth and can make small objects look much larger or large objects look much smaller than they really are.

For example, in a scene featuring a giant monster attacking a city, the filmmakers might use forced perspective to make it appear as though the monster is towering over the buildings. They might use miniatures for the buildings, and then place actors or props closer to the camera to make them appear larger and closer to the monster. By doing so, the filmmakers can create the impression of a massive creature rampaging through a city without having to build full-sized sets or use expensive CGI effects (which didn't exist in the 70s).

The process can be a challenging technique to execute, as it requires careful planning and precise camera positioning. However, when done correctly (and it is in *The Last Dinosaur*), it can be a cost-effective and creative solution for creating memorable visual effects in movies.

Before explaining the blue screen process which was relatively new to visual effects work in the mid-70s, it's important to understand the matte process and why mattes are made and their function in films *The Last Dinosaur* or even films like *The Birds* or *Earthquake*.

The matte process is an essential technique used in filmmaking to create special effects and composite different elements together to form a cohesive image. In this process, a portion of the image is masked out or removed, allowing another image to be inserted behind it.

Early forced perspective work involving mattes was done by painting on glass, which is a technique known as glass matte painting. Artists like Albert Whitlock were famous for this technique and used it extensively in films like *The Birds* and *The Magnificent Seven*.

Artist Albert Whitlock was Hollywood's "go-to guy" when it came to hand painted glass mattes. His work stretched all the way through the 80s in films like 1981's *Ghost Story* and 1983's *Psycho II.*

The glass painted matte process involved painting a detailed background onto a pane of glass, which was then placed in front of the camera. The actors would be filmed in front of the glass, and the matte painting would be combined with the live action footage in the editing room to create a seamless composite image.

A young James Cameron used this effect in John Carpenter's 1981 classic *Escape from New York* where he painted the New York City skyline as well as city buildings to be used in a daytime helicopter scene to give the illusion they were actually shooting with those buildings in the background.

As technology advanced, the process of creating mattes evolved as well. In the mid-20th century, a technique known as "traveling matte" was developed, which involved shooting a scene twice: once with the actors and once without them. The two pieces of footage were then combined, with the actors' portion of the image being masked out and replaced with the second footage. This technique was used to create a wide range of special effects, from invisibility to flying.

In the 1960s, blue screen technology was introduced, which revolutionized the matte process. In this technique, a blue screen was used as a backdrop, and actors were filmed in front of it. The blue screen could then be removed in post-production, and any background could be inserted behind the actors. Blue screen technology quickly became the industry standard and was used in many films throughout the 1970s and 1980s, including *Star Wars, Superman the Movie* and *Raiders of the Lost Ark.*

Another development in the matte process during the 1970s and 1980s was the use of front projection. This technique involved projecting an image onto a reflective screen in front of the actors, which would bounce back and be captured by the camera. This allowed the actors to interact with a projected image in real-time, creating a more convincing composite. *The Last Dinosaur* would use this in combination of rotoscoping. This was more an evolution of old school rear projection techniques.

Blue screen was relatively new at the time (debuting somewhere in the 60s). George Lucas and his effects teams revolutionized it with new camera technology allowing for amazing computerized movements with models and miniatures never seen before *Star Wars.*

The Last Dinosaur didn't have that. However the same blue screen process used for this film was used throughout the industry, including *Superman The Movie* which came on the heels of *Dinosaur.*

Blue screen visual effects, also known as chroma key compositing, is a process used in filmmaking and video production to combine two or more images or video streams together into a single shot. This process involves shooting the subject against a blue (or sometimes green) background, and then replacing the blue background with another image or footage during post-production.

The blue screen visual effects process involves several key steps:

1. Setting up the blue screen: A blue screen is set up as the background behind the subject. The blue color is chosen because it is a color that is not typically found in skin tones or clothing, making it easier to separate the subject from the background.

2. Shooting the footage: The subject is filmed against the blue screen background. The lighting must be carefully set up to ensure that the blue screen is evenly lit, and that there are no shadows or reflections on the screen.

3. Editing the footage: During post-production, the blue screen is removed from the footage using specialized software. This process involves "keying out" the blue color, which creates a transparent background. The subject is then placed onto a new background or composited with other footage.

4. Rotoscoping: Sometimes, the blue screen visual effects process may involve rotoscoping, which is the process of manually tracing around the subject frame by frame. Rotoscoping is often used when the subject has fine details or intricate movement, and can be time-consuming and labor-intensive.

The blue screen process in action.
Richard Boone and Luther Rackley are shot in a studio, acting at targets.
They are matted in later and rotoscoped for the finished piece.

Despite its many benefits, the blue screen visual effects process does have some inherent flaws. One issue is that the blue screen footage may be too light or too dark, which can make it difficult to match with the composite footage. This issue can be addressed by adjusting the lighting during the shoot and by using color grading techniques during post-production.

Another issue with the blue screen visual effects process is that the edges of the subject may appear fringed or jagged, especially if the subject has fine details or a complex outline. This issue can be addressed by using rotoscoping techniques or by using advanced software tools to refine the keying process.

The older blue screen process for visual effects was different from today's modern green screen and CGI effects in a few key ways:

1. Blue screen vs. green screen: The older blue screen process used a blue background, while modern green screen techniques use a green background. This is because green is a color that is less common in human skin tones and clothing, making it easier to separate the subject from the background.

2. Film vs. digital: The older blue screen process was typically used with film cameras, while modern green screen and CGI effects are done using digital cameras and software. This means that modern techniques can take advantage of the benefits of digital technology, such as higher resolution and greater flexibility in post-production.

3. Physical effects vs. digital effects: The older blue screen process relied heavily on physical effects such as models, miniatures, and practical effects. In contrast, modern techniques make use of digital effects created using computer software.

4. Real-time compositing vs. post-production compositing: Modern green screen techniques often use real-time compositing, where the composited image is created in real-time during filming. This allows the director and actors to see the final composite image on set, and can help to create a more seamless integration between the subject and the background.

5. Accuracy and precision: Modern green screen and CGI techniques allow for a higher degree of accuracy and precision in the compositing process. For example, modern techniques can track the movement of the camera and the subject in real-time, allowing for more realistic and seamless integration between the subject and the background.

The blue screen process conflicted with the coloring of the dinosaur itself. As noted earlier, its skin tone seems to move from grayish to bluish to purplish. The culprit was an unclear understanding of the relatively new technology.

Richard Boone and countless actors before him, almost since filmmaking began, used rear projection to provide background scenes. 1933's *King Kong* had no blue screen process. Actors stood in front of the big projection screens I talked of previously. A reverse image was then shot onto the back of thin, Muslin material to look normal behind the actor.

The process had great limitations with realism, contrasts and often washed out images behind a clear actor. No matter what the artistic intent, the audience was pretty aware they were seeing a fake, simulated background.

Wardrobe colors didn't factor into the rear projection process. Neither did dinosaur suits.

When Sagawa's team designed the suit they were working on decades of previous Kaiju movies shot on stages with hand painted backdrops. Rear projection was sometimes used, primarily for the human characters to run in front of screens showing city destruction or needing to show scale before their giant monster.

There was no rotoscoping or blue screen work. This is why Richard Boone would be peeved over this kind of stuff because he spent decades on TV not worrying about anything in front of him. If he had faced something coming at him, he could see it in real time and react in real time.

Now he was put in front of a big blue screen with some dangling ping pong ball markers and told act with nothing to act off. This was all new to an actor like Boone.

The blue screen process targeted the blue. This created major problems in the post process of color grading. It was all on film back then. There was no digital color correcting software.

Looking at behind the scenes footage of the making of this film, the dino suit looks charcoal grey. The coloring appears to have come in post, likely to rectify conflicts with the blue screen process. When film is graded, you often have to make adjustments to light and contrast which can create mismatching with the live-action footage.

There are several moments in the movie when the dinosaur is seen from afar, particularly its introductory scene, and the far shots look washed out and lighter, not matching with the real world landscape in the foreground.

This "matte" effect is compromised through what was a lack of full understanding of the blue screening technology. The problem was—you had to go with it. There was no money or time to go back and reshoot, let alone build another suit whose coloring would lend itself better.

Sagawa returned to the issue of scale. Aside from the technical aspects of the blue screen and real-action compositing, there was pleasing audiences on both sides of the world. Both liked their monsters big, but big also means big enough to wreck buildings, flip cars. Would a 20 foot high T-Rex be all that scary?

Realism had to be traded for big screen excitement and scale. A real T-Rex would come THROUGH the trees, not rise UP through tree tops. They just weren't that big. With Godzilla and *Ultraman* on the minds of both audiences, the decision was likely made to err on the side of caution and go with what you know.

2023 Miser Bros. Press/Rick Goldschmidt

The T-Rex would be BIG and we would just suspend our disbelief with the scale inconsistencies. The infamous "boulder to the head" shot with the catapult is a good example.

When the gang loads up the boulder, it's heavy and large but they all can still lift it and position it in the arm. It's not THAT big. That all changes when it whacks that monster's noggin. The boulder seemed to grow at least twice in size.

Why? Because the actual scale of the rock would be like a basketball against the scale of the dinosaur we've been given in this film. Adjustments had to be made.

It's hard to imagine Alexander Grasshoff signing off on these kinds of things as director, but if Tom Kotani is accurate in his description of the way things ended, Grasshoff washed his hands of his duties once he left Japan.

The rest was in the hands of Kotani and Sagawa.

"When you look back," Sagawa said, "There are 10 dinosaurs instead of one absolutely large monster." He lamented the chore of matching scale with multiple animals of multiple sizes. This is why all the dinosaurs all seem about the same size in the movie because it makes things easier for scaling the human characters later in post. [48]

"Actually, assuming they are 10 meters tall, it's unavoidable that they will be smaller on the scale. No matter what happens, the dinosaur and the character will always be composited for the client, but for that scene, I don't know, please shoot the character smaller when inserting it. At least from the waist or a full shot. Otherwise, it will give the impression that the dinosaur is advancing. The construction team doesn't understand this, but it can't be helped. We haven't done this before, so let's do a test first. If you don't shoot it like that, it will progress to the image of a dinosaur. Take a picture of the person in the foreground, put this dinosaur in the open, actually compose it in the background, and give it to us for temporary synthesis. This is normal." [49]

Sagawa also tried to find understanding for where the issues came from. Admitting this was all new to him and a lot of his crew, he also faulted the production's inability to think "for post" while shooting the live action material on location.

---

48 Ibid.
49 Ibid.

These limitations would create conflicts with the Western audience's demands for realism. "The director captures the audience. Who is that audience [meaning East or West]? This is a big mistake, a lousy background. Of course, that's good. Which one is your director?" [50]

Which director shoulders the issues for the background Sagawa describes. Is it Grasshoff's inexperience with effects or does it come from Kotani who didn't factor in enough with the new blue screen process, relying more on his work with painted, real and projected backgrounds?

"Making it look scary is the most important thing for the era. I think the main feeling is more important than the sense of scale. That place is gone now, but we wanted to use Toho's special effects stage, but we didn't get the budget."

Sagawa just described the tradeoff with the tone and look of the film for spectacle than the realism of scale. *Toho Studios* was famous for its giant sound stages and massive pools and sets for oceans and lakes. The budget didn't allow the production to use them for *The Last Dinosaur.*

Scale comes into play with miniature models. Many of the sets you see in the film were constructed miniatures sets. Some were created for inexplicable reasons. The opening shot of the model airplanes and fake airport runway seems unnecessary. Why wasn't a real airport used? Being this was all in Japan, why not have it that we were traveling with Masten to one of his global affiliate facilities with this one being in Japan? Why try to fake America and use miniatures that just stand out, and so early in the film, setting a B-movie tone already.

Miniature models have played a significant role in Japanese Kaiju films. These models are used to create the illusion of large-scale destruction and battles between the Kaiju and human-made structures.

---

50 Ibid.

In Japanese Kaiju films, miniature models are built at a smaller scale than the actual size of the Kaiju, and are often constructed with great attention to detail to create a realistic and convincing appearance on screen. These models can be made from a variety of materials, including plastic, foam, and resin, and are often painted and weathered to give them a more realistic appearance.

The process of building miniature models for Kaiju films typically involves several key steps. First, the filmmakers will create a design or concept for the Kaiju and any human-made structures that will be destroyed during the film. This design will then be used as the basis for creating a physical miniature model.

Once the model is built, it is filmed on a small-scale set using techniques such as forced perspective to create the illusion of a larger scale. The filmmakers will then combine the footage of the miniature model with footage of the live-action actors and any other special effects such as pyrotechnics or explosions.

The focus of the use of miniature models in Japanese Kaiju films is to create a sense of scale and spectacle that would be impossible to achieve with live-action footage alone. By using miniature models, filmmakers are able to create the illusion of large-scale destruction and battles between Kaiju and human-made structures, all while maintaining a high level of detail and realism.

The crew tried some unique things with their visuals and scale models. Thrust's jet in the opening was written and storyboarded to start close on Boone's face in the window, to have the jet careen away from camera and pull back from the real shot composited into the model jet.

We get *something* like that, and it's ambitious for a TV movie but it's nothing *Star Wars*-like or coming from the brilliance of John Dykstra.

2023 Miser Bros. Press/Rick Goldschmidt

Toho Video, 2009

The sad part is that *The Last Dinosaur* was released on the cusp of *Star Wars* and its limitations in the effects area would be accentuated by the epic space adventure.

Sagawa was obsessed with texture and look of the miniatures and how they would mesh with the suit actors and the blue screen composites.

The Polar Borer model varies in scale throughout the film. Big enough to house five people, it seems rather small in some shots, and then enlarges when the dinosaur steals it from the giant swimming pool lake.

The sets themselves are lush and intricate. Perhaps the most beautiful of the soundstage work is seen when we find the T-Rex fishing for a giant trout or Koi and Kotani allows us a long panning shot to take in the hard work of the miniature flora and landscaping. It's amazing to know this was all created for maybe a minute of screen time.

Some of the miniature models don't "hold up" as well. The helicopter shots in the arctic with very fake snow particles blown by a fan around them isn't much better than the oil rig platform shots that holds the headquarters for the mission.

It seems to me it would have been better to procure some B-roll (stock footage) of the industrial type of places and keep the dinosaur world more in the surreal territory. We know what ships, planes, airports and even oil rigs look like.

We can be more forgiving with unseen worlds. It makes a better suspension of disbelief. The lack of convincing miniatures doesn't derail the film, however I offer my suspicions that Grasshoff bristled when seeing them for the first time.

Real bones were used for the T-Rex lair. Crew and artists gathered up real bison, vulture and other bones to litter about the hellish-looking set. As a filmmaker, this is where I would've had most of the action take place.

The desolate graveyard of former adversaries and meals could've made a kind of "Hell Landscape." When Chuck Wade finds the Polar Borer down in the dinosaur's man cave, we never get any tense scene of him going down there to see if it worked.

2023 Miser Bros. Press/Rick Goldschmidt

Imagine him trying to get down there, sneaking about and getting into the machine and firing it up, the whole time not knowing when the dinosaur was going to come home.

We get a "time has passed" kind of montage or cut away and we see the Polar Borer being moved with some kind of logs and pole transport system from the lair to lake.

How they got the technology to do all this, cut all those trees without attracting the attention of the T-Rex let alone anything else and have the strength to haul that giant machine out of there is beyond me.

This beast fixated on Boone just as Boone fixated on it—they somehow managed to all get into that lair and push the Polar Borer out of there without the dino ever coming home and catching them? The damned thing has stealth technology, it didn't tip-toe into the canyon and see these pain in the ass little things burglarizing his home?

2023 Miser Bros. Press/Rick Goldschmidt

Look back to the *Tropeasaurs Rex* chapter, I guess. Instead of wasting time with the catapult scene the standoff should've been on the dinosaur's home turf, in its lair. It would have represented the ultimate invasion of the creature's world by these outsiders.

The bones in the lair were boiled, baked and stripped to weather them and give the illusion of being there for some time. Again, the texture of the props and miniatures is paramount for the illusion to be complete.

While we didn't get a final standoff in the lair, it was home to the gladiatorial fight, the image that was the stuff of kid's dinosaur books—the T-Rex and Triceratops battle. Why the three-horned lizard is buried in a mountainside INSIDE the Rex's lair is beyond me, but I went with it when I was kid. Who cares? This was fun and shit was about to go down.

Toru Kawai played the T-Rex. I have to stop here for a moment and give named credit to the two dudes inside the Triceratops suit. This is what it says on IMDb for one of them. Imagine this is your professional film credit that represents your career and work:

The first dinosaur we see is a Pterodactyl. It's almost dropped into frame to say: "See! Dinosaurs!" These animals were not true flying creatures like birds. They were gliders. From what I understand they could not hover like the beast that greets us upon the team's revival.

The background was hand painted, much like the Showa era Godzilla films and other Kaiju content. The dinosaur is a marionette, suspended on wire with a battery operated mouth that opened on intervals.

I have no idea what species of dinosaur the big charging rhino-like thing was. Steven Keats misidentifies it behind his binoculars. What I do know is the scale is way off, as any four-legged monster like this was not that huge. Again, the rules of scale will be fast and loose to provide "big monster" effects.

The creature was a single man in a suit, running on all fours. The skin looks thin, overall, but the actor was saddled with what appears to be a heavy rubber mantle to give the effect of thick elephant or rhino-like hide.

The back of the suit is somewhat bowed or humped to allow for the actor inside to walk and run with hands and feet on the floor. This would not be the same process used with the coming Triceratops scene which would employ two actors in a single suit.

2023 Miser Bros. Press/Rick Goldschmidt

The rotoscoping and matte work may be underwhelming here but it is ambitious. The first issue is the matching of the live action footage with Boone and Van Ark as the sun was bright the day they shot. The stage footage of dinosaur is more overcast and under lit, creating a major contrast in the matte process.

Van Ark's character wants to get "the shot" and puts herself in harm's way which required a combination of superimposing her from the location footage in a matte. To integrate the suitmation dinosaur with the live-action footage of Van Ark, the filmmakers used blue screen and some front projection. Van Ark was filmed in front of a blue screen, and the footage of the dinosaur was later inserted in post-production.

The blue screen allowed the actors to interact with the dinosaur and gave the filmmakers greater control over the lighting and compositing of the final shot.

It's an ambitious shot and a hell of an attempt to grip the audience as we entered this world with Boone and his intrepids. The results are mixed. It is intercut with some "through the lens" point of view footage to give us Francesca's first looks at the beast, and then editing attempts to cut fast between the live action, stage actor work and the suit actor.

It comes together but is underwhelming but props are given for attempting all of this. The wide shot of Boone moving across the front of the matte with the charging dinosaur composited in behind him and Van Ark is a damned good one. It is marred by the obvious lighting issues between the real location footage and the stage lighting shot afterward.

Boone's last second tackle of Van Ark before their "mud fest" scene where they land in the one-take mud shot all plays out in front of a blue screen.

A simple effect used to save time and money was the "Day for Night" light filtering technique.

The "day for night" lighting effect is a technique used in film-making to create the illusion of a night scene, even if it was shot during the day. It's commonly used in movies because shooting at night can be expensive and time-consuming, especially if a production has to light up large exterior sets or shoot in remote locations.

To achieve the "day for night" effect, filmmakers typically use filters or adjust the camera settings to make the daylight look like moonlight or streetlights. They also adjust the lighting on set to create long shadows and minimize the visibility of the sky. This can be done by using scrims or flags to block out the sunlight, or by lighting the scene with a blue or green gel, simulating moonlight. They may also add additional post-production effects such as color grading and compositing to enhance the final result.

The technique requires careful planning and execution, as it's important to make the scene look believable and avoid any jarring inconsistencies that could break the illusion. However, when done correctly, the "day for night" effect can be a cost-effective and practical solution for filmmakers to shoot night scenes while still maintaining creative control over the final product.

Shooting at night requires a lot of lighting and a lot of time to light properly. You've seen films where it's done right and likely didn't notice it.

The 80s gave us this weird, "night look" which we just accepted as normal (another "Film Dysmorphia" symptom). Anyone who has been in the woods at night knows it's DARK. I mean really dark. Some nights so dark you can barely see your hand before your face.

In 80s horror, particularly, we got this electric blue gel tint and the background lit by spotlights clouded in foggy haze to give a dreamlike look that pervaded everything from *Friday the* 13th slashers to *ET: The Extraterrestrial.*

Most would say that despite the unreal look, that was lighting done right. The fact that we just accepted and went with and even came to love it says it was done correctly with artistic flare.

When it's done wrong, you definitely notice it. Badly lit scenes in lower budgeted films look like naked, bright spotlights are used to just flood the area, often washing out the actors. It is something that can't be "fixed in post."

It's an old effect. It also saves actors on what we call "Overnight Grinds." Your entire sleep cycle is screwed because you arrive on set by early evening before sunset and shoot right through until sunrise. It's grueling.

Spielberg used "Day for Night" in the opening of *Jaws* as well as the scene where the shark rips off the dock with the two men fishing for it with a holiday roast.

The Last Dinosaur used this technique for most, if not all of its night time shots. In a way it helped to blend the live location footage a bit better with the stage work. The first time we see it in action is when a Pterodactyl swoops down on the team's camp and Bunta confronts it.

The lighting almost works, but the awkward matte and blue screen work takes us out of it. Luther Rackley was looking in the wrong direction for the flying dinosaur, a hazard of wrong focal points in the blue screen process.

2023 Miser Bros. Press/Rick Goldschmidt

Joan Van Ark saddles up her turtle.

Joan Van Ark's funny turtle effect recount was a total practical effect. As she pointed out, a team of small crew members were stuck beneath a large fake turtle shell that she would stand on. They'd get under it, likely holding their breath and rock the shell underneath her.

When we get the shot of the animal moving, the head loggers about, operated in a hand puppet way by an actor beneath the shell. The turtle does not open its mouth, with the large head a stiff plastic sculpture affixed with a long neck that ran under the shell with someone just rolling and joggling it about to give it some movement.

When the reptile sets sail down the lake, the team of small crewmen moved as Joan described, in tandem to give the effect of the thing swimming or propelling itself with its legs.

The T-Rex reveal is a big scene with editing taking us back and forth between the dino suit actor, blue screen compositing and live action on location humans. This is where the scale of the beast comes into play and will be a running issue for reviewers to this day. This is also where the flapping jaw issue is apparent.

I will point out later that the scale of the water and the physics of the water stand out as "not natural." There is a point in mentioning this.

Bunta's spearing of the beast is a collage of live action, blue screen, suitmation and stage work. The T-Rex bends its head to snap off Bunta's spear thrown into its chest. This was a combination of hand puppet head against a false chest as the suit itself was incapable of such physical action. The scale is also way off here when you compare the size of the spear in Luther Rackley's hand to its size embedded in the dinosaur's flesh.

Close ups of dinosaur eyes and their movements were done with puppet action pieces. The suits themselves did not have this kind of detailed function. When we see the eye rolls or eyes looking in a certain direction, they are part of a small piece mechanism for the camera to go tight and catch that action to add for dramatic effect.

The Triceratops was done like the old Vaudeville horse costume gag. Two men were the same creature. The head was up front and drove the action of the front legs while the guy stuck behind him had to work in tandem with the hind end to make it all look like one singular action.

The guy who played the ass end of the Triceratops has no credit though and he had the thankless job of having head and face in the ass of Mr. Nimiamoto during all of that. Imagine being inside that suit for hours—under hot lights, sweating, and smelling nothing but ass the whole time you're being beaten, tossed and hurled to the ground.

There should be some kind of award for that.

2023 Miser Bros. Press/Rick Goldschmidt

2023 Miser Bros. Press/Rick Goldschmidt

Sagawa said this is where the production wanted to see a little more violence and gore, likely for whatever non-US theatrical releases. That would give it a bigger screen feel than a made for TV feel.

The actors inside the Triceratops dealt with incredible heat as the suits were not well-ventilated. The head of the suit had heavy horns and it was assisted by piano wire to keep it up. Remember, the front end actor was hunched over, his legs the front legs of the beast.

This meant the heavy apparatus of the dinosaur's head carried mechanics for the actor to puppet the opening and closing of the mouth. The whole thing was heavy as hell, so wires were attached that ran to grids above with technicians following along catwalks off camera above the set to make sure it all worked in a single movement.

It seems so archaic by today's standards.

The T-Rex is gored in the fight, with two horns plunging into its belly. Sagawa recalled, "The claws went in and there was a lot of blood." He referred to the T-Rex striking back, clawing the Triceratops's belly as it lie on its side after being bitten in the neck.

The blood effects were done with several large tubes of fake blood hand pumped from behind a fake section of skin matching the suit. A prosthetic T-Rex foot with sharper toe nails digs into the material and artists pumped the blood from large syringes into tubes inserted into the material.

During some of the close-ups of the two beasts clashing, the front actor came partially out of the suit to operate the head puppet with his arms and hands. The stage backdrop switches between the hand painted backdrop to real sky with a low angle looking up from the ground to the two suit actors towering above to give epic scale.

This use of real outdoor light started appearing more frequently by the end of the Showa era with 1975's *Terror of Mecha Godzilla.*

Saliva was created from a variety of gelatins and glycerin, mixed in huge buckets with power tools and by hand, and then slopped onto the suit actors—the horns, the jaws, the bodies to give that textured realism that Sagawa knew American audiences expected.

Copious amounts of this material were used in the T-Rex's introduction, the Triceratops fight and throughout the film's action scenes as an extra "texture" for detail.

Dust and air blasts from the fighting titans were provided by large fans aimed toward the actors to add more of that sought after visual texture and create that haze or pall that hung over the T-Rex's den of death.

When that Triceratops fell over, mortally wounded, the first half went down first. The hind end was delayed. Was it because the actor couldn't hear direction, or maybe the front actor broke wind? The final cut has the dinosaur's body falling front half first, then a delayed reaction as its entire back half realizes and falls down as well.

The miniature work was sketched out in both detailed concept art as well as storyboards. I've read one review and listened to a podcast dedicated to the works of Rankin/Bass that floated the idea that the model of the Polar Borer used at Masten's press conference scene is the actual miniature model used in the film.

It's possible.

Sagawa extrapolated about audience vision and expectation for effects work, hinting that maybe it was more than just a cultural difference. "First, we have to match the sizes - large, medium, and small - with the monsters. That's it. In other words, what do you call a long shot? Start with the background. Is it the image that emerges with intelligence? That's it. Artistic people can't do it, and they can't gain experience with special effects."

Sagawa hints that maybe appreciation for the surreal can be impaired by ignorance or an unopened mind. [51]

"We use special effects for this, right? This is the one that matches the monster. It's not something underneath, it's something you want to run or sink on its own. The texture of this miniature is important, isn't it?" Sagawa talked of the Polar Borer and how it floated in the water.

In our sense of light, buildings and houses, for example, are actually seen from different angles. When it rains and the wind blows, and it gets dirty, it becomes like this and naturally enters our natural environment. This is the first time we can pay attention to such things." [52]

The small things matter in miniature design.

Sagawa laid out the process with the scaling of the models according to the size of the monster. A major criticism of the later Godzilla films is how attention to detail was supplanted by budget restrictions. When the Godzilla films hit their peak, the city build-ings were built of solid materials that would simulate real crumbling structures more realistically. If you go back and look at the films between 1954 through roughly 1966, you'll see the mini buildings were packed with inside rooms, even furniture.

As the budgets tightened by the late 60s, the skyscrapers were just cheap, thin materials with little detail. They could be built quicker and the scenes could be shot, and as Joan Van Ark said, "Moving on."

---

51 Ibid.
52 Ibid.

This type of cut in quality was seen by many fans as originating with Jan Fakuda films that really got a drubbing with *Godzilla vs. Megalon.* One effect goes against this in that film and I waited until we got to the stage and miniature work to mention it.

One scene in *Godzilla vs. Megalon* sees the villainous Megalon approach a giant hydro electric power dam. The set was built on an outside lot with natural lighting. The scale is spot on and the detail or "texture" (as Sagawa likes to say) was intricate. The matte work was almost seamless. The live action actor was rotoscoped right in behind the dam and for a beautiful moment in that film, you have what might be one of the best miniature effects in the original Godzilla Showa era series.

Megalon smashes the dam and water gushes through and the scale of the water and its physics look real. It all worked for that brief moment in that movie.

Sagawa talked of the issues with the physics of water and fire. Both elements work on their frequency. No matter how good your miniature sets are, fire or water effects will never look the way you want them too. This is where CGI excels.

Water and fire have their own rules. Despite how big the set is, they will always look small. They look like small fires and the water never makes waves properly. A monster that's supposed to me pushing through the ocean looks like a big guy wading through a bigger pool.

That's why film is shot at a faster speed to slow down the image in playback to make everything move slower because it seems to make the image more massive. The slower the monster moves, the more powerful the image appears to be.

Let me divert for one second to a personal story about scale. Back in my middle school days I would hit our library to devour any books on cryptids: The Loch Ness Monster, Bigfoot, whatever.

I think it was seventh grade and I found this large, black and white photo of the famous "Surgeon's Photo" of the Loch Ness Monster. At my young age of 12 I knew the photo was bogus. I WANTED it to be real. It sure looked like a dinosaur, a Plesiosaur to be exact, but I knew it was bullshit.

It was the scale of the displacement of water around the creature's body in the water. The rings of water weren't waves, but rather looked like the small ripples a stone makes when you plop it into a pond. Having grown up in the country, I knew what it was like to throw rocks into a lake or pond and that's what that photo looked like.

The famous photo was debunked in the early 90s when the photographer admitted it was nothing more than a kid's toy submarine affixed with wood putty or something like that modeled into a dinosaur neck and head. They floated it out a few feet from shore at sunset and the picture was taken.

I was right…those ripples told me everything. I couldn't believe scientists or even physicists never noticed it. The scale was all off.

That's the same thing that happens in movies. The water never moves right because it can't. It's not the real volume and the physics are off. The same with fire. A fire on a model set looks like a fire on a model set no matter how great the models look.

"Water and fire. They're the two elements that take three days to get right. It's all about how you show them. That's why it's so difficult to create waves. It's fine because there aren't any waves at the moment, but if we had to create them, it would be all about the size of the waves." Sagawa backed up everything I just said with that quote. [53]

Some fine matte work was used when Boone, Keats and Rackley go to rescue Van Ark from the cave. The T-Rex has her trapped and in one shot they rush up to an embankment where the matte line blends well with the live action location. Everyone is looking in the right direction and the lighting and exposure of the dino stage footage matches pretty well with the live action footage.

The Wile E. Coyote boulder and vine gag is another ambitious choice by the director(s). While the vine itself is clearly a rope with some plastic leaves affixed, the concept is cool—lassoing the T-Rex's tail to attach it to the boulder.

You can almost see Boone drawing out the plan like the famed Looney Tunes coyote in his plans to catch the Roadrunner:

------

53 Ibid.

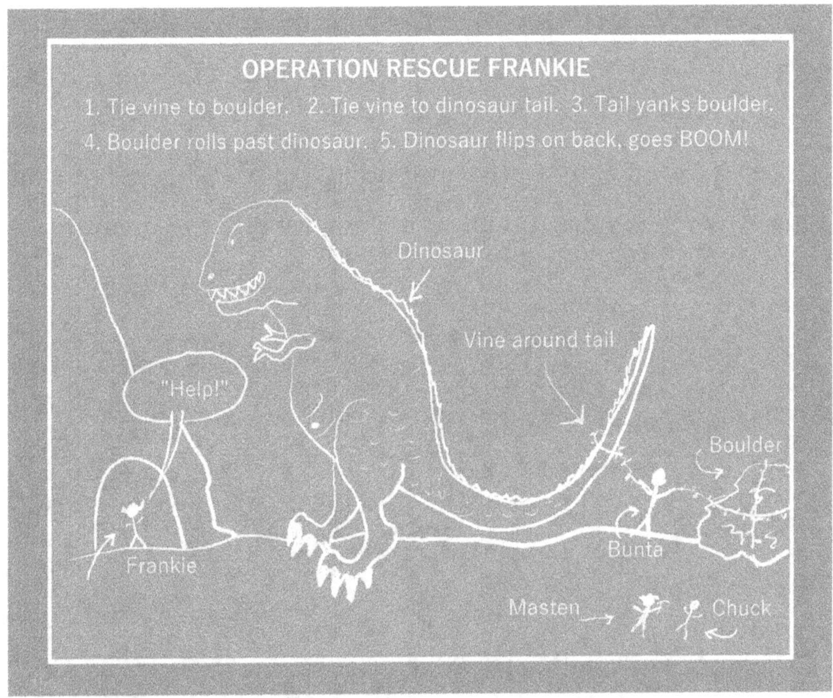

The effect has a miniature boulder yanked into motion, rolling downhill, passing the confused T-Rex then going tight, yanking the big old lizard slapstick-like into the air, crashing down on his ass. You can hear a cartoon "flip" sound effect with this in your head.

The boulder drags the beast down the hillside, crashing both into a lake or stream below.

As Boone and the crew watch the dinosaur leave, we get a shot of a hand drawn matte painting in front of them showing the pathway of destruction the creature cleared on its way down the hill.

The matte is hand painted, not too convincing and composited in, not painted on glass.

The scale of fire to the dinosaur is seen when Boone lets loose with handmade grenades against the dinosaur in the final confrontation. These are small gourds, no bigger than a pineapple yet when they explode they seem like small artillery blasts.

In the end, *Tsuburaya Productions* met their deadlines and the film was finished. Most would think that would be it. Now it's done. Not quite.

There's now the process of promoting and releasing the film and this is where the Internet today is still torn over those intentions.

**A giant prosthetic foot for the "T-Rex Stomp" scenes
that crush the doctor and Bunta.**

2023 Miser Bros. Press/Rick Goldschmidt

**The infamous boulder/catapult scene shows the issues with scale.
Not the size of the boulder in the shot above next to the dinosaur
but then its size next page in the arm of the catapult above
Boone and Van Ark.**

**The explosions above are off scale.
Giant explosions from hand-sized bombs.**

2023 Miser Bros. Press/Rick Goldschmidt

2023 Miser Bros. Press/Rick Goldschmidt

A SPECIAL PRESENTATION

Dozens of reviews proclaim that *The Last Dinosaur* was intended for a US or North American theatrical release, but when the American execs saw the final film, they changed their minds. This fits with the online narrative that the film was just so awful, *ABC* backed out of any theatrical release.

The argument against this has a lot of evidence--the first being that *ABC* was a *television* network. Their directive was to bring on Rankin and Bass for televised content, not feature theatrical releases. Those too young to remember, particularly the snarky viewers who hate on everything for those clicks and comments, never examine this fact.

ABC was not in the business of making movies for theaters. The cost to release a film, per screen was cost prohibitive for many, especially independent filmmakers. This was still a day before VCRs and even widespread cable television. Theatrical would be a terrific thing but often the money spent could not be justified.

There were still "Movies of the Week." These were star-studded made for TV films that that the networks made directly for their channels. They were made out to be big events. They would do the same for landing the rights to big theatrical blockbusters by creating "Network Premiere" showcases on a weekend evening.

The Last Dinosaur was always planned to be a prime time, big event for TV for the network's *ABC Friday Night Movie*.

The film would get a theatrical in Japan and Europe, but that was always the plan for the Eastern side of the co-production.

"The decision to not release *The Last Dinosaur* in the United States was a decision made solely by *ABC*," producer Benni Korzen told me. The reason behind that was they were ones who paid, financed and owned it. The decision had something to do with the expense of a theatrical release. If the cost seems too high for the anticipated return, then you find another way to get audiences to see it. That's the same for today.

The three networks back in the day commanded a huge amount of power in programming. "The reason why *ABC* kept coming back to Rankin and Bass was because they felt the investment in them was really smart. The product they got from them was good and the network made money off of it," Korzen stated. "If the cost of *The Last Dinosaur* was under two million dollars why spend five million to put it into theaters when you were *ABC* and had a massive audience with paid advertisers right there in front of you?"

Sounded like a no-brainer to me.

For Korzen, Rankin/Bass were good at what they were doing and profitable. Their formula was solid and they had proved to themselves that they knew what they were doing. The project was created for television, pitched to television, and released to television.

Just as the two producers planned from the start.

"Japan was Arthur's [Rankin] turf and he knew everything about the big monster movie background. The reason why this movie and all they had been doing had something to do with the fact that he figured out how he could tap the most important elements of how things worked in Japan and make it perfect for an American audience." Korzen had the utmost admiration for the way these two men did their thing.

"They didn't need to have a theatrical release for a movie because everything they had done at that time was as good as it could be."

"The difference between what Jules and Arthur did, there was never any desperation, no "Shit, we have a problem here that cannot easily be resolved." Korzen laid out how calm both men were under pressure. They would have a crisis, solve it and then wonder what was for dinner that evening. "They operated very differently from most other productions I was involved with over the years. They didn't have to invent anything. They already had things behind them."

They had a pedigree.

Rankin/Bass were able to function with less effort than other production companies because of the power they amassed in their filmmaking stable. They had a network financing their live-action feature films, they had decades of holiday material still pulling in the same popular numbers and advertising dollars and their name was synonymous with quality entertainment.

"There was a model in place back then where the studios and the industry knew where it was going. You could count on movies of the week for revenue, then cable sales then video sales. Now nobody knows where it is going. Nobody knows what the industry will be like in three years."

The revenue streams are muddied now with the loss of guaranteed video sales and network licensing. Networks are eroded and streaming does not yield the incredible cash windfalls like the days of cassette and DVD sales.

I said to Korzen as we wound things that down, that despite its limitations, despite Van Ark's correct assessment of kitsch and jokiness, *The Last Dinosaur* is fun. It may be fun in a *Mystery Science Theater* kind of way. It may be fun even as a college drinking game night.

The bottom line is it was made by people who loved what they were doing. It was made with people who decided to give it their all regardless of whatever the final result would be. Joan Van Ark made that clear. While she may not see the film as anything serious or noteworthy on her resume, she gave it her all, she gave it 150% when "Action!" was yelled. The same with Richard Boone. The same with everyone. Those suit designers, model builders, set designers--they made the best movie they could under the conditions they were in.

In short, they were professionals.

That's something we don't see a lot of these days. It's about "good enough." Why bother? It's good enough. I had a friend who was into home construction who treated each build with a "whatever" attitude.

"It's not a church," he would say to me with a grin and a shrug. It was good enough for the money he was making.

Joan Van Ark, Richard Boone, Arthur Rankin and Jules Bass, Benni Korzen…they treated this project as if it WAS a church. The end result might not have been so imperial, but they knew they put their absolute best into it.

It wasn't just "good enough" for them.

Jules Bass, a man of few words, once said of the film, ""I was amazed that it got such a cult following. There were a lot of people who seemed to enjoy it. So who am I to judge?"

A classy statement from a classy guy.

The film might not be the best film ever made but it was made by people who gave it their best.

Perhaps their time has passed.

Perhaps there are no more.

They were the last dinosaurs.

SPECIAL THANKS

There are quite a few people to thank. Joan Van Ark—for her time and her candor. No, Joan does not find the film to be a masterpiece or even close to good, but as I wrote, this diva gave her all when she was making it like she does with everything she decides to do.

Benni Korzen—the associate producer demurred when first approached, believing he wouldn't remember enough about a movie made so long ago. That was not the case. He was a landfill of deep, rich information and memories. He contributed to Joan's adamant positive assessment of Richard Boone. This all helped to dispel the present unfounded online nastiness by reviewers who want so hard to believe Boone and the cast didn't get along, the actor was drunk and barely coherent and fought with the directors and crew. Tom Kotani in post-*Dinosaur* interviews expressed not just his respect for Boone but a genuine affection for the man himself.

Rick Goldschmidt—the official *Rankin/Bass* historian who knows pretty much everything there is to know about the dynamic producing duo. He outfitted and licensed to me a number of unseen and official production photos, slides and materials that have enriched this book and made it something special.

Goldschmidt was the right choice to write the foreword for this book as Rankin/Bass's ambassador.

Richard Boone—I wish I had known him. I thank him for that letter he wrote on behalf of all artists. I thank him for providing me with some fun, childhood memories and entertainment with this film. I would like to point out my own perception. If the stories are true that Boone's experiences in World War II scarred and haunted him, he never let it become a personal vendetta against the Japanese people or their culture.

Japanese crew accounts, including Tom Kotani talk of their love for him, his friendliness and respect for them while shooting *The Last Dinosaur*. There are those stories of him learning enough Japanese to help Kotani interact with the American actors.

Boone went on to make another Japanese co-production, *The Bushido Blade*, which would be the last film of his life. The horrors of war never interfered with his love and respect for the Japanese people. "Gentle," was how Masumi Sekiya described him.

Whatever monster he battled in real-life, he battled it alone and silently.

Special thanks to all of you who love this film--who understand what it really is and love it anyway. We are in cynical times and attention now comes from inflaming, trolling, nastiness and online vitriol.

Mystery Science Theater has kept the light burning for us, to guide us toward films that might not be classics, but are far more entertaining than their present day counterparts with digital effects and named stars that are "good enough."

Passion runs short these days in the creative process. We have witnessed the dawn of AI, Artificial Intelligence that in my assessment will impact the human race in ways greater than the splitting of the atom. Soon whole scripts will be written from requested prompts: "Give me a film with this, with an element of that and make it like this with dialogue like that..." and the studios will reach their holy grail of algorithms and create the perfect, generic blockbuster to be consumed like fast food.

Thank you to all of you who know big monster movies aren't cuisine, but instead, big, sloppy desserts or gravy-laden mounds of fries and melted cheese. They are to not just eat, but enjoy, savor and sometimes at the end let out a gratifying belch or fart.

When done, we punctuate it with a satisfied exhale of "Ahhh-hhh…."

Thanks to people who know their movies and know the difference between "So bad it's good" and just plain bad. The line that separates grows blurrier and less defined with every film release.

Thank you to *Toho Studios* for giving us such fun for almost a hundred years.

Last but not least, thanks to YOU for wanting buy or listen to this book. You get it. You love this kind of stuff or you wouldn't have picked this up.

The world needs more of you.

Don't go extinct.

B Harrison Smith

2023 Miser Bros. Press/Rick Goldschmidt

A German press ad for *The Last Dinosaur*

THE LAST DINOSAUR

CREDITS

1. An Arthur Rankin, Jr./Jules Bass Film

2. Richard Boone

3. The Last Dinosaur
    (c) Rankin/Bass Productions, Inc. 1977

4. Co-Starring
    Joan van Ark

5. Steven Keats

6. Luther Rackley

7. Music by Maury Laws
    Arranged and Conducted by Ken Hirose

8. "The Last Dinosaur"
    Title Song Sung by Nancy Wilson

    Music by Maury Laws

    Lyrics by Jules Bass
    Arranged and Conducted by Bernard Hoffer

9. Associate Producer Benni Korzen
    Special Effects Kazuo Sagawa

10. Tsuburaya Productions Producer Noboru Tsuburaya

11. Screenplay by William Overgard

12. Produced by Arthur Rankin, Jr. and Jules Bass

13. Directed by Alex Grasshoff and Tom Kotani

THE LAST DINOSAUR

Directed by

Alexander Grasshoff and Tsugunobu "Tom" Kotani

Writing Credits (in alphabetical order)

William Overgard

Cast

Richard Boone ... Masten Thrust Jr.

Joan Van Ark ... Francesca 'Frankie' Banks

Steven Keats ... Chuck Wade

Luther Rackley ... Bunta

Masumi Sekiya ... Hazel

William Ross ... Hal - Mother 1 Chief Technician

Carl Hansen ... Barney

Tetsu Nakamura ... Dr. Kawamoto

Nancy Magsig ... Thrust's Girl on Plane

Don Maloney ... Mother 1 Captain

Vanessa Cristina ... Reporter

James Dale

Hyôe Enoki

Shunsuke Kariya ... Caveman Leader

Gary Gundersen

Toru Kawai ... Tyrannosaurus

Katsumi Nimiamoto ... Triceratops (front half)

Produced by

Jules Bass ... producer

Kazuyoshi Kasai ... associate producer

Benni Korzen ... associate producer

Kinshiro Ohkubo ... associate producer

Arthur Rankin Jr. ... producer

Noboru Tsuburaya ... producer: Tsuburaya Productions

Masaki Îzuka ... associate producer

Music by

Maury Laws

Cinematography by

Shôji Ueda ... (as Shoji Ueda)

Film Editing by

Minoru Kozono

Yoshitami Kuroiwa

Tatsuji Nakashizu

Production Management

Minoru Kurita ... production manager

Second Unit Director or Assistant Director

Shohei Tôjô ... assistant director (as Shohei Tojyo)

Art Department

Kazuhiko Fujiwara ... art designer

Sound Department

Yuji Hiyoshi ... sound mixer

Special Effects by

Kazuo Ohashi ... production manager: special effects

Kazuo Sagawa ... special effects

Moriake Uematsu ... special effects specialist

Yoshiyuki Yoshimura ... assistant director: special effects

Tetsuzô Ôsawa ... art designer: special effects (as Tetsuzo Ohsawa)

Visual Effects by

Yasuo Kitazawa ... lighting: special effects

Michihisa Miyashige ... optical specialist: special effects

Minoru Nakano ... optical specialist: special effects

Sadao Sato ... cameraman: special effects

Camera and Electrical Department

Hisaaki Yoneyama ... lighting technician

Music Department

Kenjiro Hirose ... conductor (as Ken Hirose) / music arranger
(as Ken Hirose)

Bernard Hoffer ... arranger: theme song / conductor: theme song

Nancy Wilson ... theme song: sung by

Additional Crew

Kiyotaka Ugawa ... coordinator

2023 Miser Bros. Press/Rick Goldschmidt